ARTHUR R. ASHE, JR.

A HARD
ROAD
TO GLORY

BOXING

The African-American Athlete
in Boxing

Other titles in the *Hard Road to Glory* series

BASEBALL
BASKETBALL
FOOTBALL
TRACK & FIELD
A HISTORY OF THE AFRICAN-AMERICAN ATHLETE
  Volume 1, 1619–1918
  Volume 2, 1919–1945
  Volume 3, Since 1946

ARTHUR R. ASHE, JR.

A HARD ROAD TO GLORY

BOXING

The African-American Athlete in Boxing

WITH THE ASSISTANCE OF
KIP BRANCH, OCANIA CHALK, AND FRANCIS HARRIS

Amistad

NEW YORK, NEW YORK

"Views of Sport: Taking the Hard Road With Black Athletes" by Arthur R. Ashe, Jr., © 1988 by The New York Times Company. Reprinted by permission.

Amistad Press, Inc.
1271 Avenue of the Americas
New York, New York 10020

Distributed by:
Penguin USA
375 Hudson Street
New York, New York 10014

Produced by March Tenth, Inc.

1 2 3 4 5 6 7 8 9 10

Library of Congress Cataloging-in-Publication Data
Ashe, Arthur.
        A hard road to glory—boxing : the African-American athlete in
    boxing / Arthur R. Ashe, Jr. ; with the assistance of Kip Branch,
    Ocania Chalk, and Francis Harris.
            p.   cm.
        "The text of this book was taken from the three-volume set of A
    hard road to glory and combined into one compendium on boxing"
    —CIP data sheet.
        Includes bibliographical references (p.) and index.
        ISBN 1-56743-036-8 : $9.95
        1. Boxing—United States—History.   2. Afro-American boxers—
    Statistics.   I. Ashe, Arthur.   Hard road to glory.   II. Title.
    GV1125.A84   1993
    796.8'3'0973—dc20   93-37951
                                                              CIP

Contents

To my wife, Jeanne, and my daughter, Camera

Publisher's Statement

The untimely passing of Arthur Ashe on February 6, 1993, requires telling the story of how *A Hard Road to Glory* came to be. It is a story that echoes its title, a tale that takes place in the publishing world and yet, not surprisingly, contains similar elements to those found in the world of sports: extraordinary individual effort, unified teamwork, setbacks, defeats, and eventual victory. It is only a partial testimony to a courageous man whom I was proud to have as a colleague and a friend.

Ten years earlier, in February 1983, while I was executive director of Howard University Press in Washington, DC, I received a telephone call from Arthur Ashe. He had heard of my interest in seeing that a work on the history of the Black athlete be published. He had expressed a similar desire to Marie Brown, a literary agent, who had referred him to me. He asked me when I planned to visit New York City again, and I told him it just so happened that I had to be there the next day.

That was not completely true. However, this subject was of such burning interest to me and I was so excited that a person of Arthur's stature was interested in writing such a book that I felt I should move expeditiously.

The following day I met him at his apartment on East 72nd Street, where we had a brief discussion. Then we went to his agent, Fifi Oscard, and met with her and Kevin McShane of the Oscard Agency. Arthur presented a general outline of the book that became the basis of our discussion, which in turn led to the negotiation of a contract.

On April 5, 1983, with the approval of the Executive Committee of the Commission on Management and Operations of Howard University Press, we formally executed a contract for a book that was tentatively titled *A History of the Black Athlete in America.* In May 1983 Arthur came to Washington, where we held a press conference and a ceremonial signing of the contract at the Palm Restaurant. I felt ecstatic that we were making the kind of history that would influence generations.

It should be noted that Arthur came to Howard University Press because, of the more than twenty commercial publishers in New York that he had approached, not one had seen the value or viability of a book on the history of Black athletes.

As he was soon to learn, however, Arthur and I had much more in common. We shared similar backgrounds of growing up in Virginia: He was from Richmond and I am from Portsmouth. We both attended schools (Maggie L. Walker High School and I. C. Norcom High School) that although segregated had outstanding teachers who nurtured Black students, instilled in them the desire to achieve, and provided important contacts to do so in the wider world. We were proud to be working together.

In June 1983, Arthur underwent double-bypass heart surgery. Miraculously, in a matter of weeks he was back at work on this project. His commitment went far beyond intellectual curiosity and enthusiasm. By this time Arthur had already assembled the nucleus of his research team, which included Ocania Chalk, Kip Branch, Derilene McCloud, and Sandra Jamison. (Rod Howard later replaced Ms. Jamison.) My son Francis Harris was to join this team in September 1983. (Doug Smith, of *USA Today*, assisted in this edition.)

In December 1985, I resigned from my position at Howard University Press, effective June 1986. I then began the preliminary stages of forming Amistad Press, Inc. as an independent publishing house managed and controlled by African Americans. After fifteen years at a university press, which had followed fifteen years with commercial publishers in New York, I was ready to move on to the professional challenge of my life.

There were still, however, some loose ends at Howard. Sensing a lack of scholarly and administrative support, Arthur asked university officials in January 1986 if they still had a commitment to publish his book. Within twenty-four hours of his question he was informed by an officer of the university that they had no further interest in his work. They were agreeable to his finding another publisher, and on February 21, 1986, Howard University released Arthur from his contract. By this time he had compiled about 75 percent of the material found in the present volumes. It was inconceivable that the project should stop at this point. We had come too far.

Arthur and I agreed that he would explore opportunities with other publishing houses

for his work while I was attempting to raise capital to launch Amistad Press. In May 1986, I met Lynne Lumsden and Jon Harden, who had recently purchased Dodd, Mead and Company, Inc., a venerable New York firm with a reputation for publishing influential African-American authors. We began negotiations for a joint venture in book publishing. By the middle of June 1986, we had settled on the legal parameters for this relationship. On July 1, 1986, Amistad Press, Inc. was incorporated in the State of New York. On August 22, 1986, Arthur Ashe signed a contract with Dodd, Mead and Amistad Press to publish *A Hard Road to Glory: A History of the African-American Athlete.* He had decided on this evocative title, and we all agreed that the work, based on original and extensive research, would necessarily consist of several volumes.

The entire team was working well. We had negotiated another critical turn in the development of this project, and we were feeling elated, for we had finally found a supportive atmosphere in the private sector. We shared an enthusiasm and a commitment to see this work through to its successful publication.

We planned to publish the work in the fall of 1987. To this end, Arthur appeared on the Author's Breakfast Program of the annual meeting of the American Booksellers Association, which was held in Washington, DC, at the end of May.

A Hard Road to Glory was announced with great fanfare and extensive promotional material, and it was received with equally positive interest.

In November 1987, while we were furiously engaged in the tasks of copyediting, proofreading, and typesetting, we learned that Dodd, Mead was experiencing financial difficulty. By February 1988, when it was confirmed that Dodd, Mead would not be able to proceed with this project, Amistad was offered the opportunity to purchase the Dodd,

Mead interest in the contracts that we owned jointly, including that of *A Hard Road to Glory.* I accepted with great pleasure and some trepidation. We still had to find a way to get the books out.

I initiated discussions with several publishing houses to explore their interests in a joint venture relationship similar to the one that Amistad had had with Dodd, Mead. In the spring of 1988 discussions began with Larry Kirshbaum, president of Warner Books. Simultaneously, through the efforts of Clarence Avant, I met Martin D. Payson, who at the time was general counsel of Warner Communications, Inc., which owned Warner Books. Marty Payson, who worked closely with Warner Communications's chairman, Steve Ross, became enthralled with the idea of *A Hard Road to Glory* and thought it would be a significant project for Warner Books and Warner Communications. A joint venture between Amistad Press and Warner Books began in April 1988. We then set a new publication date for November. Our spirits were lifted again.

While completing the final stages of reviewing galleys and sample page proofs, Arthur began having trouble using his right hand. Ultimately, he underwent brain surgery. As a result of this operation, he learned that he had been infected with HIV, the virus which was to take his life.

The publication of *A Hard Road to Glory* was a major achievement for a man who had had many triumphs. Arthur was intimately involved in the work at every stage of its development, from proposal to manuscript to bound books. He had been released from the hospital only a few days before the books arrived from the printer in October 1988. He asked his wife, Jeanne, to drive him from their home in Mt. Kisco, New York, to my apartment in Manhattan, where he saw the finished copies for the first time.

The first books had come from the bindery on a Friday and were sent directly to my home so that I would not have to wait until Monday to see them. I had received the books on Saturday, when I telephoned Arthur. His first reaction upon seeing them was similar to mine: He simply stared at them. We both looked at each other and smiled continuously. Because their daughter, Camera, was asleep, Jeanne had remained in the car and waited until my wife, Sammie, and I came back with Arthur and his first set of books. I think we were all nearly speechless because we realized what a tremendous ordeal and success we had experienced together.

This edition of *A Hard Road to Glory* names a single publisher of the work, Amistad Press, Inc. My wife and I started this company with our own personal financial resources. We were able to keep the company going in lean early years because Arthur became the first outside investor and supported us in attracting other investors. He personally guaranteed a bank loan that had been difficult to obtain, since the company had not yet published any books. Fortunately, we paid off that loan many years ago. Through Arthur's efforts we were able not only to publish his work, but we were also able to bring other important works to the public. We are on the road to achieving the goals for which Amistad Press was founded.

Present and future generations of writers will owe a great debt to a great man, Arthur R. Ashe, Jr., for helping make it possible for them to have a platform from which to present their creativity to the world.

Charles F. Harris
President and Publisher
Amistad Press, Inc.
March 1993

Views of Sport:

Taking the Hard Road With Black Athletes

by Arthur R. Ashe, Jr.

My three-volume book, *A Hard Road to Glory: A History of the African-American Athlete*, began almost as an afterthought to a seminar class I was asked to give on the historical and sociological role of the African-American athlete. Though I had never seen it, I assumed some esteemed black historian, sociologist or sports reporter had compiled the entire story of the black athlete in one volume. A search found only "The Negro in Sports," by Edwin B. Henderson, written in 1938 and slightly updated in 1948.

After three months of preliminary research, three inhibiting factors emerged for anyone wishing to put it all together: it would take more money than any reasonable publisher's advance would cover; black historians never deemed sports serious enough for their scarce time; and these same historians had underestimated the socio-historical impact of the black athlete in black American life. But the truth is that the psychic value of success in sports was and is higher in the black community than among any other American subculture.

This high psychic reward is not a contemporary phenomenon. Just after the Civil War when sports clubs were formed and rules were written, athletes became the most well known and among the richest of black Americans. Isaac Murphy, perhaps the greatest American jockey of the 19th century, earned more than $25,000. A black newspaper, the Baltimore Afro-American, complained in an editorial in 1902 that Joe Gans, the black world lightweight boxing champion, got more publicity than Booker T. Washington. It is no different today; Mike Tyson is better known around the world than Jesse Jackson.

In spite of the obstacles, I decided to proceed with the book because I became obsessed with so many unanswered questions. How did black America manage to create such a favorable environment for its athletes? Why did so many blacks excel so early on with so little training, poor facilities and mediocre coaching? Why did the civil rights organizations of the time complain so little about the discrimination against black athletes? And why were white athletes so afraid of competing on an equal basis with blacks? I just had to have my own answers to these and other puzzling sets of facts.

For 120 years, white America has gone to extraordinary lengths to discredit and discourage black participation in sports because black athletes have been so accomplished. The saddest case is that of the black jockeys. When the first Kentucky Derby was run in 1875, 15 thoroughbreds were entered and 14 of their riders were black. Black domination of horse racing then was analogous to the domination of the National Basketball Association today. Subsequently, the Jockey Club was formed in the early 1890's to regulate and license all jockeys. Then one by one the blacks were denied their license renewals. By 1911 they had all but disappeared.

This example appears in Volume I, which covers the years 1619–1918. It is the slimmest of the three volumes but took the most time, effort and cross-referencing of facts. Starting with official record books of all the sports, I sought to find out who was black, where he (there was no appreciable female involvement until World War I) came from, and where he learned his skills. I encountered two major obstacles: no American or world record was recognized unless it was under the auspices of a white college or the Amateur Athletic Union (simply put, no records set at black colleges or black club events counted to national or international governing bodies); and some early black newspapers published accounts that were frequently, if unintentionally, just plain wrong.

In the 27 years between the end of the two World Wars (the period covered by Volume II), the foundation for the quantum leaps made by black athletes after 1950 was laid. Again there were several cogent factors that influenced both the pace and progress of the black athlete. The one institution that provided minimum competition and facilities was the black college. But many of these schools still had white presidents and the small cadre of black presidents were hesitant to spend money on athletics for fear of alienating white donors who may have preferred an emphasis on academics.

A very positive factor was the formation of the black college conferences. But to white America, these conferences were nearly nonentities. They never got to see Alfred (Jazz) Bird of Lincoln University in Pennsylvania, or Ben Stevenson of Tuskegee Institute, who is by consensus the greatest black college football player before World War II. They never saw Ora Washington of Philadelphia, who may have been the best female athlete ever. Of course everyone knew and saw Jack Johnson, Jesse Owens and Joe Louis. They were, and still are, household names.

There were other famous names who because of their own naivete, bitterness and ignorance suffered indignities that brought me and my staff to tears of sadness and tears of rage. In 1805, for example, according to an account in The Times of London, Tom Molineaux, a black American from Richmond, Va., actually won the English (and world) heavyweight boxing title in the 27th round against Tom Cribb, but the paper quotes the English referee as saying to the prostrate Cribb, "Get up Tom, don't let the nigger win." Cribb was given four extra minutes to recover and eventually won.

. . .

There were times, to be sure, when white America got a glimpse of our premiere black athletes. The first black All-American football player, William H. Lewis, surfaced in 1892. Lewis was followed 25 years later by Paul Robeson and Fritz Pollard. But the most heralded confrontations took place on the baseball diamond when black teams played white major league all-star aggregations. The black squads won almost 75 percent of the time. The same for basketball. In the late 1920's and 1930's the original Celtics refused to join the whites-only professional leagues so they could continue to play against two black teams: the New York Rens and the Harlem Globetrotters.

Between 1945 and 1950, the athletic establishment was upended when all the major sports were integrated, in some places. What the black athlete did in the next 38 years is nothing less than stupendous. In particular, he (and she) brought speed to every activity. With fewer and fewer exceptions, whites were not to be seen in the sprints on the tracks or in the backfield on the gridiron.

Which brings us to the primary unanswered question of the project. Do black Americans have some genetic edge in physical activities involving running and jumping? My reply is that nature, our unique history in America, and our exclusion from other occupations have produced the psychic addiction to success in sports and entertainment. Once the momentum was established, continuing success became a matter of cultural pride. And yes, we do feel certain positions in sports belong to us. Quick, name a white halfback in the National Football League? Who was the last white sprinter to run 100 meters under 10 seconds?

Records aside, black athletes have had a major impact on black American history. In the early 1940's, for example, the black labor leader A. Phillip Randolph made the integration of major league baseball a test of the nation's intentions regarding discrimination in employment. The phrase "If he's [a black man] good enough for the Navy, he's good enough for the majors" became an oft-heard slogan for many. And when the opportunity finally came, it seemed almost predictable that black America would produce a Jim Brown, a Wilt Chamberlain, an Althea Gibson, a Bill Russell, a Gale Sayers, a Muhammed Ali, a Lee Evans, a Carl Lewis, and yes, a Tommie Smith and a John Carlos.

Proportionately, the black athlete has been more successful than any other group in any other endeavor in American life. And he and she did it despite legal and social discrimination that would have dampened the ardor of most participants. The relative domination of blacks in American sports will continue into the foreseeable future. Enough momentum has been attained to insure maximum sacrifice for athletic glory. Now is the time for our esteemed sports historians to take another hard look at our early athletic life, and revise what is at present an incomplete version of what really took place.

This essay first appeared in the New York Times *on Sunday, November 13, 1988, one day before* A Hard Road to Glory *was first published. We reprint it here as Arthur Ashe's reflections on the necessity and significance of this work.*

Foreword

Boxing is no game. It is more than and less than a game, but not simply a game. Even to call it "sport" stretches credulity. Boxing is both an *obsession* and *a reminder*, having to do with man's ability to survive, and to defend himself against the savages lurking within, and eventually to best himself, and *It*. This can lead to ennobling ideas from those observing, but is most often simply dangerous and discouraging work in the ring. No wonder African Americans have been so proficient at it. Hard? Oh yes.

From the slaves to the barge-loaders, the bridge-builders, the volunteers of the infantry, the crop-gatherers, the "Buffalo Soldiers," the pathfinders of the West, and heroes like those who saved Teddy Roosevelt's "Roughriders" on San Juan Hill during the Spanish-American war, Black men have always been given suicide duty in the New World, and it was no different inside the ring. Arthur Ashe, Jr. has compiled a dispassionate, intimate look at that history, that anti-legacy, showing us how the taming of a wilderness is always the work of doomed men who must get the work done quickly, before the work does them.

Boxing must have had an appeal even to a gentleman such as Ashe, who also played a remorseless "sport." At times, it comes down not to ability, because of the top twenty per-

formers of any craft, they are all human beings, more or less. The abilities between opponents are sometimes equal. It is the one who applies the most *will* that has the something extra. In fact, these are the best matches, they say, when the result comes down to what opponents are made of—what they will endure to stay on their feet.

I'm pleased to note that this volume is made up of such stern stuff. Arthur and his magnificent researchers have pulled a range of classic and esoteric sources, from the first elder of boxing literature in this language, Pierce Egan, to the gnome griot and boxing editor, Nat Fleischer, to sundry newspaper and magazine clippings, to W.E.B. Du Bois himself: They have combined to capture not only records and histories of fighters, but to put them in unbiased historical and psychological context in America.

The result is this. You can not only find out about Tom Molineaux, but glean that old Tom might not have been near the fighter that Harry Wills was later. You can learn how well Jack Dempsey ducked the 6'2", 220-pound Wills (not to mention Jack Johnson). Wills may well have been the uncrowned heavyweight champion of the world in the Roaring Twenties, when America tried to whitewash the knowledge of its debt to African Americans, indigenous peoples, and immigrants too, especially to the children of its own blood.

Ignoring a truth does not make it disappear. Deep in the northern cities, during the 1940s, the worlds filled by workers of the Great Migration would spawn Joe Louis, Henry Armstrong, and Sugar Ray Robinson—all born in the South, then forged in Detroit, St. Louis, New York. The like hasn't been seen before, or since.

The grace note of the ring history of African Americans is Muhammad Ali, who foreshadowed another coming epoch when he became heavyweight champion in 1964. Ali heralded an exhilarating reality of Black Americans beginning to sense who they were, and how strong, and beautiful. They were borne off by the tumultuous 1960s as Ali was barred from the ring for three years.

Here, in the 1990s, we have Mike Tyson, the defrocked champion, sitting in an Indiana penitentiary, barred from the ring for three years, convicted of raping a Black woman under the most hazy of circumstances. I've never heard of a White man in America being convicted of raping a Black woman, under the clearest of circumstances. Perhaps it did happen somewhere, but I have never heard of it. What better mirror then, for a society that claims, almost proudly, to have one of four

young Black men in prisons, or with prison records, making it impossible for them to become apprentices to any craft?

Boxing has to do with the taming of a frontier inside men that causes man's inhumanity to man. It is the reminder of the choking overgrowth of that wilderness, and it can be one triumph over it, a cutting instrument, a precious tool of the hand. What value is a life without struggle? African Americans certainly do not know; hence, a list of great champions. Boxing is a *reminder:* The world is not so civilized that it no longer requires the more thorough work of men who know, deep inside, that they are believed to be expendable. Doomed men always get the most dangerous duty.

They say the light that burns brightest lasts only half as long. But somehow, we are still here, hewing out the darkness.

Ralph Wiley
October 1993

Ralph Wiley writes for *Sports Illustrated* and lives in Washington, D.C. He is the author of *Serenity: A Boxing Memoir. Serenity* is a search for the boxer's peace of mind, from Joe Louis to Mike Tyson. Wiley is also the author of the books *What Black People Should Do Now* and *Why Black People Tend To Shout.*

Foreword

TO

A Hard Road to Glory:
A History of the African-American Athlete, Volumes 1–3

This book began in a classroom at Florida Memorial College in Miami, Florida, in 1981. I was asked to teach a course, The Black Athlete in Contemporary Society, by Jefferson Rogers of the school's Center for Community Change. When I tried to find a book detailing what has surely been the African-American's most startling saga of successes, I found that the last attempt had been made exactly twenty years before.

I then felt compelled to write this story, for I literally grew up on a sports field. My father was the caretaker of the largest public park for blacks in Richmond, Virginia. Set out in a fanlike pattern at Brookfield Playground was an Olympic-size pool, a basketball court, four tennis courts, three baseball diamonds, and two football fields. Our five-room home was actually on these premises. Little wonder I later became a professional athlete.

My boyhood idol was Jackie Robinson, as was the case with every black kid in America in the late 1940s and early 1950s. But I had no appreciation of what he went through or, more importantly, what others like him had endured. I had never heard of Jack Johnson, Marshall Taylor, Isaac Murphy, or Howard P. Drew—icons in athletics but seldom heralded in the post-World War II period.

These and others have been the most accomplished figures in the African-American subculture. They were vastly better known in their times than people such as Booker T. Washington, William E.B. Du Bois, or Marcus Garvey. They inspired idolatry bordering on deification, and thousands more wanted to follow. Indeed, in the pretelevision days of radio, Joe Louis's bouts occasioned impromptu celebration because, between 1934 and 1949, Louis lost only once.

But if contemporary black athletes' exploits are more well known, few fully appreciate their true Hard Road to Glory. Discrimination, vilification, incarceration, dissipation, ruination, and ultimate despair have dogged the steps of the mightiest of these heroes. And, only a handful in the last 179 years have been able to live out their post-athletic lives in peace and prosperity.

This book traces the development of African-American athletes from their ancestral African homelands in the seventeenth century through the present era. Their exploits are explored in a historical context, as all African-American successes were constrained by discriminatory laws, customs, and traditions.

As I began to complete my research, I realized that the subject was more extensive than I had thought. All of the material would not fit into one volume. Therefore, I have divided the work as follows:

Volume I covers the emergence of sports as adjuncts to daily life from the time of ancient civilizations like Egypt through World War I. Wars tend to compartmentalize eras and this story is no different. Major successes of African-Americans occurred in the nineteenth century, for example, which are simply glossed over in most examinations of the period.

Volume II examines black athletics during that vital twenty-year period between the World Wars. No greater contrast exists than that between the 1920s—the Golden Decade of Sports—and the Depression-plagued 1930s. The infrastructure of American athletics as we know it today was set during these crucial years, and the civil rights apparatus that would lead to integration in the post–World War II era was formalized. Popular African-American literature and its press augmented the already cosmic fame of athletes such as Jesse Owens and Joe Louis, who were the first black athletes to be admired by all Americans.

Volume III is set between World War II and the present. It begins with an unprecedented five-year period—1946 through 1950—in which football, baseball, basketball, tennis, golf, and bowling became integrated. These breakthroughs, coupled with the already heady showings in track and boxing, provided enough incentive for African-Americans to embark on nothing less than an all-out effort for athletic fame and fortune.

The reference sections in each volume document the major successes of these gladiators. These records are proof positive of effort and dedication on the playing field. More importantly, they are proof of what the African-American can do when allowed to compete equally in a framework governed by a set of rules.

Each volume is divided into individual sport histories. Primary source materials were not to be found in the local public library and not even in New York City's Fifth Avenue Public Library. Chroniclers of America's early sports heroes simply left out most of their darker brothers and sisters except when they participated in white-controlled events. Much had to be gleaned, therefore, from the basements, attics, and closets of African-Americans themselves.

Interviews were invaluable in cross-referencing dubious written records. Where discrepancies occurred, I have stated so; but I have tried to reach the most logical conclusion. Some unintentional errors are inevitable. The author welcomes confirmed corrections and additions. If validated, they will be included in the next edition of this work.

Today, thousands of young African-Americans continue to seek their places in the sun through athletics. For some African-Americans the dream has bordered on a pathological obsession. But unless matters change, the majority may end up like their predecessors. Perhaps this history will ease the journey with sober reflections of how difficult and improbable the Hard Road really is. In no way, however, do I care to dissuade any young athlete from dreaming of athletic glory. Surely every American at some time has done so.

A word about nomenclature. Sociologists have referred to nearly all immigrant groups in hyphenated form: Irish-Americans, Italian-Americans, and Jewish-Americans. African-Americans are no different, and this term is correct. Throughout this book, I shall, however, use the modern designation *"black"* to refer to African-Americans. The appellations *Negro* and *colored* may also appear, but usually in quotes and only when I thought such usage may be more appropriate in a particular context.

November 1988

Acknowledgments

A Hard Road to Glory would have been impossible without the help, assistance, contributions, and encouragement of many people. Initial moral support came from Reverend Jefferson Rogers, formerly of Florida Memorial College; Professor Henry Louis "Skip" Gates of Cornell University; Howard Cosell; Marie Brown; my editor, Charles F. Harris; and my literary agent, Fifi Oscard. All made me believe it could be done. An inspiring letter urging me to press on also came from Professor John Hope Franklin of Duke University, who advised that this body of work was needed to fill a gap in African-American history.

My staff has been loyal and faithful to the end these past four years. I have been more than ably assisted by Kip Branch, who has stood by me from the first day; and by Ocania Chalk, whose two previous books on black collegiate athletes and other black athletic pioneers provided so much of the core material for *A Hard Road to Glory*. To my personal assistant, Derilene McCloud, go special thanks for coordinating, typing, filing, phoning, and organizing the information and interviews, as well as keeping my day-to-day affairs in order. Sandra Jamison's skills in library science were invaluable in the beginning. Her successor, Rod Howard, is now a virtual walking encyclopedia of information about black athletes, especially those in college. To Francis Harris, who almost single-handedly constructed the reference sections, I am truly grateful. And to Deborah McRae, who sat through hundreds of hours of typing—her assistance is not forgotten.

Institutions have been very helpful and forthcoming. The people at the New York Public Annex went out of their way to search for books. *The New York Times* provided access to back issues. The Norfolk, Virginia, Public Library was kind and considerate. This book could not have been done without the kind help of the Schomburg Library for Research in Black Culture in Harlem, New York. Its photography curator, Deborah Willis Thomas, found many photographs for me, and Ernest Kaiser followed my work with interest.

The Enoch Pratt Free Library in Baltimore, Maryland; the Moorland-Spingarn Library at Howard University in Washington, D.C.; and the Library of Congress not only assisted but were encouraging and courteous. The offices of the Central Intercollegiate Athletic Association, the Southern Intercollegiate Athletic Conference, the Mideastern Athletic Conference, and the Southwestern Athletic Conference dug deep to find information on past black college sports. The National Collegiate Athletic Association and the National Association for Intercollegiate Athletics were quick with information about past and present athletes. The home offices of major league baseball, the National Basketball Association, the National Football League, and their archivists and Halls of Fame were eager to provide assistance. Joe Corrigan went out of his way to lend a hand.

The staffs at Tuskegee University and Tennessee State University were particularly kind. Wallace Jackson at Alabama A&M was helpful with information on the Southern Intercollegiate Athletic Conference. Alvin Hollins at Florida A&M University was eager to assist. Lynn Abraham of New York City found a rare set of boxing books for me. Lou Robinson of Claremont, California, came through in a pinch with information on black Olympians, and Margaret Gordon of the American Tennis Association offered her assistance.

Many people offered to be interviewed for this project—especially Eyre Saitch, Nell Jackson, Dr. Reginald Weir and Ric Roberts—and I am truly grateful for their recollections. (Eyre Saitch and Ric Roberts have since passed away.) Others who agreed to sit and talk with Kip Branch, Ocania Chalk, or me include William "Pop" Gates, Elgin Baylor, Oscar Robertson, Anita DeFranz, Nikki Franke, Peter Westbrook, Paul Robeson, Jr., Afro-American sportswriter Sam Lacy, A.S. "Doc" Young, Frederick "Fritz" Pollard, Jr., Mel Glover, Calvin Peete, Oscar Johnson, Althea Gibson, Mrs. Ted Paige, Charles Sifford, Howard Gentry, Milt Campbell, Otis Troupe, Beau Jack, Coach and Mrs. Jake Gaither, Lynn Swann, Franco Harris, Dr. Richard Long of Atlanta University, Dr. Leonard Jeffries of the City College of New York, Dr. Elliot Skinner of Columbia University, and Dr. Ben Jochannon.

Dr. Maulana Karenga of Los Angeles and Dr. William J. Baker of the University of Maine offered material and guidance on African sports. Dr. Ofuatey Kodjo of Queens College in New York City helped edit this same information. Norris Horton of the United Golfers Association provided records, and Margaret Lee of the National Bowling Association answered every inquiry with interest. To Nick Seitz of *Golf Digest* and *Tennis*, I offer thanks for his efforts. Professors Barbara Cooke, Patsy B. Perry, Kenneth Chambers, Floyd Ferebee, and Tom Scheft of North Carolina Central University were kind enough to read parts of the manuscript, as did Mr. and Mrs. Donald Baker. Professor Eugene Beecher of Wilson College, an unabashed sports fan, shuttled many clippings our way.

To the dozens of people who heard about my book on Bob Law's *Night Talk* radio show and sent unsolicited but extremely valuable information, I cannot thank you enough. And to the hundreds of unsung African-American athletes who played under conditions of segregation and whose skills and talents were never known to the general public, I salute you and hope this body of work in some measure vindicates and redresses that gross miscarriage of our American ideals.

Finally, to my wife Jeanne Moutoussamy-Ashe, I owe gratitude and tremendous appreciation for her understanding, patience, tolerance, and sacrifice of time so I could complete this book.

Arthur R. Ashe, Jr.
1988

ARTHUR R. ASHE, JR.

A HARD ROAD TO GLORY

BOXING

The African-American Athlete
in Boxing

CHAPTER 1

The Beginnings to 1918

Beginnings

No sport has had as profound an effect on the lives of African-Americans as boxing. Professional bouts have led to racial murders, and injuries to fighters have caused permanent physical and mental harm. Yet the sport retains a viselike grip on the imagination of all of us. There seems to be something primeval about hand-to-hand combat in the ring that makes sober people sit up and pay attention. No athletic event—not the Olympics, the World Series, or the Super Bowl—can match the drama of a world heavyweight title fight between two charismatic boxers.

Boxing now is not the same activity one sees depicted on ancient art pieces. That man began fighting for entertainment early is proved by scenes of boxers on objets d'art of the Egyptian civilization during the time of the pharaohs. The tomb of Beni-Hasan in particular is quite graphic in its wall paintings of boxings. At the time, boxing was a controlled contest in which blood flowed freely and swings were more of the roundhouse variety than jabs or uppercuts. An ancient match would look very crude by today's standards.

The Greeks introduced their own brand of fighting into the Olympic Games, which began in 776 B.C. Boxing started in 632 B.C. and was called *pancration*. It was much gorier than it should have been since no one wore gloves. The Romans followed the Greeks and added what are called battles royal. These spectacles entailed putting several gladiators together in one arena and having them fight it out until only one remained.

There was some opposition to these Roman shows from small Christian sects. Clement of Rome and Ignatius (later sainted) were just two who publicly condemned the bouts to no avail. But after A.D. 400, the gladiatorial bouts stopped. Fighting for sport then fell into a period of disorganization for almost 1,300 years. Then English and French nobles decided that an aristocratic gentleman's education was incomplete unless he could defend himself. What proceeded was a more scientific approach to fighting and the first true break from no-holds-barred brawling.

William Richmond and Tom Molineaux

James Figg capitalized on the English gentry's demand for quality instruction in self-defense. In 1719 he set up his School of Arms and Self-Defense, and he was his

1

nation's first boxing champion. Soon he had a waiting list, and even King George I attended. Interest grew briskly until Jack Broughton—a Figg pupil—formalized the first set of rules for the sport, now known simply as Broughton's Rules.

These guidelines included no hitting below the belt, no hitting an opponent when he was already down, and no holding below the waist, and they standardized the ring. The ring itself—from which the term for boxing matches derived—was round and about twenty-five feet in diameter with a firm dirt floor. A line or mark three feet long was drawn down the middle by the referee to serve as the place the boxers had to return to after a knockdown. Hence the phrases *toe the mark* and *come up to scratch*, in use today. No gloves were used, and blood still flowed—that was what the public wanted. Although boxing was banned in England from 1750 to 1790 because of the number of deaths in the ring, it remained popular nonetheless.

Into this scheme of things came William Richmond of Staten Island, New York, who was born free on August 5, 1763. His mother was an ex-slave belonging to Reverend George E. Charlton, who, after moving to Staten Island from the South, set her free. Growing up along the docks of New York City harbor during the British occupation, Richmond frequently got into bouts with sailors and seldom lost. One day he was noticed by the British Manhattan commander, Hugh Percy, who took an immediate liking to the youngster.

In 1778, Percy was recalled to England. He asked Richmond's mother to let him take her son to England. Richmond's mother reluctantly agreed, and he settled in the English county of Yorkshire to learn cabinet-making. He got into his first fight there by accident. At the horse races near York on August 25, 1791, he was accosted by George "Docky" Moore and subsequently gave him a sound thrashing in a makeshift ring nearby. He immediately received more challenges, since the sport was gaining in popularity. David Mendoza had just been crowned as the first Jewish champion of England in 1792, and his style of fighting was termed "scientific"—meaning he tried to avoid being hit rather than going toe-to-toe with opponents.

By 1800, Richmond was a semi-professional boxer and had an impressive list of wins to his credit. His success attracted wealthy patrons, and he decided to move to London, where he opened a tavern called the Horse and Dolphin on St. Martin's Lane in Leicester Square. After his first publicized loss to George Maddox, he scored enough wins to earn a title berth against the then champion, Tom Cribb. They agreed to fight on October 8, 1805, at Halsham (near Eastbourne) on the village green.

The stakes were high for Cribb in particular: his title, English honor, and the supposed superiority of the white race. For Richmond it was the first time a black American athlete had contested for a national or world title in any sport. The monetary purse was nominal: twenty-five guineas. The atmosphere surrounding the bout was festive. A crowd in the thousands was present, and dukes and other nobles appeared on horseback. No one paid to see fights then; it was first come, first serve for the choice views.

The newspapers had already hired boxing journalists to cover bouts, and their opinions were frequently more credible than those given by referees, who could be bought off at times. The most influential paper was the *London Times*. Its edition of October 9, 1805, reported on the outcome of the bout: "A...battle for twenty-five guineas was fought between Cribb and Richmond 'The Black.' It would [be] insipid for us to enter into particulars respecting the fight, which, if it may be so called, lasted nearly an hour and a half. It was altogether tiresome; the black danced about the ring, fell down, etc., while Cribb, through fear, or some other motive, declined going in, and beating him off hard. It was altogether an unequal match; and an interval of twenty minutes together elapsed without a blow of any consequence being struck. Cribb beat him without hurt. The business of the day was not over until near five o'clock in the evening." The crowd was pleased that, for the second time, a black man had been put in his place.

Cribb formally claimed the heavyweight title in 1807—the same year Britain abolished the slave trade (in law, not in fact)—and then retired. But he was forced to come back and defend English honor in 1810 when one of Richmond's protégés, Tom Molineaux, challenged him. His two bouts against Molineaux were the most famous of the early nineteenth century.

Tom Molineaux came from an unlikely place and an uncommon family. He was born a slave in Georgetown (now part of Washington, D.C.) on March 23, 1874. His father, Zachariah, was a boxer, as were his brothers. His master, Algernon Molineaux,

moved with them to a Richmond, Virginia, plantation and frequently arranged for bouts between his slaves and those on neighboring plantations. This was a rather commonplace occurrence, and fortunes were won or lost on the outcomes.

The average price of a healthy, male, field-hand slave around 1800 was roughly a thousand dollars. But the Molineaux boys could command a premium of nearly a hundred percent in a bout if the right deal were struck, and caution was surely taken with them. It just so happened that within a few miles of the Molineaux farm there took place one of the most famous slave revolts on record. Tom Molineaux must have heard about it through the slave grapevine.

Richmond, Virginia, in 1800 had thirty-two thousand slaves and eight thousand whites. On the night of August 31 a very charismatic slave, Gabriel Prosser, and his followers went on a killing spree of revenge and liberation. They murdered as many whites as possible—sparing only Quakers—in hopes that other slaves from nearby plantations would join to take over the city. Prosser's plan was betrayed by other slaves, and he was captured in Henrico County and publicly hanged on October 7. Tom Molineaux was only sixteen years old.

Molineaux's master had won so much on Tom by 1809, that he promised him his freedom if he won one last bout against a slave named Abe. This, too, was not uncommon, as slaves were often set free by benevolent masters for performing some extraordinary service. Molineaux handily defeated Abe, his master won his rather large wager, and Molineaux was set free as promised. With five hundred dollars in his pocket he headed for New York City and soon boarded the H.M.S. *Bristol* for London, England, where he came under the influence of William Richmond.

Under Richmond's tutelage Molineaux began serious training. He won his first bout against Jack Burrows, whose ring name was "The Bristol Unknown." White boxers in England frequently adopted false names so that losses to people like Molineaux would not be so embarrassing. The record books are laden with monikers of fighters who sought to protect their reputations. His next victory, for example, was against "Tom Tough," née Tom Blake.

After six more wins Richmond felt that Molineaux was ready to challenge Cribb to "unretire" and face his pupil. This challenge was printed in the *London Times*. Cribb finally agreed to "meet the Moor." Cribb was three years older than Molineaux and had gained a few extra pounds in his retirement, but the fight was nonetheless set for December 10, 1810, at Copthall Common in Sussex. No fight in memory had attracted so much attention and anticipation. A special attendee was the aging Baron Hugh Percy.

The day of the fight was perfectly miserable. It was raining and cold, and the referee, Ap Rhys Price, had a difficult time getting the ring cleared for the bout. Most reliable reports put at least ten thousand people at ringside. (There were no seats; everyone stood or sat on makeshift benches.) As the fight began, Molineaux quickly established his dominance, but Cribb held his ground. After twenty-seven rounds the bout was still in doubt.

In the twenty-eighth round Molineaux suddenly caught Cribb with a hard right. The Englishman went down, and Price started his count of thirty seconds. (A fighter had thirty seconds to "toe the mark" after a knockdown. A round ended when any fighter went down.) When Cribb failed to "come to scratch," Molineaux and Richmond began a gleeful victory dance. But Joe Ward, Cribb's aide, leaped into the ring in clear violation of the rules and accused Richmond of hiding weights in Molineaux's hands. All the while the timekeeper, Sir Thomas Apreece, kept yelling *"Time! Time!"*

Incredibly, Price waived the rules and allowed Cribb a full two minutes to revive. He went on to win sixteen rounds later over a dejected Molineaux. Richmond was furious but helpless as a blatantly partisan Price bent the rules to defend white English honor. Cribb collected two thousand dollars for his win, and a subscription on the grounds was collected for Molineaux. Richmond immediately demanded a rematch, which was printed in the *Times* on December 25, 1810.

In part, Molineaux wrote, "To Mr. Thomas Cribb...my friends think that had the weather on last Tuesday...not been so unfavorable, I should have won the battle....I therefore, challenge you to a second meeting....I cannot omit the opportunity of expressing a confident hope that the circumstance of my being of a different color to that of a people amongst whom I have sought protection will not in any way operate to my prejudice....Your most humble and obedient servant. T. Molineaux." Molineaux was not an educated man, but this challenge written for him did express his true sentiments and contained a subtle but pointed reference to his previous discriminatory treatment.

Cribb accepted the second challenge, but Molineaux then began taking his return bout too casually. He started drinking heavily and got into an argument with Richmond, which caused their estrangement. When the day of the bout arrived, September 28, 1811, Molineaux reportedly consumed a whole chicken and a quart of ale just before going into the ring. Cribb won in eleven easy rounds.

Molineaux fought three more official bouts and then joined a boxing troupe that traveled through the British Isles. He died penniless, alcoholic, and despondent on August 14, 1818, in Galway, Ireland. He never returned to America and never did see any of his family after his departure from New York.

Richmond continued boxing, giving lessons at his school at Number 6 Whitcomb Street in London, and minding his tavern. He fought his last round at age fifty-two against Tom Shelton. He had a hand in the careers of several other black fighters, including Sam Robinson of New York, "Sutton," Joseph Stephenson of Havre de Grace, Maryland, "Massa Kendricks," "Bristow," and "Johnson." The very first black fighter on record was Joe Lashley, who fought in England in 1791, but it is not known where he was born.

Richmond settled in well in his role as teacher, saying, "[I]f a man of color cannot fight for the English title, then at least I can be a servant [teacher]."[1] He died on December 28, 1829. The *London Times* mentioned that he succumbed to a fit of cough-ing after spending the evening with Tom Cribb. Richmond and Cribb must have remained friends despite Molineaux's foul treatment.

Pierce Egan, the esteemed chronicler of the sport in his era, had the last and best eulogy for William Richmond: "In the ring, in the point of activity, he stands nearly unrivaled, and is considered to excel every other pugilist in hitting and getting away, and dealing out severe punishment with his left hand." Athlete, merchant, teacher—Richmond was the first in a long line of African-American boxing wonders.

The Anglo-Africans

From the era of the War of 1812 until after the Civil War, boxing had a precarious toehold in America. Religious objections were strong and peaked in the 1840s during the evangelical movement. Bouts were clandestinely held on barges or in private clubs. Slaves continued to box when they got the chance. There was much intraracial opposition. William Johnson, the free black from Natchez, Mississippi, who kept a personal diary from 1835 until 1852, described several public fights between slaves.

But the most cogent thoughts came from the pen of black abolitionist Frederick Douglass. In his autobiography he mentions the holidays at Christmas as a time when "the sober, thinking, industrious ones would employ themselves in manufacturing..."[2] He also believed that southern plantation owners used "those wild and low sports" to keep blacks semicivilized.[3] Perhaps he was correct, but boxing re-mained popular nonetheless.

After the Civil War social acceptance of boxing gained some adherents, in part due to the passage of the new Queensberry Rules in 1869. Fights called for three-minute rounds, ten-second counts after knockdowns, and mufflers or gloves. Into this new atmosphere came the first black world champion from our neighbor to the north. George Dixon was the first of three great Anglo-Africans to reign in their weight classes.

Dixon was born at Leston's Lane in Halifax, Nova Scotia, Canada, on July 29, 1870. His family had originally settled in Nova Scotia when large groups of blacks loyal to King George III during the Revolutionary War decided to leave the colonies. In the opinion of ring expert Nat Fleischer, "for all his ounces and inches, there never was a lad his equal."[4] Sam Austin, the editor of *The Police Gazette* (the major sports paper of the late 1800s), added that Dixon had no flaws.

He moved to Boston with his parents and became interested in boxing while working as an apprentice to a photographer who specialized in pugilists' photos. After training in a local gym the 5'3", 100-pound Dixon was spotted by Tom O'Rourke, who became his manager. He turned professional at age sixteen during a glorious time for the black athlete. Black jockeys were winning nearly all the important races like the Kentucky Derby; baseball players were still in the International League; and William H. Lewis was just six years away from becoming the first black All-America football player.

Dixon quickly learned the art of the body feint. Fans loved seeing him dart his head and upper body in and out to draw his opponents off guard. He fought three years before losing to another Canadian, George Wright. But soon he had financial backers and was able to post larger side-bets. (In these times, without a commissioner to regulate the sport, opposing boxers generally had to publicly state how much of their own money was put up for a fight. Though these sums usually came from patrons, it let the public know the gravity of a bout. The more important the bout, the higher the side-bet.)

On May 10, 1888, Dixon fought a nine-round draw against Tommy Kelly for the paperweight (105-pound limit) title but was denied it. So he sought the American bantamweight title against Cal McCarthy. This championship fight occurred on February 7, 1890, and ended in a no-contest decision after seventy rounds at the Union Athletic Club in Boston. In a second bout for this title on March 31, 1891, Dixon became the first black man to hold an American title in any sport by knocking out McCarthy in the twenty-second round. He had already become the first black boxer to win an international title when he KO'd the British featherweight champion, Nunc Wallace, on June 27, 1890.

But 1892 was an even more momentous year for Dixon and the sport. On June 27 he KO'd Fred Johnson in fourteen rounds at Coney Island, New York, to become the first black world titleholder—the new featherweight king—and $4,500 richer. And his bout on September 6 of that year was perhaps the most discussed of the decade and had social repercussions far beyond the boxing ring.

Dixon had never fought in the South. Of the three bouts he had fought in Washington, D.C., two were against other blacks. Now he was offered a bout in New Orleans at the private Olympia Club as part of a three-day boxing carnival. The main feature was the heavyweight title affair between the champion, John L. Sullivan, and "Gentleman" Jim Corbett on September 7. Dixon would fight white amateur Jack Skelly on September 6.

In 1892 New Orleans was very racially divided in the post-Reconstruction period. Racist Jim Crow laws prevailed, and no racially mixed public bouts were legal. But as the Olympia Club was private, no laws would be broken. In addition, a global flu epidemic was just receding and large gatherings were discouraged. Dixon secured a promise from the promoters to set aside seven hundred tickets for "people of color" to witness his performance. And what a performance it was!

His bout was billed as the world featherweight championship and is so listed in the record books. Dixon weighed 115 pounds to Skelly's 116.5. New electric indoor lights were used for the first time, and a winner-take-all purse of $17,500 awaited the winner, which could go only to Dixon if he won because Skelly was an amateur.

In the first round Skelly was peppered with shots from the more experienced champion as the white local fans winced in dismay. It was assumed that any experienced white boxer in peak condition could prevail over any black fighter. The promoters were almost sure Skelly was going to win, although Dixon was the reigning champion. But through the last four rounds it became "simply a question of how much punishment Skelly could absorb....Dixon broke Skelly's nose with a right-hand swing.

The blood came spurting from the injury....The sight was sickening....Finally in the eighth round, after a minute's work, Dixon crashed a right swing to the point of the jaw....Skelly...was counted out."[5] In some quarters of the city black citizens celebrated for two days.

But the morning papers on September 7 were swift and brutally frank in their assessment. From the *Chicago Tribune*: "white fans winced every time Dixon landed on Skelly. The sight was repugnant to some of the men from the South. A darky is alright in his place here, but the idea of sitting quietly by and seeing a colored boy pommel a white lad grates on Southerners."

From the *New Orleans Times-Democrat*: "What with bruises, lacerations and coagulated blood, Skelly's nose, mouth, and eye presented a horrible spectacle....some even turned away their heads in disgust...at that face already disfigured past recognition....It was a mistake to match a negro and a white man, a mistake to bring the races together on any terms of equality, even in the prize ring....It was not pleasant to see a white man applaud a negro for knocking another white man out."

Evidently nearly all the white spectators had come to the Olympia Club fully expecting a white amateur to handle a world champion, no matter what his color. The club itself, according to the September 11 *New Orleans Daily Picayune*, decided to "permit no more matches to be fought there, which ignore a respect for the color line." For his part, "Little Chocolate," as Dixon was called, said he would fight in New Orleans again if asked.

Dixon's win and the resulting racial animosity from whites was a prime factor in limiting access for blacks to heavyweight title bouts. It encouraged white boxers to draw the color line, and it meant the absolute end of any more fights of its kind in the segregated South.

On October 4, 1897, Dixon finally lost his world featherweight title at Woodward's Pavilion in San Francisco to Solly Smith, whom he had previously beaten. He regained it over Dave Sullivan on November 11, 1898, on a disqualification in the tenth round. Dixon thus became the first black fighter to gain, lose, and regain a world title. He lost it for good on January 9, 1900, to Terry McGovern in New York on an eighth-round knockout.

At the end Dixon was without friends or his manager, O'Rourke. He had lost all his ring earnings and admitted as much. He was quoted as saying, "I hope that my career will be a good lesson for others....I hope that they will remember my plight and not follow the—Easy come, Easy go Methods—which has put me in the position where I now find myself."[6]

He died January 6, 1909, in New York City. His body lay in state at the Longacre Athletic Club for two days until funds could be amassed to send his remains to Boston. George Dixon, the first black world boxing champion, was buried in Mount Hope Cemetery.

Dixon's stablemate under the managership of O'Rourke was Joe Walcott, sometimes known as "The Barbados Demon." Walcott was born March 13, 1873, in Barbados, West Indies. Built like a fireplug, he was only five feet, one and a half inches tall and weighed 145 pounds at his best.

But what a fighter he was! Walcott simply loved to mix it up in the ring. He won the New England wrestling titles in the lightweight and middleweight classes—in the same night!

Walcott was added to O'Rourke's roster of boxers from his position in Boston as an elevator operator at the American House Hotel. He hung around Jack Sheehan's gymnasium and was soon beating everyone in his weight class. He turned professional at age seventeen in 1890 and won his first bout, which netted him $2.50 at the Music Hall. On August 22, 1893, he KO'd the Australian lightweight champion, Jack Hall.

But Walcott was a natural welterweight. In a match against George "Kid" Lavigne, Walcott had to "train down" to the lightweight limit. In fact, Lavigne's manager, Sam Fitzpatrick, forced O'Rourke to agree that if Walcott did not stop Lavigne inside of fifteen rounds, Walcott would lose the bout. He did lose in fifteen rounds, though he bloodied Lavigne unmercifully. Special provisions like the foregoing were common then.

After losing a bid for the world lightweight title against Lavigne on October 29, 1897, and a welterweight title bid to "Mysterious" Billy Smith in 1898, Walcott seemed poised for his chance in 1900. But part of his chance to fight for the welterweight title again may have been an agreement to "take a dive," or deliberately lose a few chosen bouts. An eleventh-round loss to Tommy West on August 27 certainly was fixed because he feared for his life. With no central organization to control the sport, gamblers bought and sold boxers at will. No black fighter between 1895 and 1906 could go undefeated, no matter how good he was.

Walcott's problem was that he did nothing to publicly disguise his blatantly inept performance. Nat Fleischer recalls that O'Rourke personally told him that "Walcott didn't dare to win that night. I got the tip...he must lose....If West had been stopped in that twelfth round...I'd probably have been laying nice, peaceful and natural on the next slab."[7]

New York had passed the Horton Law in 1896 rather than ban boxing outright. This law allowed private clubs to stage bouts, provided both the clubs and the boxers were registered by the state. It also lifted restrictions on the numbers of rounds and decisions by referees, and it forbade side-bets. But because of Walcott's showing, the Horton Law was replaced on August 30 by the Lewis Law, which mandated professional boxing on a club-membership basis only. That remained in effect until 1911. Despite these problems Walcott earned and defeated Jim "Rube" Ferns for the welterweight title on December 18, 1901. He won every round until it was stopped in the fifth after a KO. Walcott thus became the second black champion, but his laurel was not a world title.

After losing his welterweight crown to Aaron "Dixie Kid" Brown on April 30, 1904—the first time a title held by a black boxer was lost to another black boxer— Walcott fought a draw with Joe Gans for the world title on September 30 of that year. Brown had outgrown the welterweight class and abdicated his championship, so Wal-

cott claimed it, and his claim was generally recognized. He finally lost it to Billy "Honey" Mellody after recovering from a gun accident that left his friend dead and his right hand shattered.

Walcott fought on until 1911. He later became a fireman on a freighter, a porter at New York City's Majestic Theater, and a handyman at Madison Square Garden. He had spent all his earnings and died in an automobile accident in Massillon, Ohio, in 1935.

"The Dixie Kid" held the welterweight title only six months—from April 30, 1904, until October 4 of that year, when he abdicated. He fought on through 1914 as a middleweight.

The last of the black champions from the British Commonwealth was another Virgin Islander, Peter Jackson. Jackson came from Fredericksted, where he was born on July 3, 1861. At age six he was taken to Australia to live and began taking boxing lessons at age seventeen from Larry Foley. He won the Australian heavyweight title on September 25, 1886, from Tom Leeds in thirty seconds of the first round. He thus became the first black man to win a national boxing crown.

Jackson sailed for America in 1888 to fight the leading heavyweights, but racism immediately halted his plans. He had to settle for fighting George Godfrey, who was *The Police Gazette's* "Colored Champion." *The Police Gazette* named colored champions in almost every weight class, in part to stimulate interest among its black readers and in part to appease the racist sentiments of its other ethnic readers. Baseball was squeezing the last blacks out of the major leagues, and the *Gazette* merely reflected the general feelings of antipathy toward black athletes.

Already twenty-eight in 1889, the 6' 1½", 192-pound boxer was running out of time if he hoped to annex the world title. As good as he was and with the Australian title to his credit, he could find few whites to fight. He decided to go to England, but not before expressing the hope that "here in your America, the opportunity which I have been seeking will come to me."[8] He was so wrong. Few periods in American history can match the racism toward blacks and Orientals of the late nineteenth century.

One white man who pointedly refused to meet Jackson was America's first national sports hero, John L. Sullivan, better known as "The Boston Strong Boy." Sullivan was the world heavyweight champion in 1889, but when approached about fights with blacks, he said, "I will not fight a negro. I never have, and I never shall."[9] But in truth Sullivan *had* fought a black man in Tombstone, Arizona.

In 1884, a year before he won the title, Sullivan was touring the Southwest and challenging all comers to stay in the ring with him for two rounds for five hundred dollars. A "near giant [black] named Jim, who rode for John H. Slaughter" took up the challenge. The *Tombstone Epitaph* recalls that Sullivan and Jim met in Schiefflin Hall, and when the fight began, Jim got in the first lick, "a looping round house swing that caught Sullivan high on the head and threw him off balance." But that was it. Sullivan finished him off handily, and Jim was "carried out feet first like a ton of coal."[10] This

encounter may not have been official, but it happened nonetheless.

Jackson captured the British title from Jim Smith on November 11, 1889, on a foul in the second round. (British boxers were evidently still using dirty tactics seventy-nine years after the Tom Cribb–Tom Molineaux bout.) On May 21, 1891, the thirty-year-old Jackson had his most famous bout, with a future champion, James Corbett. At the California Athletic Club in San Francisco, the two boxers fought a sixty-one round draw. Experts rate this as one of the sport's most acclaimed fights. A year later, Corbett won the world championship from Sullivan at the aforementioned boxing carnival in New Orleans.

Sadly, after winning the heavyweight title, Corbett also drew the color line, thus depriving younger black heavyweights of a chance for glory. In a possible attempt at atonement for this, Corbett wrote in his autobiography that Jackson was the best fighter he had ever seen. Jackson's most poignant plea came in a lengthy letter published in the July 3, 1893, *Rocky Mountain News* of Denver, Colorado.

It said, in part, "Before age has impaired my powers I hope to have the pleasure of again meeting James J. Corbett in the ring. Not that I have a feelng of animosity for him. On the contrary, I like him very much.... Corbett defeated the best fighter that ever lived, John L. Sullivan.... So it comes about that Corbett, being champion of America, and your humble servant practically holding the championship of England and Australia, the three fight-countries of the universe, either of us, should one defeat the other, would be the champion pugilist of the world....I was very sorry when he took on Charles Mitchell of England and passed me by....The champion's proposition that I put myself in condition and be prepared to take Mitchell's place...is foolish.

"I ask in all fairness, what earthly chance have I of meeting the champion next December?...I have never challenged Corbett and I never will....Age is now coming on me—I am thirty-two....I hope to get on a match with him....Boxing I think, is a manly sport....It is not for every man to be a fighter....If a man is fainthearted he should never step over the ropes....The man whose heart fails him suffers...like the poor wretch on the way to the galllows."

It is clear that Corbett promised Jackson a rematch but that someone persuaded him to renege. Even Corbett's conscience as a sportsman was not strong enough to meet the Australian and English champion, embodied in Jackson. Racial antagonism in America was that strong in the early 1890s. Equally as poignant, two years later in 1895, was another open letter, written this time by the white sports editor of the influential New York *Sun*, Charles A. Dana. His missive was the most provocative piece of racist sports journalism yet seen in America and caused a sensation that lasted for years afterward.

Dana wrote, "We are in the midst of a growing menace. The black man is rapidly forging to the front ranks in athletics, especially in the field of fisticuffs. We are in the midst of a black rise against white supremacy....Less than a year ago Peter Jackson could have whipped the world—Corbett, [Robert] Fitzsimmons,...but the white race is saved from having at the head of pugilism a Negro....There are two Negroes in the ring today who can thrash any white man breathing in their respective classes...George Dixon...and Joe Walcott....If the Negro is capable of developing such prowess in those divisions of boxing, what is going to stop him from making the same progress in the heavier ranks?

"What America needs now is another John L. Sullivan....How is it that these sable champions spring up all at once? Is it because they are far better than their white brethren or is the white race deteriorating?...Wake up, you pugilists of the white race! Are you going to permit yourself to be passed by the black race?...Some say that the 'colored brother' is not a man of the highest courage, but I doubt that....He has always been made to believe that he belongs to an inferior race....But...the Negro has evinced as much courage in combat as the white man."

Because the New York *Sun* was one of the sports world's most-read papers, Dana's commentary was a bombshell. He openly appealed to the worst in the white sporting public and reinforced the popular notion that black athletes in all sports lacked heart. Fifteen years after Dana's piece appeared, his racist theories caused the downfall of the most acclaimed white heavyweight champion since Sullivan.

With few opportunities, Peter Jackson's career was short and bittersweet. He had thirty-five wins, three losses, and one draw. He returned to Australia and died of tuberculosis on July 13, 1901, at forty-one.

He was buried with honor at Toowong Cemetery in Roma, Queensland, and his gravestone is engraved with words that wished for him eternal peace:

SLEEP, PETER, SLEEP, *brave champion.*
   All hushed,
will gather around where snow-white
      flowers, moist-eyed,
we fling within the grave.
The fight is done.
Sleep, Peter, Sleep.
The hero's rest is there
in mother earth's broad breast.

Joe Gans

The first African-American to win a world title was born in Baltimore, Maryland, on November 25, 1874. His name at birth was Joseph Gaines, but it was later shortened to Joe Gans. At full maturity he stood 5'6¼" and weighed 133 pounds. His nickname at the height of his powers was "The Old Master."

Gans was found along the docks of Baltimore, where he first toiled as an oyster shucker. Like other black boys his age, he went to the Monumental Theater to see whatever was on the program. One night the theater featured a battle royal in which several youngsters were all put in the ring at one time and told to fight it out until only one remained. Gans won this affair and attracted the attention of boxing enthusiast and restaurant owner Al Hereford.

The gentle Gans was genuinely surprised that someone like Hereford showed interest in him. Hereford supposedly replied, "That's my funeral, not yours. I'm satisfied to take a chance."[1] Turning profes-

sional in 1891, Gans was one of the busiest fighters on record. In his first nine years he lost only twice. One of these losses was to another famous black boxer, Bobby Dobbs, who, although a natural welterweight, fought anybody and everybody. Dobbs had been born a slave in Knoxville, Tennessee in 1858.

After the loss to Dobbs in 1897, Gans was thought to be champion material with a string of victories laced with knockouts. He landed a shot at the world lightweight title against Frank Erne on March 23, 1900, but was KO'd in the twelfth round. His fighting skills were nevertheless obvious. He piled up more knockouts until he fought a bout on December 13 of that year against Terry McGovern in Chicago. Gans "took a dive" and lost in the second round to blows that observers declared would not harm an infant. It was obviously a fixed bout, and the resulting stink caused the Chicago City Council to ban the sport. He deserved the shame he felt, although he may have feared for his life just as Joe Walcott had before him. Some even felt he had taken a dive against Erne as well.

A year and a half after his disgraceful display against McGovern, Gans got his second chance at the world lightweight crown. Fighting in Fort Erie, Ontario, Canada, he KO'd Erne in the first round to become the first native-born African-American to win a world crown. A right to the chin caught Erne off balance, followed by a left to the jaw and another right to the jaw, and down went Erne for good. Erne was still on the canvas when referee Johnny White counted him out.

Gans then began gaining weight. He fought as a welterweight although he would lose the weight to defend his lightweight title. This up and down in weight took its toll. He was forced to defend the title against Jimmy Britt, who was not above using foul tactics to his advantage. In the second round Gans went down and was delivered a low blow, which drew a warning from referee Ed Graney. Britt ignored the warning. In the fifth round Gans again went down, and Britt clouted Gans on the side of the head while he was on his knees. Instead of going to a neutral corner as Graney instructed, Britt hovered atop Gans and struck when he could.

Finally, Graney would take no more and disqualified Britt for repeated fouls. Then all hell broke loose. Britt took swings at Graney, and they both hit the deck until police arrived to separate them. So Gans retained his title on a foul. But to remove any doubt about his superiority, Gans defeated Britt in 1907 in six rounds. The tactics used by Britt would have been unthinkable for a black boxer to use against a white opponent in a championship fight.

Gans was then challenged by Oscar M. "Battling Nelson" Nielson of Denmark, who was the new world lightweight champion. After the Britt win in 1904, Gans relinquished his world lightweight title and actually won the vacant world welterweight title from Mike Sullivan on January 19, 1906. Gans could hardly refuse—the money was so tempting. Nelson and Gans then agreed to a "fight to a finish" at Goldfield, Nevada, on September 3. The promoter was Tex Rickard, who would figure very prominently in a later bout between Jack Johnson and Jim Jeffries.

The $34,000 purse was divided into $11,000 for Gans and $23,000 for Nelson. Billy Nolan, Nelson's manager, insisted on this split because he knew Gans was short

of money. In addition, Gans had to reduce to the 133-pound limit at age thirty-two. Furthermore, Nolan insisted that Gans had to make the weight on the day of the fight in his boxing clothes. Gans had to agree because he needed the money. No matter; the fight was a classic.

Under a brutal Nevada sun, Gans reportedly vomited four times and broke his right hand in the thirty-third round. Ever the model of sportsmanship, he twice bent over to pick up Nelson after knocking him down. Nelson was not so kind. In the forty-second round, by then half blind from punches, Nelson lashed out with a vicious blow to the groin. Without hesitation, referee George Siler ordered Nelson to his corner and awarded Gans the fight on a foul. Gans thus regained his old world lightweight title.

However, his victory caused the first serious outbreaks of racial violence against blacks as a result of a boxing match. Police reported incidents across the country attributed to the bout. William Conway, a black bar patron in Flushing, New York, had his skull fractured by three white customers. Anthony Roberts, a black doorman at the St. Urban Apartments on New York City's Central Park West, told police he fought off two white attackers with a razor and a small pistol.

Gans regained his title, but he was losing another battle. He had tuberculosis and knew he was going to die. He retained his world lightweight crown with four successful defenses and ordered his manager to book another match with Nelson. With a wife and two children, he wanted to provide for their future. Gans and Nelson met on Independence Day in 1908, and although Gans was "The Old Master" for five rounds, he could not hang on. He went down three times in the seventeenth and final round as Nelson regained his lost title. They met one last time in Colma, California, on September 9, and Nelson again prevailed with a knockout in the twenty-first round.

In the spring of 1909 Gans went to Prescott, Arizona, to try to arrest his deadly affliction. But realizing intuitively that he was near death, he asked his friend Kid North to take him home before he expired. He just made it, dying in his mother's arms as his wife and children stood nearby. Joseph (Gaines) Gans was buried in the Mount Auburn Cemetery in Baltimore on August 13, 1910. He left his family financially secure and his reputation restored.

Gans was not alone among black boxers in the lower weight classes. The aforementioned Aaron "Dixie Kid" Brown was widely respected, although he had a pitiful end. Brown committed suicide by jumping from a hotel window. Frank "The Harlem Coffee Cooler" Craig hailed from New York City and fought as a middleweight around 1900. Sim Thompkins adopted the nickname "Young Peter Jackson" and was a Baltimore-based welterweight during the Joe Gans era. Charles Henry "Jack" Blackburn was known as "The Philadelphia Comet" and mixed it up with Sam Langford and Gans several times. Blackburn became best known as Joe Louis' trainer after spending some prison time for a shooting.

Sam Langford was one of the best of his time and could have been world middleweight champion. He was born in Nova Scotia, Canada, on March 4, 1886, and fought in more different weight classes than anyone else. Though only 5'6" his weight varied between 150 and 190 pounds. Be-

cause black fighters had such difficulty booking bouts against whites, he fought other blacks over and over: Joe Jeanette eighteen times, Sam McVey fifteen times, Jim Barry twelve times, Jack Johnson once. It was strongly rumored that Jack Johnson reneged on an oral promise to fight him when he became heavyweight champion. Langford and others like him before World War I had to endure discriminatory treatment not meted out to other ethnic groups.

Gans' death closed out the second era of the African-American boxer that had begun with the Tom Cribb–William Richmond fight in 1805. Authorities allowed blacks to contest for world titles in all weight classes but the heavyweight division before 1908. Gans and his contemporaries—George Dixon, Joe Walcott, Peter Jackson, Bobby Dobbs, and many others—proved to all that blacks could garner their share of honors if given the chance. It was well into the first decade of the century before the first black heavyweight challenger for the world crown could prove his worth. And the sport has not been the same since then.

John Arthur Johnson

Athletes from myriad sports acquired monikers or nicknames that enlivened their marquee value and described some obvious talent or celebrated their hometown. Not so with John Arthur Johnson, who was born in Galveston, Texas, on March 31, 1878. He was known simply as "L'il Arthur" as a boy and Jack Johnson as a man. History invested him with the opportunity to batter down the last serious barrier to blacks in sports.

Starting with John L. Sullivan and ending with Jim Jeffries on his retirement in 1905, white world heavyweight champions cooperated with boxing officials to maintain it as a bastion of white supremacy. Looking back on what motives could have driven them to take this approach, it seems contradictory to at once deny the black man the chance to prove himself while espousing the notion that he was innately a coward. Surely a coward would have been no competition against a world champion. The most plausible answer was the general feeling throughout the nation around 1900 that blacks were socially, physically, and mentally inferior to whites, even divinely ordained so.

Major league baseball had barred blacks since 1885. The jockeys had been denied their license renewals. Marshall Taylor was literally run off some of the velodromes. College football teams had quotas for blacks. Black tennis players were not acceptable on the grass courts of Newport, Rhode Island. In this supportive atmosphere, it was palpably easy for white heavyweight champions to draw the color line and not be accused of ducking a likely black contender. For white America truly believed then that no black man had a chance anyway, though some sports writers had their doubts.

Johnson came from a family of three boys and three girls and was a favored child. His mother, Tina, and sister Lucy were especially fond of him. His father was much more strict, insisting that he work alongside him at his janitorial duties. After finishing the fifth grade, Johnson quit school and embarked on a string of jobs that took him far beyond Galveston. He worked on a milk wagon for $1.25 per week; in Gregory's Livery Stables; as a baker's apprentice. At thirteen he tried to run away from Galveston as a stowaway aboard a moving freight train, only to find out later that the train had just shifted around in the yard itself.

He heard about Steve Brodie, the man who jumped off the Brooklyn Bridge and lived to tell about it, and yearned to meet him. Johnson finally did meet Brodie after smuggling himself onto a steamship. When caught, he had to work as a cook's helper to pay for his trip. But the ill treatment he received at the hands of whites in many occupations left a vein of resentment and repressed anger and frustration in him. Later, as one of his biographers, Finis Farr, noted, "He could make people angry by the expression on his face."[12]

From New York his wanderlust took him to Boston, where his leg was broken by a horse while he was working at the racetrack. He was still only fifteen. Homesick, he headed back to Galveston for a job on the docks as a stevedore. There he had to fight just to keep his place. After taking a few lickings, his sister Lucy shamed him into defending himself, and he eventually prevailed against the bully of the wharf.

At sixteen he headed for Dallas, where his boss in a carriage shop, Walter Lewis, happened to be an ex-boxer. Offered free lessons, Johnson took them and tested his new skills against Bob Thompson, who traveled as part of a troupe of boxers. Although he took a licking for the required four rounds, he collected twenty-five dollars for his time and decided fighting was more profitable than building buggies. From 1895 through 1897 he traveled and boxed for a living. He even suffered the indignity of battles royal and spent some time as Joe Walcott's sparring partner.

Back home in Galveston in 1897, he married Mary Austin, a black woman, and had his first serious bout against Joe Choynsky, a noted Polish-Jewish heavyweight, on February 25, 1901. He was KO'd in three rounds. Both fighters spent three weeks in jail since boxing was illegal in Texas. Johnson, however, used his time incarcerated wisely, taking more lessons from Choynsky. It would not be his last time in jail.

Johnson and Austin were divorced in 1902. He took up with Clara Kerr, another black woman. By then a determined fighter, he signed on with Frank Corella as his manager, who arranged vaudeville appearances as well. It was quite common for black boxers to augment their ring earnings with theatrical exhibitions when traveling across the country. Johnson's stint included a harmonica solo, a bass fiddle routine, a dance routine, and the wide smile of his that bared a bright golden tooth.

In the ring Johnson was acclaimed the best black boxer alive on February 3, 1903, when he defeated "Denver" Ed Martin for the Negro heavyweight crown. The average white fight fan, however, knew very little of these affairs. In 1903 and 1904, for instance, all his opponents were black. Few whites desiring a shot at the world title would bother boxing a noted black heavyweight, for they had everything to lose. If they won, the public would say, "So what." If they lost, the public would say, "You must not be very good to lose to a black fighter."

Black heavyweights of the period tended to be older than their white counterparts. First, it took longer for them to establish their reputations. Second, a good young fighter without early backing or promotion usually quit and learned a trade. Third, they had to have white managers to book their bouts, and these managers were willing to take on only proven properties. Fourth, some of them were part-timers. And fifth, many of them had committed themselves to boxing before Sullivan and company began drawing the color line.

In 1903 world champion Jim Jeffries echoed the old Sullivan line by declaring, "I will not fight a negro! If the public demands that I should fight Johnson I will surely have to decline. If Johnson wants to fight for the championship he will have to fight somebody besides me. If I am defeated, the championship will go to a white man, for I will not fight a colored man. Now mind, I am not shrinking from this match because I am afraid of Johnson, for I think I could lick him as I have the rest."[13] Jeffries was not maligned for thinking this way. It looked hopeless for any black heavyweight to dream of fighting for the world title at the end of 1903.

The following year Johnson started to publicly question Jeffries's abilities, which Johnson claimed were hidden behind "the color line." It was the image of the uppity black man challenging the strongest white man in the world to a fight. But Jeffries would not be budged. He retired in May 1905, citing a lack of competition—white competition, that is. Johnson then turned his attention to Marvin Hart, the new world titleholder, though he had lost to Hart four months before Hart became champion. He also lost on a second-round foul to Joe Jeanette, a black heavyweight.

Hart then lost to the Canadian Tommy Burns, so Johnson again readjusted his aim. But the retired Jeffries was still on his mind. Burns, like the other champions before him, drew the color line, although his reputation was not nearly as dynamic. He stood 5′ 7″ and weighed only 175 pounds. Johnson had to establish a record that was uncontestable. He was undefeated in 1906 and 1907.

One of his wins was over Bob Fitzsimmons, the former world champion. Johnson was thus the first black man to score a victory over a world heavyweight champion. Meanwhile, his new manager Sam Fitzpatrick sought every means possible to arrange a date with Burns. Burns kept refusing, so Fitzpatrick and Johnson decided to literally chase Burns wherever he went. Burns made plans to go to Australia, so Johnson got there ahead of time. When Burns found out that Johnson was already in Australia, he stayed in the United States.

Several newspapers—including the St. Louis *Post-Dispatch* and the New York *Sun*—now demanded Burns defend himself and his title against Johnson. Another former world champion, James Corbett, said, "Tommy Burns would lick Jack Johnson if they ever came together."[14] From England, Burns had to say something, so he boasted that "I'll take care of Johnson when I return to the United States."[15] Johnson, though, had no intention of letting Burns return to the United States before fighting him.

London's National Sporting Club wanted to stage the fight, and Johnson and Fitzpatrick went there to open discussions. But Johnson was made to wait out on the sidewalk while Fitzpatrick was ushered inside. Johnson was furious but Burns mooted the discussions when he departed for France. Johnson followed. Burns then departed for Australia; Johnson followed after hearing King Edward VII refer to Burns as a Yankee bluffer—which must have been doubly damning since Burns was a Canadian, not an American.

Finally Burns could run no more, and he agreed to meet his black challenger. Actually, if some wise and clairvoyant seer had been asked to name the most logical place for the first world heavyweight title bout between a white and a black boxer, Australia would have been it. Still largely unexplored and underpopulated and possessing a rugged frontier spirit, the Aussies were quite hospitable to black athletes. Peter Jackson had been popular there, and so was cyclist Marshall Taylor.

The fight date was set for December 26, 1908, with a purse of $40,000, split $35,000 for Burns and $5,000 for Johnson. Hugh "Huge Deal" McIntosh was the promoter of this bout at Rushcutter's Bay in Sydney. Before the fight Burns said to a New York *World* reporter, "I will bet a few plunks that the colored man will not make good! I'll fight him and whip him, as sure as my name is Tommy Burns."[16] Burns still believed that black fighters were basically cowards.

Johnson was more measured in his response. "Burns has embedded in his brain the belief that I have a yellow streak, that I am not game....I am here to assure the sporting patrons of Australia that nothing like that will happen. I have not lost heart."[17] Johnson even opened his training to the public and delighted some startled reporters when he bet a friend that he could outrun a kangaroo and did so. By his own admission he did lots of road work but comparatively little boxing, giving my attention to ball and bag punching."[18] Still, just before round one Burns was a 3-to-2 favorite.

Twenty-six thousand fans, reporters, sportswriters, and local notables and two women attended the fight. Johnson, thirty, and Burns, twenty-seven, weighed 195 and 180 pounds, respectively, although Johnson was almost six inches taller at 6' 1¾". The opening bell sounded at 11:15 A.M., and Johnson immediately began berating his opponent, "Who told you I was yellow? You're white Tommy—white as the flag of surrender!"[19] And down went Burns from a right uppercut.

After the first round, bettors started hedging their wagers. Following round two the odds were even. By the eighth round Burns' eyes were almost closed, and he was bleeding from the mouth. No mouthpieces were worn in those days. Johnson talked constantly, inviting Burns to approach and take his best shot. After the thirteenth round, McIntosh consulted with police about stopping the fight. But Burns' aides said he would fight on. In the fourteenth round Burns was staggered twice by rights to the head and combinations. The police finally called a halt, and John Arthur Johnson, a descendant of the Koromantee tribe of West Africa, was the new world heavyweight champion.

While the *Washington Post*'s J. Ed Grillo reported Johnson's victory as a popular one, Johnson himself was frank and forthright: "I never doubted the issue from the beginning. I knew I was too good for Burns. I have forgotten more about fighting than Burns ever knew."[20]

Tommy Burns was also honest. He said, "Race prejudice was rampant in my mind. The idea of a black man challenging me was beyond enduring. Hatred made me tense."[21] Johnson had startled Burns and Fitzpatrick before the fight by asking Burns if he and McIntosh were good friends. When Burns replied that "there are none better,"[22] Johnson insisted McIntosh referee the match. Fitzpatrick gulped, but Johnson held his ground. Johnson wanted to make sure there would be no problems afterward on this matter.

Two other ringside commentators made noteworthy pronouncements. One was former heavyweight champion John L. Sullivan, a guest columnist for the *New York Times*. He cynically said that "the negro can't assume that title [heavyweight champion]....I can't see where Johnson will be given a high position in the general public."[23]

The other commentator wrote one of the most famous passages ever penned in sports. He was author Jack London, of *Call Of The Wild* fame. London must have felt sorely piqued at Johnson's victory because his tone was emotional yet conciliatory. He wrote, "The fight!—There was no fight!...It had all the seeming of a playful Ethiopian at loggerheads with a small white man—of a grown man cuffing a naughty child....But one thing now remains. Jim Jeffries must emerge from his alfalfa farm and remove the golden smile from Jack Johnson's face. Jeff, it's up to you!"[24]

So Jim Jeffries became the "Great White Hope" to save his race. But he was four and a half years retired and overweight. Johnson had his own troubles. Following his breakup with Clara Kerr, he had forsworn black women, thinking they could not be trusted. In her place came Belle Schrieber, a white woman. In Australia, however, he was accompanied by Hattie McClay, whom the Aussie press referred to as "that New York Irish girl." Back home in Galveston, the local black community had planned a welcome reception, but they asked Johnson not to bring McClay. Johnson told them to go to hell.

In New York City, blacks had no such southern qualms and welcomed him with a brass band at Grand Central Station. The black press wanted Johnson to defend his title against a black challenger. But he refused, as Jeffries began softening his opposition to a bout. Johnson then fired Fitzpatrick and took on George Little and Sig Hart as his new managers. Sam Berger, Jeffries' manager, thought a Johnson-Jeffries fight was as good as a license to print money.

Jeffries was finally persuaded to come out of retirement, and the two parties met on December 1, 1909, at the Albany Hotel in New York City to work out the largest and richest proposition in sports history. Johnson had to agree to fight in the United States, to limit the bout to from twenty to one hundred rounds, to allow clubs to bid for the site rights, to post—along with Jeffries—a five-thousand-dollar good faith bond, and to allow Jeffries to split the proceeds either sixty-forty or seventy-five-twenty-five as he saw fit.

Six of the world's best-known promoters offered sealed bids with a five-thousand-dollar nonrefundable bid fee. They were Ed Graney, Jack Gleason, Jimmy Coffroth and Tom McCary, Hugh "Huge Deal" McIntosh, and George Lewis "Tex" Rickard. It came down to McCary and Rickard. McCary offered the fighters the entire purse plus $110,000, but they had to sign in twenty-four hours. Rickard then explained his bid of $101,000, including $20,000 immediately, $20,000 sixty days thence, and another $50,000 forty-eight hours before the bout. Jeffries and Johnson asked for twenty-four hours to think about it.

The next day Rickard showed up with $20,000 in solid gold to show he meant business, and he won the bid. But just before they were about to sign, the police intervened and threatened to jail anyone who signed anything because of the Lewis Law, which allowed only club bouts. The group simply got up, took a ferry across the Hudson River to the Naegeli Hotel in Hoboken, New Jersey, and signed the papers. After considering Salt Lake City, San Francisco was chosen as the site for July 4, 1910. This proposal constituted the largest legitimate business deal ever consummated by an African-American to that time.

The thirty-four-year old Jeffries began his weight-reducing regimen in Carlsbad, California, and then at the Rowardennan Hotel near San Francisco. Johnson and Duryea went to spend Christmas in London to fulfill vaudeville engagements, and he managed to get into all sorts of trouble.

After being arrested in London twice for "breaking furniture" and "using foul language," Johnson made his way to San Francisco. The psyching began at once. Jim Corbett, a part of Jeffries' camp, said "Take it from me, the black boy has a yellow streak, and Jeff will bring it out when he gets him into the ring."[25] The February 5, 1910, *Chicago Defender*, a black paper, said,

"The Future Welfare of His People Forms a Part of the Stake."

Problems then came in bunches. On March 24 Johnson was jailed in New York City's Tombs prison for roughing up another black man, Norman Pinder. He then fired George Little, one of his managers. On June 15 the Governor of California, James C. Gillette, bowed to pressure from religious groups and canceled California as the venue. Fortunately Rickard had a friend in Nevada Governor Denver Dickerson, who agreed to Reno as a site. Once the materials were in place the arena was built in three days.

Jeffries began getting nervous. He changed the money split to sixty-forty, although he had a confirmed offer of $608,000 for a "Grand Tour of Champions" beginning July 8—if he won. Johnson was offered no such tour. Upon arriving in Reno, Jeffries made the following statement: "When the gloves are knotted on my hands, and I stand ready to defend what is really my title, it will be at the request of the public, which forced me out of retirement. I realize full well what depends on me, and I am not going to disappoint the public. That portion of the white race that has been looking to me to defend its athletic superiority may feel assured that I am fit to do my very best. If Johnson defeats me, I will shake his hand and declare him the greatest fighter the world has ever known."[26] It was an extraordinarily racist statement from a man who hadn't fought in five years.

Johnson's entourage included Billy Delaney, his trainer and former trainer for both Jeffries and Corbett; Tom Flannigan; "Professor" Burns; Sig Hart; Barney "Doc" Furey; George "Kid" Cotton; Dave Mills;

Stanley Ketchel, the former world middleweight champion; and Frank Sutton. In his prefight comments he said, "Every fighter on the eve of his fight declares that he hopes the best man wins.... if Mr. Jeffries knocks me out or gains a decision over me, I will go into his corner and congratulate him as soon as I am able.... I mean it...I will proclaim Mr. Jeffries king of them all."[27] The world's press was sending out over a million words a day from Reno just before the bout. Thirty thousand people showed up for a place in an arena that held only eighteen thousand.

Official ticket prices ranged from ten to fifty dollars, and there were few scalpers. Curiously, two black boxers, Bob Armstrong and Sam Langford, joined the Jeffries camp. Langford was surely jealous and wanted a bit of revenge from Johnson for reneging on an agreement to fight him after becoming champion.

John L. Sullivan was once again a *New York Times* guest columnist but was afraid to say publicly beforehand that he thought Johnson would win. Joe Choynsky and Tommy Burns opted for Jeffries. Battling Nelson picked Johnson. On Saturday, July 2, Rickard duly paid the $101,000 to former New York Congressman Tim Sullivan for safekeeping. The fighters were ready and the war of words was over.

Writer Norman Mailer once penned a book about a bout between Muhammad Ali and Joe Frazier called *The Fight*. But that fight did not even closely approximate the Johnson-Jeffries bout in overall athletic, social, and racial importance. The morning of July 4 was a clear, powder blue. For breakfast Johnson had four lamb cutlets, three scrambled eggs, and several slices of steak. Jeffries had fruit, toast, and tea. They agreed to dispense with the traditional pre-fight handshake—an obvious insult to Johnson, which he calmly ignored.

Johnson entered the ring wearing a floor-length robe with velvet lining; Jeffries wore street clothes minus a shirt. Johnson bowed to all four sides of the ring. When asked to call a flip of a coin to see who would get the shady corner looking away from the sun, Johnson interrupted and told Jeffries he could take any corner he desired. Jeffries chose the shady side. When they doffed their outer garments, Jeffries was wearing purple trunks; Johnson wore navy blue trunks with an American flag draped through the belt loops. Jeffries was attempting the near impossible. He had not fought in nearly six years but was unbeaten in twenty-one fights. Still, he was a solid 5-to-3 favorite.

The fight began one hour late, at three o'clock. A serious Johnson easily won the first two rounds as Jeffries clinched at every opportunity. In round four Jack suffered a cut lip from an uppercut as both fighters talked incessantly. Rickard reminded them that this "was a fight not a talkfest."[28] At the end of the fifth round most experts believed Jeffries had little chance. His punches had no crispness and were off target and generally ineffective, and he was tiring.

Johnson taunted not only Jeffries but his backers at ringside as well. To Sullivan he said while clinching, "John, I thought this fellow could hit."[29] To Corbett at the end of the seventh round, he bellowed over Jeffries' shoulder, "Too late now to do anything, Jim; your man's all in."[30] The ninth and tenth rounds were all Johnson as he did his heaviest damage with uppercuts. (In those days fighters did not wear mouthpieces.) In the eleventh Jeffries was spitting blood and hugged at every opportunity.

Jeffries knew that if he fell at the feet of a black man it would symbolize the failure of the white race. The myth of the natural superiority of the white man over the black man had brought Jeffries out of retirement in the first place, and now he was paying the price. In round thirteen Jeffries was a pitiful sight as Johnson allowed Jeffries to hit him at will while laughing at the feeble attempts.

The end came at two minutes twenty-five seconds into the fifteenth round. A left uppercut sent Jeffries down on both knees near the west side of the ring. The referee counted. Jeffries rested one foot on the canvas and was up at the count of nine. Johnson hit him with a left at point-blank range "full on the face," which sent him through the ropes. Again Jeffries came back to be met with a right to the ear. Corbett cried out, "Oh don't Jack; don't hit him!"[31] Johnson ignored him and sent another left home. Jeffries sank to the floor sideways.

Rickard counted again. Eight seconds later Jeffries' seconds rushed into the ring—in clear violation of the rules—to help him. Delaney broke through and demanded that Rickard give the fight to Johnson. Delaney did not realize that Jeffries' camp was throwing in the towel. John Arthur Johnson was now the undisputed world heavyweight champion.

Johnson was uncompromising in his postfight comments. "I won from Mr. Jeffries because I outclassed him in every department....I was certain I would be the victor. I never changed my mind at any time....I believe we both fought fairly....He joked me and I joked him. I told him I knew he was a bear but I was a gorilla and would defeat him."[32]

From Jeffries: "I lost my fight... because I did not have the snap of youth.... I believed in my own heart that all the old-time dash was there. ... It simply was not there and that's all there is to it.... I guess it's my own fault....They started calling for me and mentioning me as 'the white man's hope.' I guess my pride got the better of my judgement."[33] Later Jeffries admitted that "I never could have whipped Johnson at my best. I couldn't have hit him."[34]

The fighters cleaned up financially. Johnson got $110,600—$50,000 for the movie rights and $60,600 as his share of the proceeds. Jeffries got $90,400—$50,000 for the movie rights and $40,400 as his share. There was no federal or state income tax at all. Forty years later, Jeffries still regretted his comeback attempt. He died a wealthy man at seventy-seven.

While the crowds dispersed peacefully in Reno, there was pandemonium and bloodshed elsewhere over Johnson's unpopular victory. Page four of the July 5 *New York Times* read like a police precinct bulletin board: "THREE KILLED IN VIDALIA [Georgia] ... OMAHA NEGRO KILLED ... TWO NEGROES SLAIN ... BLACKS SHOOT UP TOWN ... HOUSTON MAN KILLS NEGRO ... NEGRO SHOOTS WHITE MAN ... NEGRO HURT IN PHILADELPHIA ... OUTBREAKS IN NEW ORLEANS ... POLICE CLUB RIOTING NEGROES ... MOB BEATS NEGROES IN MACON [Georgia] ... 70 ARRESTED IN BALTIMORE ... ALMOST LYNCH NEGRO." In all, thirteen blacks were killed and hundreds were wounded as angry whites retaliated over the loss of their Great White Hope.

White town councils in Washington, D.C., Atlanta, Baltimore, St. Louis, Cincinnati, and other cities banned films of the fight. Congress passed a quickie law banning the distribution of the films across state lines for commercial purposes. One can only wonder what the reaction would have been had Jeffries won. As Talladega College Professor Wil Pickens wrote in the July 29, 1910, *Chicago Defender*, "[I]f Jeffries had won the fight, it would have aroused no resentment in the Negro race against the white race. The Negroes would have forgotten it in about fifteen minutes."

Travels and Travails

Johnson did not enjoy a period of idolatry or social acceptance. Whites considered him too uppity, mainly because he had a white wife. So he headed for Europe and some vaudeville engagements managed by his nephew Gus Rhodes. He did not fight at all in 1911. He married Etta Duryea and opened his own saloon called Café de Champion at 42 West Thirty-first Street in Chicago, which featured famous black chanteuse Bricktop. He just refused to change his lifestyle. He had one fight in 1912, a ninth-round KO over Jim Flynn.

On September 11, 1912, Etta committed suicide by shooting herself. A month later Johnson himself was shot in the foot by one of his musicians over another white woman, Lucille Cameron, who later became his secretary. Cameron's mother threatened to charge Johnson with abduction. Cameron was held in late October for questioning under the Mann Act, which made it a crime to transport anyone across state lines for immoral purposes. On November 1, 1912, his café's liquor license was revoked. On November 7, Johnson was formally indicted by a grand jury of violating the Mann Act. (The presiding judge, of all people, was Kennesaw Mountain Landis, who would be singularly responsible for keeping blacks out of major league baseball when he became the commissioner.) But the person in question was not Cameron; it was Belle Schrieber, who had agreed to serve as a government witness. White America meant to punish Johnson one way or another.

Said Charles Erberstein, Schrieber's lawyer, "Jack Johnson has insulted every white woman in the United States."[35] Booker T. Washington was even asked to give a statement. He replied through his secretary, Emmett J. Scott, "Jack Johnson's case will be settled in due time in the courts....this is another illustration of the most irreparable injury that a wrong action on the part of a single individual may do to a whole race. It shows the folly of those who think that they alone will be held responsible for the evil that they do....No one can do so much injury to the Negro race as the Negro himself....I do not believe it is necessary for me to say that the honest, sober elements of the Negro people of the United States is severe in condemnation of the kind of immorality which Jack Johnson is at present charged....I do not mean to, as I said at the beginning, say how far Jack Johnson is or is not guilty of the charges."[36]

Johnson was handcuffed, jailed, and released on bail of $32,000 in collateral property. His indictment listed eleven counts: three counts of prostitution; two counts of debauchery; three counts of unlawful sexual intercourse; two counts of crimes against nature; and one count of inducement to prostitution. Schrieber must have been quite graphic in her evidence. Johnson married the eighteen-year-old Cameron eight days after her release on November 25. But at his trial on May 13, 1913, the jury returned a guilty verdict after deliberating only one hour and forty-five minutes. On June 4 he was sentenced to a year and a day and was fined a thousand dollars by Judge George Carpenter.

To evade jail for these ridiculous charges, Johnson hatched an escape worthy of a John Le Carré novel. He sent his wife to Toronto and arranged a swap with Andrew "Rube" Foster, the black owner of the Chicago American Giants baseball team. (Both Foster and Johnson were big, dark-complexioned, and bald-headed.) Disguised as a member of Foster's squad, Johnson slipped by American authorities in Hamilton, Ontario, on a train that left from Chicago's Englewood Station. Johnson got Foster to agree to switch the train's route to Buffalo through Canada, although Foster never knew about Johnson's escape plans.

When the train got to Hamilton, Johnson and his nephew off-loaded. They were met by his former manager, Tom Flanagan, who drove them to Toronto to meet his wife. Johnson, his wife, and his nephew left Canada on June 29, 1913, aboard the steamer *Corinthian*. Although he did not know it at the time, he would remain outside the United States just three weeks short of seven years—all because of the racism in his native country.

Johnson Loses His Title

His European theatrical engagements were
canceled. In Paris he wound up fighting Jim
Johnson, a black boxer, in his only serious
bout of 1913. This was the first world heavyweight title fight between two black
fighters. Johnson broke his arm in this ten-
round draw. He was not paid for fighting
Frank Moran the following year because
World War I broke out the next day, June 28,
1914. On to Russia where, after meeting
Rasputin, he was asked to leave. Back to
Paris, where he was unwelcome. So he
headed for England. They asked him to
leave. He was, for a time, a man without a
country.

Back home, the black press kept up
with him. In the August issue of *Crisis*, the
official organ of the National Association
for the Advancement of Colored People
(NAACP), the esteemed W.E.B. DuBois offered this assessment: "Some pretend to
object to Mr. Johnson's character. But we
have yet to hear, in the case of white
America, that marital troubles have disqualified prizefighters or ball players or
even statesmen. It comes down then, after
all, to this unforgiveable blackness. Where-
fore we conclude that at present prizefight-
ing is very, very immoral, and that we must
rely on football and war for pastimes until
Mr. Johnson retires or permits himself to be
'knocked out.'" Immoral or not, the average
black man in the street was still very much
a Johnson fan.

To help Johnson—supposedly—Jack
Curley proposed to Johnson in late 1914
that he fight Jess Willard, a 6'6", 250-pound
giant. Curley intimated that if Johnson accepted his thirty-thousand-dollar offer, he
might be able to return home to see his
mother without a jail sentence. Unfortunately, Curley's partner, Tom Jones, was
Willard's manager. Johnson agreed, and
after being turned down by Pancho Villa in
Mexico, he persuaded the president of
Cuba, General Mario Menocal, to agree to
stage the fight at the Oriental Racetrack in
Havana.

Johnson and Willard met on April 5,
1915, in front of thirty-two thousand fans,
for which the fighters were paid thirty thousand and ten thousand dollars, respectively. Willard, from Pottawatomie County,
Kansas, brought an 18-to-3-to-1 record into
the ring. He had never so much as donned
a pair of gloves until he was twenty-four.
Johnson was then thirty-seven years old.

Johnson won the first four rounds,
laughing at his clumsy opponent's efforts.
The crowd, which contained the largest
group of blacks ever to watch a title fight,
was for Johnson. Round eight was Willard's
best, but nothing of consequence happened for another seventeen rounds. The
twenty-sixth round, though, was one of the
most analyzed in all of boxing history.

Johnson was way ahead on points.
Willard shot a left jab to Johnson's face and
then a right to the stomach. After a clinch,
referee Jack Welch ordered a "break," and
then Willard rushed and scored with a left
to the body. Another jab at Johnson's head,
and he was no longer the heavyweight
champion. He was counted out with his
knees bent in the air and his hands shading
his eyes from the sun. After the count of
ten, he was up immediately and left the
ring.

It appeared that Johnson "threw" the
fight in the twenty-sixth round. During that

last clinch Johnson supposedly looked over Willard's shoulder and signaled to his wife to leave with Curley. The thirty thousand dollars due him was not paid in full before the bout, and as the story goes, the rest was paid during the last round. In his autobiography he wrote of an "additional percentage which Willard's manager (Curley's partner) owed me if I lived up to my agreement to lie down."[37] Most boxing historians believe Johnson did indeed tank the bout—a disgraceful performance from a world champion in any sport. Historians are also in agreement that Johnson won every round except possibly the twenty-fifth.

Johnson probably lied to reporters afterward, saying, "Willard was too much for me. I just didn't have it."[38] Nat Fleischer said he had Johnson's affidavit in a safe in his office, in which he "declares he faked the knockout according to arrangement with Curley."[39] Finis Farr thought that "Jack's tale of being advised to throw the fight to Willard was fantasy."[40] In any event he lost, and a riot followed at the racetrack. To worsen matters, Willard announced two days later that he, too, would thereafter draw the color line.

Prison and the End

Curley was not able to secure a jailproof return to the United States for Johnson. Johnson returned to England, where he was fined 1,075 pounds for punching a theater owner in the eye over the rental of the fight films. He was expelled in January 1916 and went to Spain for three years, where he fought bulls and played in a movie, *False*

Nobility. His mother died in 1917, and he pined over her loss.

He then headed for Mexico again and tried to make a go of it as a wrestler, bullfighter, and boxer. He was even accused at one point by American authorities of spreading social equality propaganda among blacks down there. Finally, Johnson convinced himself that he could run no more. A Chicago politician, Tom Cary, persuaded him to give himself up.

So on July 20, 1920—six years, eleven months, and ten days after leaving—Johnson surrendered to U.S. authorities in San Diego, California. At Leavenworth Prison, he served only eight months of his original sentence because of good behavior. (The warden there was his old friend Denver Dickerson, the ex-Governor of Nevada.) He was even made the prison's physical director. He was released on July 9, 1921, after delivering an inspirational address to the inmates.

Back in Chicago he was accorded a warm welcome, and he made speeches for a living on various subjects. In 1924 he even spoke at a Ku Klux Klan rally in Danville, Illinois. In 1925 he was divorced from Lucille Cameron and married Irene Marie Pineau, his fourth wife and third white wife.

He was the most dominant force in all of boxing for the first twenty years of this century. Nearly every nonpartisan expert agrees that had he not been forced into exile, he would have had as fine a record as Joe Louis. That he was hounded for his choice in women was, on the one hand, unfortunate for him but, on the other hand, more a testament to the miscarriages of America's ideals of equality, fair play, and justice.

John Arthur Johnson died in a car accident on June 10, 1946, near Raleigh, North Carolina. He was, in this author's opinion, the most significant black athlete in history.

Notes

1. Chalk Monograph, p. 23.
2. Frederick Douglass, op. cit., p. 145.
3. Ibid., p. 148.
4. Nat Fleischer, *Black Dynamite*. vol. 3., p. 6.
5. Ibid., p. 45.
6. Ibid., p. 121.
7. Ibid., p. 235.
8. Ibid., vol. 1., p. 139.
9. Chalk, *Pioneers in Black Sport*, p. 142.
10. Durham and Jones, op. cit., p. 111–12.
11. Fleischer, op. cit., vol. 3, p.131.
12. Finis Farr, p. 39.
13. Chalk, op. cit., p. 240.
14. Quoted in Farr, op. cit., p. 49.
15. Ibid.
16. Quoted in ibid., p. 56.
17. Quoted in ibid., p. 58.
18. Jack Johnson, *In the Ring and Out.*
(Chicago: National Sports Publishing, 1927), p. 160.
19. *The New York Times*, December 27, 1908.
20. Ibid.
21. Farr, op. cit., p. 61.
22. Johnson, op. cit., p. 164.
23. *The New York Times*, op. cit.
24. Quoted in Farr, op. cit., p. 61.
25. Quoted in Farr, op. cit., p. 82.
26. Quoted in ibid., p. 107.
27. Quoted in ibid., p. 107.
28. *The New York Times*, July 5, 1910.
29. Quoted in ibid.
30. Quoted in ibid.
31. Quoted in ibid.
32. Quoted in ibid.
33. Quoted in ibid.
34. Quoted in Farr, op. cit., p. 119.
35. Quoted in Chalk, op. cit., p. 154.
36. Telegram from the Tuskegee Institute, October 23, 1912.
37. Jack Johnson, *Johnson Is a Dandy*, p. 199.
38. Quoted in Farr, op. cit., p. 204.
39. Fleischer, op. cit., vol. 4, p. 116.
40. Farr, op. cit., p. 199.

CHAPTER 2

1919–1945

Jack Johnson's Legacy

America's boxing authorities after the First World War believed they had rid themselves of blacks as contenders for the heavyweight title. Jack Johnson had lost his world heavyweight title to Jess Willard while in exile in 1915. Noted black heavyweights like Joe Jeanette, Sam Langford, Sam McVey, et al., were getting old or, at best, not worthy of title contention—so authorities thought. There was no longer a need for a "white hope."

William Henry "Jack" Dempsey stepped up in the racially torn summer of 1919 and won the world heavyweight crown from Willard on July 4. He followed his victory with only two defenses in 1920. He also let it be known that he would draw the color line and refuse to fight blacks. Such was the bitter taste that Jack Johnson's flamboyance and flouting of social convention left in the mouths of white America. In his wake, other black heavyweights paid a heavy price for his iconoclasm.

The first to suffer was Harry Wills, born on May 15, 1892, in New Orleans. Like Jack Johnson before him, Wills was a stevedore and stood a massive six feet two inches and weighed 220 pounds. Because

he had refused to fight the same blacks over and over, he spent much of his time before the war in Panama, where race was not so large a factor. He returned to the United States and on July 26, 1920, he became the legal number one contender for Dempsey when he scored a third-round knockout over Fred Fulton at New York City's First Regiment Armory. Dempsey himself was present to see Wills' victory.

Knowing of Dempsey's prior decision to decline fights with blacks, Paddy Mullins, Wills' manager, decided to stick to his long-range plans for a title shot. He would have Wills fight Dempsey or no one else. Mullins knew the law was on his side. Boxing had been legalized once again in New York State in 1920, because of lobbying by such influential groups as the American Legion. It was difficult to say "no" to such a publicly patriotic group. But when Dempsey refused to fight, Mullins was forced to book fights wherever he could find them—including Cuba. Wills even became the Colored heavyweight champion in 1922 when he defeated Bill Tate.

Finally, so the story goes, Wills was signed by George Lewis "Tex" Rickard, the major domo of boxing promoters, to fight Dempsey in 1923, but Rickard reneged. A year later, James Farley, the chairman of the New York State Athletic Commission, ordered Dempsey to select Wills as his next opponent but Rickard refused to promote it, claiming that "higher ups" in Albany (the state capital) instructed him to leave it alone.

Some believed Rickard, who controlled the sport at Madison Square Garden, was afraid Dempsey might lose. But Nat Fleischer wrote that Rickard had no choice. "There was nothing personal in the denial to Wills of a chance to battle for the heavyweight championship."[1] Rickard was doing what his political superiors told him to do, according to Fleischer. However, the October 5, 1918, *New York Age*, a black newspaper that followed Wills's fortunes closely, had quoted Dempsey's manager, Jack Kearns, as saying, "I never was in favor of mixed bouts...Willard squelched the Colored heavyweight division when he squelched Jack Johnson in Cuba. Why resurrect it again?" That certainly sounded like Kearns too meant to keep blacks out of title contention. Still Rickard announced on May 1, 1924, that Wills and Dempsey would fight on September 6 of that year, but it never came to pass.

Wills and Mullins sat through two years of frustration and were finally offered a bout with a white contender, Gene Tunney, to "clear up" the matter. Mullins, according to Fleischer, screamed, "NO!" It would be "Dempsey or nobody."[2] Wills was then told by Rickard that if he refused to fight Tunney he would forfeit his title chances. Mullins' demands to Farley went unheeded. Rickard then staged the first million-dollar fight in history between Dempsey and Tunney—in Philadelphia. This

bout went to the City of Brotherly Love because Dempsey was legally bound in New York State to fight Wills. Wills' demise was one of the most blatantly discriminatory maneuvers in sports history.

Wills was reportedly paid $50,000 for his forfeit, but the Dempsey–Tunney bout grossed $1,895,733; the richest ever. Wills ended 1926 with a loss to Jack Sharkey at Ebbetts Field in Brooklyn and later fought a twelve-round no-decision bout against Louis Firpo at Boyle's Thirty Acres in Jersey City, New Jersey. Nicknamed "the Brown panther," Wills fought Sam Langford fourteen times, Sam McVey four times, and Joe Jeanette twice. He did, however, retire financially secure with major holdings in several Harlem apartment buildings.

In the lower weight classes after the war, opposition to advancement was not nearly as severe. Louis "Battling Siki" Phal of Senegal became the first black holder of the world light-heavyweight title in 1922, but three years later, on December 15, 1925, he died of gunshot wounds in the back. On August 19, 1926, Theodore "Tiger" Flowers, better known as "the Georgia Deacon" because he was constantly seen reading Bible verses, won the world middleweight title over Harry Greb at Madison Square Garden. This first-ever middleweight crown for a native-born black American drew a gate of $101,134.70, and a crowd of 16,311. But in a freakish accident, Flowers died following a routine eye operation on November 11, 1927.

It was during this era of the festive 1920s, and the literary flowering of the Harlem Renaissance, that some blacks began attending the fights at Madison Square Garden in their finest sartorial splendor.

Madison Square Garden was relatively new and after the bouts, hordes of fans—black and white—headed "uptown" to Harlem seeking fun and cabaret entertainment. New York was *the* sports capital of America and the modern Madison Square Garden was the most famous indoor arena extant. Yankee Stadium was the most well-known outdoor sports palace.

There was still a dark side to the boxing business and that remained the ever-present influence of organized crime and their betting schemes and parlors. George Godfrey (a.k.a. Feabe Smith Williams), the black heavyweight, was forced to "throw" a fight against the Italian, Primo Carnera, on June 23, 1930. While everyone knew that Carnera's life was controlled by underworld figures, timely hints to other fighters worked just as well. As Nat Fleischer noted, "Carnera's fight with Godfrey was fixed for the former to win."[3]

Other blacks who sought glory in the ring in this era include, among others, Joe Johnson and Bruce Flowers in the lightweight division, Jack McVey and Lee Anderson in the middleweight class, Buddy Sanders among the welterweights, and Ace Clark and Black Bill in the heavyweight division. Some who fought in several weight classes were Jack Thompson, Larry Johnson, John Lester Johnson, Kid Norfolk, "Baby" Joe Gans, Chick Suggs, Harry Sellers, Larry Gaines, Billy Jones, and Frankie Ansel. All of them laced up their gloves hoping for a way out of their ghetto existence. The best way to start was to first try their luck in the amateur Golden Gloves competitions.

The Golden Gloves, which began in 1923, were staged in the beginning by *Chicago Tribune* sports editor Arch Ward to test Illinois' anti-boxing law. Scheduled for a three-night run, it was so popular that it had to be held over because 424 boxers showed up to register. Groups such as the National Reform Association tried to stop the tournament but a court injunction kept them at bay. In 1926, boxing was legalized in Illinois. Not to be outdone in New York City, the *Daily News* began a New York version in 1927. A year later, the *Tribune* invited boxers from a wider area of the Midwest than just Chicago and thus was born The Golden Gloves Tournament of Champions, which debuted on March 24, 1928.

With successful events in both Chicago and New York, it was only natural that the respective winners meet in a National Tournament of Champions. This format thrived and afforded many young fighters their opportunities for supervision and instruction. Blacks were welcomed from the very beginning and the Golden Gloves became their most important steppingstone to professional success. It also helped to partially remove the sport from the cloistered and unprotected clubs to the public arenas where the light of thoughtful scrutiny prevailed. Its rise occurred just in time, for Tex Rickard died in 1929 during an appendicitis attack, and left the sport floundering as the Great Depression began.

For some black fighters, these hard times were only slightly more discernible than their pre-Depression existence. Two blacks won world titles. Cecil Lewis "Young Jack" Thompson, who was born in San Francisco in 1904, defeated Jackie Fields on May 9, 1930, at The Olympia in Detroit in fifteen rounds to capture the welterweight crown. Thompson weighed in at 142¾

pounds to Fields' 145¾ pounds. He lost his
crown four months later to Tommie Freeman at the Public Hall in Cleveland, Ohio,
and then regained it in twelve rounds from
Freeman at the same place on April 14,
1931. Thompson died prematurely of a
heart attack in 1946 at age forty-two.

The other black world titleholder was
William "Gorilla" Jones, who was born on
May 12, 1906, in Memphis, Tennessee. A
prolific boxer, he once had sixty-two bouts
in a three-year period. Jones won one of
two competing elimination tournaments to
choose a successor to Mickey Walker, who
resigned the middleweight title in early
1931. Jones defeated Tiger Thomas in Milwaukee on August 25, 1931, in ten rounds,
to win the National Boxing Association
(NBA) version of the crown. He lost the title
when he was beaten by the Frenchman
Marcel Thil on a foul in the eleventh round
in Paris on June 11, 1932. Jones finished
with a record of ninety-seven wins, twenty-
three losses, thirteen draws, three no-con-
tests (exhibitions), and five no-decisions
(no verdicts).

However successful the lighter classes
may have been, the heavyweight division
was a mess after Rickard's death. There
were few quality boxers around in that
class and, beginning in 1930, there were
five different winners in as many years. A
new hero was needed; someone who captured the public's imagination like Babe
Ruth in baseball and Red Grange in football. The elements were in place, the time
was propitious, and the Depression
provided an added incentive. Out of the
feeder system of the recently organized
Golden Gloves and Amateur Athletic Union

(AAU) came the savior of the entire sport.
And he was black. His name was Joseph
Louis Barrow.

The Brown Bomber

No era of sporting excellence for blacks
had such an inauspicious beginning as the
one defined by the rise and fall of Joseph
Louis Barrow. Boxing was more affected by
the Depression than most other sports because its very existence depended upon the
thousands of employed, single men who
lived in northern urban areas like New York
City, Chicago, Philadelphia, Detroit, and
Baltimore. With fewer dollars in their
pockets, they were more choosy about
entertainment.

While great numbers of whites found
themselves in similar predicaments, they
could afford to be more optimistic about
the future; they would be first in line if the
economy improved. No such optimism
floated about the black communities of
America. They could only aspire to so
much before hitting an artificial ceiling
placed there by racism. Consequently,
many young blacks sought a quick way out
of their predicaments. The fastest route
seemed to pass through the boxing ring
where, in spite of the Depression, boxers
made more money in less time than in any
legitimate enterprise known to the average
black American. Joe Louis did just that and
became the most famous black man on
earth since Jack Johnson.

Johnson had many detractors; Louis
had no more than a handful. Johnson was
born in the South and migrated northward;

Louis was born on May 13, 1914, in Lafayette, Alabama, and eventually settled in a northern ghetto in Detroit. Johnson had to chase his quarry all over the world to get a chance for the world heavyweight title; Louis could try right here at home. But most important, Johnson took a not-so-secret delight in piquing white America with his white wives; Louis heeded his counsel to avoid even being photographed alone with a white woman.

Joe Louis started out as Joe Barrow to a father, Munro, who was committed to a state hospital for the mentally ill. His mother Lily, hearing that her husband had died, married Patrick Brooks who had eight children of his own. The Barrow-Brooks clan soon moved to Detroit to work in the automobile industry. The poorly educated young Louis was brought face to face with harsh racial and urban realities like ethnic street gangs, flushing toilets, brick school-houses, and trolley cars. Of his prior life, he said, "There didn't seem to be anything bad between whites and blacks in Alabama but you have to remember I was a little boy...I never heard about lynchings; nobody ever called me a nigger until I got to Detroit."[4]

In the matter of education, Louis had more in common with another future champion, Floyd Patterson, who ducked school because he did not want anyone to see him in dirty clothes. At Detroit's Duffield Elementary School, though he was twelve years old, he was placed in the fifth grade, but he never cultivated any special interest in books. Because of his insecurities, he developed a stutter. Patterson avoided school by hiding in subway tunnels all day. At the Bronson Trade School, Louis became a fairly good catcher on the baseball team and a teacher prophetically noted he was "Good in manual training. This boy some day should be able to do something with his hands."[5] Quite an understatement.

In 1931 when he was seventeen, Louis was out of school and working in the Briggs Automobile Factory for a dollar a day. He also hauled ice blocks—as did Jack Johnson—and began taking violin lessons. After being badgered by a friend, Thurston McKinney, to take boxing lessons, he finally gave it a try at the Brewster East Side Gymnasium. With the fifty cents his mother gave him for his violin lessons he rented a locker and borrowed a pair of trunks and some ill-fitting shoes. He never took another violin lesson.

Louis entered a world already traipsed by hundreds of blacks before him. Radio broadcasts of the big fights were in their infancy and the sports sheets catered to fans everywhere. "Jack Dempsey was the one hero that I had when I was a kid," said Louis. "We listened to his fights on the radio. It was always Dempsey does this, Dempsey does that."[6] Louis did not realize that he idolized a man who refused to fight blacks after winning the title.

Atler Ellis arranged for Louis' training and placed him on the Brewster team. He promptly lost his first sanctioned bout to Johnny Miler at the Detroit Athletic Club in the fall of 1932. He remembered that he "...was a badly beaten and bruised boy when I slipped into the house that night. I didn't want anyone to see me, so I ducked upstairs."[7] He had been knocked down seven times and was given a merchandise check for seven dollars.

Though he was by then working for Ford Motor Company and training at the same time, he steadily improved and managed to reach the finals of the 1933 AAU National Light-heavyweight Tournament in Boston. He lost to Max Marek. A year later on May 13, he won this crown in St. Louis. After an amateur career of fifty-four bouts, which included AAU and Golden Gloves titles, he was ready to turn professional.

No matter how good he was, he needed connections with managers and promoters to advance his career. Boxing's reputation in the early 1930s was not the best around and blacks were particularly vulnerable because they placed a higher personal psychic value upon sports than did whites. Consequently, they could be persuaded more easily with less temptation. Louis wanted a black manager but was not sophisticated enough at the beginning to know that that was not enough for a heavyweight. No black boxer had fought for the heavyweight title since Jack Johnson in 1915—almost twenty years before.

In 1933, Louis happened to meet John Roxborough, a black Detroit businessman and a friend of local sports clubs for blacks. He was also the king of the illegal numbers rackets in the city's black neighborhoods. But to Louis, Roxborough became "...the best friend I ever had."[8] Roxborough agreed to manage Louis and enlisted the help of a black Chicago-based mortician, Julian Black, who was in the numbers rackets as well. Black also owned an eatery, Elite Number Two, which was a much frequented watering hole for Chicago's sports set.

Black knew the best trainers in the Midwest and called upon one of them, an ex-fighter named Jack Blackburn, to help the young AAU champion become a professional. The resulting bond between Louis and Blackburn became one of the strongest, warmest, and most trusting in all of sports history. Since Louis weighed only 175 pounds in 1934, he faced an uphill struggle and needed all the help he could get. But he soaked up the advice from the former boxer which began with lessons on balance. "If you're off balance after you throw a punch, then it wasn't thrown right," noted Blackburn.[9] They also worked on adding more poundage. Most important, Louis was taught how to become a model black American heavyweight because of the residue of white disdain from the Jack Johnson era. If Louis were to get his shot at the title, he could not take any unnecessary chances.

Louis was literally groomed to be a champion. He was told he had to knock out opponents rather than risk the judges' decisions, for judges were routinely "bought off" by organized crime. Roxborough gave him lessons on personal hygiene and proper table manners. Russ Cowans, a sports reporter for the *Michigan Chronicle*, provided English lessons to improve his diction, and all concerned advised him "...for God's sake, after you beat a white opponent, don't smile."[10] With these cues and a powerful punch, he turned professional on July 4, 1934, after an amateur record of fifty-four wins and four losses.

In his first professional bout he scored a first-round knockout of Jack Kracken and earned $59—almost three week's wages at Ford Motor Company. By May 5, 1935, his record was twenty-two wins, no losses, and no bout went past ten rounds. But he had not fought in New York City, the nation's boxing capital. Ordinarily a black fighter had to "throw" a few fights—like Joe Gans, Joe Walcott, and George Godfrey—if he wanted to get ahead, but so far Roxborough and Black had been able to resist these demands. As one promoter said to Roxborough, "I can help your boy, but you understand he's a nigger and can't win every time he goes into the ring."[11]

Roxborough and Black needed a New York connection and they found one in Michael "Uncle Mike" Strauss Jacobs, a promoter and ticket agent. They agreed that Jacobs would promote Louis' fights and his managers would take 50 percent of Louis' share for ten years. (It was not atypical for managers then to take half a fighter's purses. They figured they were taking a big chance and they had to pay off the organized crime mobsters from their share. But 50 percent of a national champion's earnings seemed excessive.) Jacobs then assured Roxborough and Black that Louis would not have to throw any bouts; that he "...can win every fight he has, knock'em out in the first round if possible. I promise if Joe ever gets to the top, he'll get the shot at the title."[12] Jacobs kept his promise and twenty years after Jacobs had died, Louis said he was "...one of the finest men I ever knew."[13]

Primo Carnera was chosen for Louis' New York debut. The hulking six-feet-seven-inch, 275-pound Italian was, of course, completely controlled by the Mafia and had hit an opponent so hard on February 10, 1933, that he died five days later. Carnera would simply do whatever his handlers wanted if he could. However, in their bout on June 25, 1935, Louis knocked him to the floor in the sixth round. But there was more to this bout than the win. It almost did not happen.

Front-page stories blared the news that Italy, under fascist dictator Benito Mussolini, was preparing to invade Ethiopia, ruled by its monarch Haile Selassie I. Newspaper publisher William Randolph Hearst wanted to have the bout cancelled because his wife's Milk Fund charity was a recipient of some of the fight proceeds. Louis was obviously seen by some as a symbol of the oppressed Ethiopians in his bout against the Italian giant. The distinguished black historian Rayford W. Logan of Atlanta University commented that "I am afraid that the defeat of Carnera by Louis will be interpreted as an additional insult to the Italian flag, which will promote Mussolini to start again the recent attempt by Italy to annihilate Abyssinia [Ethiopia]."[14] A compromise was reached by having a pre-fight announcement made at ringside that urged all concerned to view the bout as a contest between two fighters and nothing more. But to many observers it was an example of American democracy versus Italian fascism.

After Louis' victory over Carnera, his stock in the black community soared. He was as popular as Satchel Paige at a time when, as one black newspaper noted, "It takes twice as much effort to turn ordinary colored citizens into fight fans...when they hear of hard striving boys of their race being robbed of decisions by crooked referees, or forced to lay down to inferior white opponents...."[15] The primary obstacle was the powerful black church which was generally not in favor of boxing as a profession. Intellectuals like W.E.B. Du Bois were strongly against boxing.

Louis seemed befuddled by all this attention at first. After church services with his mother following the Carnera win, he said, "When I walked in the church, you'd have thought I was the second coming of Christ...Rev. J.H. Maston...talked about how God gave certain people gifts...and through my fighting I was to uplift the spirit of my race. I must make the whole world know that Negro people were strong, fair, and decent....He said I was one of the chosen. I thought to myself, 'Jesus Christ, am I all that?'"[16]

Next, Louis defeated another ex-champion, Maximillian Adalbert "Max" Baer who stood six feet two and a half inches and weighed 220 pounds. Baer fell in four rounds at Yankee Stadium. But just four hours before this bout, Louis had impulsively married nineteen-year-old Marva Trotter, his girlfriend for some time. He was now nearly twenty-five pounds heavier than his professional debut weight and already one of the wealthiest black men in America. For his last two fights alone, he had grossed $300,000.

Louis finally received his comeuppance on June 19, 1936. In a bout for which he used a future heavyweight champion, "Jersey" Joe Walcott, as a sparring partner, he lost in another controversial bout to the German Max Schmeling in a twelfth-round knockout. Some say he had not trained according to Blackburn's instructions, he had played too much golf, and was not in proper shape. In addition, his trainer Blackburn, who was an alcoholic, was involved in a shootout in late 1935 in which an elderly man had died. Though he was acquitted, Blackburn had to be watched.

The Nazis in Adolf Hitler's Germany were jubilant over Schmeling's victory. One of their writers, George Spandau, called it a cultural achievement for the white race.

The October 1936 issue of the National Association for the Advancement of Colored People's magazine, *Crisis*, reprinted a complete transcription of an article from the German magazine, *Der Weltkampf*. In part, it read: "The Negro is of a slave nature, but woe unto us if this slave nature is unbridled, for then arrogance and cruelty show themselves in the most bestial way...these three countries—France, England, and white North America—cannot thank Schmeling enough for his victory, for he checked the arrogance of the Negro and clearly demonstrated to them the superiority of white intelligence." Earlier that year in August, Jesse Owens had burst Hitler's racist balloon by winning four gold medals at the Olympic Games in Berlin.

Like a rider thrown from a horse, Louis was back in the ring in less than two months with a third-round knockout of Jack Sharkey, another ex-champion. The world now knew that Louis deserved a shot at the title. No more excuses. No more alibis. No more flimsy subterfuge as was the case with Harry Wills. As promised by Jacobs, he got it on June 22, 1937, at Chicago's Comiskey Park against the current champion, James J. Braddock.

This bout against Braddock almost failed to come about because Braddock had signed to fight Schmeling. But Joe Gould, Braddock's manager, figured that Louis would be easier since he had lost to Schmeling and that Braddock would not have to run the gauntlet of anti Nazi Jewish demonstrators. In reality, the issue was over who would promote the bout, Jacobs or Madison Square Garden. Jacobs won when Judge Guy T. Fake ruled that the only valid agreement was Louis-Braddock. (It is interesting that Madison Square Garden allowed semi-naked black boxers to fight there yet denied black college basketball teams berths in their much heralded doubleheaders on Saturday afternoons.)

The twenty-three-year-old Louis never trained harder for a bout in his life. He had six tune-up bouts since his Sharkey win, and at his Kenosha, Wisconsin, camp, he scheduled nineteen sessions of boxing with workouts on Saturdays, Sundays, Tuesdays, and Thursdays. Braddock, thirty-two, came into the ring not having fought in two years, so Louis was a 2-to-1 betting favorite. On fight night, 20,000 of the 45,000 in attendance were black—the largest number of blacks ever to see a live bout.

In the first round Louis was dropped by a right hand, but bounced up quickly and waited for time to take its toll. The champion had obviously counted on a quick knockout for he knew he could not go the distance. By the eighth round it was clear to all that, barring an act of God, Louis would win. Blacks in the crowd were delirious with joy. Some of them began crying, hugging one another, holding hands, laughing, mimicking Louis' every blow, wincing with every blow he took. They were witnessing a historic occasion, as no black person present had traveled to Sydney, Australia, in 1908 to see Jack Johnson win his title. These 20,000 were the chosen few.

At one minute, ten seconds into the eighth round, referee Tommy Thomas counted out James Braddock and Joseph Louis was the new world heavyweight champion.

But Louis would not feel complete until he conquered Max Schmeling. As Jacobs ironed out the details of a Louis-Schmeling rematch, he was aware of the increasing tensions between Germany and Austria and the atrocities against the Jews there. As a Jew himself, Jacobs knew there would be trouble, which was partially dampened by a friendly meeting Louis had with President Franklin D. Roosevelt. The President told the new champion, "Joe, we need muscles like yours to beat Germany."[17] It was also at this time he found out his father, Munro, was not dead as presupposed, and the champion subsequently arranged for his care until his passing in 1938.

The date for Schmeling was set for June 22, 1938, at Yankee Stadium, just as word of Nazi concentration camps for Jews was spreading. Many now worried about a Louis loss to Schmeling. In short, Louis had to win or all of America would suffer the psychological consequences of more Nazi drivel about racial supremacy over blacks and Jews. If Louis lost, Jacobs, himself, would be considered a traitor to *his* own people. But Louis reportedly told Jacobs that he had no plans to return to Ford Motor Company and that he, Jacobs, would not have to go back to selling lemon drops on the Staten Island Ferry.

In mid-May, Louis' camp in Pompton Lakes, New Jersey, was picketed by pro-Nazi sympathizers. When Louis was asked if he was scared, he replied, "Yeah, I'm scared. I'm scared I might kill Schmeling."[18] The source of Louis' anger was a late hit by Schmeling in their first bout and he meant to get even.

Never before, save possibly the Jack Johnson fight with Jim Jeffries, had black America been so consumed by a single event. No political happening, no other sports occasion, no war, no imminent passing of any law could compare with the possibility of a Louis victory. Ask any black person who was alive and over ten years of age when Joe Louis fought Max Schmeling, and he or she would remember it clearly. Neither Jesse Owens' four Olympic gold medals nor Jackie Robinson's signing with the Brooklyn Dodgers equaled the elation of this night. The emotional immediacy of a Louis victory over the "Nazi" Schmeling was wildly compelling.

Two other factors made this bout special: direct radio broadcasts and the accreditation of black journalists. Jacobs initially believed that live radio would hurt the live gate and had not allowed it. The inability of black sports reporters getting credentials was another matter. Joe Bostic of the *New York Age* explained, "They [major stadium and arena managers] would turn us off by saying that working press tickets were only for people from the daily press....We would get what they called tax tickets; you still had to pay a tax but there was no admission price. The seats were far from ringside. After Louis fought [Jorge] Brescia [October 9, 1936], we got our first boxing press credentials."[19]

On the day of the fight, an unusually calm Louis weighed 198 to 193 pounds for Schmeling. "This is it Chappie. It's your chance to prove you're a real champ," explained Blackburn, who had Louis trained to his outer limits as they entered the ring. Referee Arthur Donovan brought the two boxers together and afterwards, Louis stood in his corner rather than rest on his stool a few extra minutes. He was

critically aware of the burden he was shouldering. Never before had as many Americans—all Americans—pulled for a reigning champion as they were for Louis. It was a rerun of the Louis–Carnera bout but with far graver circumstances. Before he sat down again, he would erase all doubts that he was the best in the world.

At the sound of the opening bell, Louis charged across the ring and began assaulting Schmeling with stinging left jabs that found their marks. Schmeling got in one right hand that did little damage. Four more Louis left jabs and then he saw an opening for a right to the jaw. Hit flush on the left side of his face just below his ear, Schmeling caromed off the ropes to be met with a right to the body which, Louis said later, made the German squeal "..like a stuck pig."[20] Donovan scored it a knockdown.

After a count of one, the challenger was back in the center of the ring and another right to the jaw put him on the floor for a three-count. Up again, he took a left and a right to the head and fell to his knees for a count of two—solely because his mind could not follow the referee's count. His fighter's training forced him up a third time, and Louis let fly with a left hook and a right to the jaw. It was over. In two minutes, four seconds of the first round, the Brown Bomber had convinced all doubters that, racial theories to the contrary, he was the undisputed world champion.

The entire nation celebrated but blacks were euphoric. No need to hide their joy this time. There were no murders or retributive acts of racial revenge, as was the case when Jack Johnson defeated "the white hope" Jim Jeffries in 1910. Louis was, at that moment, more idolized than any black athlete had ever been before, until the prime of Muhammad Ali. He took seven months off to enjoy himself before granting the black world light-heavyweight champion, John Henry Lewis, a title shot. In this second heavyweight title bout between two blacks—the first was Jack Johnson versus Jim Johnson—Louis mercifully knocked out Lewis after two minutes, twenty-nine seconds into the first round.

Though no one any longer questioned his fistic talents, he did pile up some personal problems. His marriage began to fail, he lost thousands of dollars on the golf course, and he gave money away to friends and relatives. As late as 1942 when he enlisted in the army, his bouts since 1934 had grossed nearly $2 million and certified Treasury records showed a federal and state tax bite of $227,746. Yet his net income totaled only $84,500 for the period, as his managers were taking 50 percent and training expenses came out of his own share. Louis did not comprehend the tax consequences of his actions.

After the second Schmeling bout, Louis fought four times in 1939 and four times in 1940. He then began what was called a "bum-of-the-month" tour from January through November in 1941. Only one opponent lasted the fifteen-round limit and that was Arturo Godoy who afterwards rushed over to Louis and kissed him on the mouth. The bum-of-the-month tour barely covered expenses but Louis kept spending. In 1942, he donated the entire proceeds of his fight with Buddy Baer—$89,092—Max's brother, to the navy Relief Fund, though the navy, which includes the marines, was clearly the most discriminatory of the armed forces branches. The marines were also the last of the armed forces to integrate.

Two months later, on March 27, he donated another $36,146 to the Army Relief Fund from his fight with Abe Simon. He did not fully understand that these sums were still considered income by the government. Actually, Louis was left to his own devices by Roxborough and Black after they tried to get him to temper his spending. But Roxborough was sent to prison, in 1941, for two and a half years for operating a numbers business. By the end of 1942, Louis' beloved Blackburn had died of heart disease. He was by then in the army and owed the government $117,000 in back taxes, Roxborough $41,000, and the Twentieth Century Sporting Club $60,000. Given a chance to clear up some of this debt with a $300,000 payday in September 1942, Sergeant Joe Louis was denied the opportunity to fight by Secretary of War Henry Stimson.

When Louis received his honorable discharge from the army in October 1945, he was broke though he had fought ninety-six exhibitions, traveled 70,000 miles, and had done all he was asked. His wife Marva was divorcing him and when she agreed to accept a $25,000 cash settlement, he did not have it to pay. But he was still the world heavyweight champion and everybody loved him.

It was a wonderfully expectant time to be a talented black athlete. Jackie Robinson had signed with the Brooklyn Dodgers to break the color line in team sports, and basketball and football were ready to admit blacks as well. Much of the goodwill for black athletes generated in the dozen years leading to the end of the war was due to the positive image that Louis had created. He could build on that reputation to see his way out.

Those Other Black Champions

Joe Louis so dominated the 1930s and 1940s that his fellow black boxers in lower weight classes sometimes failed to attract their just due. But they all shared the same condition as members of the black underclass making their way during the Depression, since few middle-class young men, black or white, aspired to be professional boxers.

The aforementioned John Henry Lewis became the world light-heavyweight champion on October 31, 1935, when he defeated Bob Olin in St. Louis in fifteen rounds. He started out in Los Angeles where he was born on May 1, 1914, just thirteen days before Joe Louis. It is claimed that he was a great-great nephew of Tom Molineaux, the early nineteenth-century boxing contender, but, true or not, his boxing skills were certainly respected.

Lewis' father was a boxer who taught his son in Phoenix, Arizona, where the family had moved so the elder Lewis could work as a trainer at a local college. John Henry turned professional at sixteen, and thirteen of his first fourteen fights were won by knockouts before the seventh round. One of these opponents, Sam Terrain, died as a result. Lewis, at five feet eleven inches and 174 pounds, was a powerful puncher. But the big purses were in the heavyweight division. So he fought constantly. In June

1936 and April 1937, he fought four times in each thirty-day period.

At one time Lewis was managed by Gus Greenlee who was responsible for the resurrection of baseball's Negro National Leagues in 1933. His prior manager, Ernie Lira, arranged both light-heavyweight and heavyweight opponents. His first loss came on November 16, 1932, to "Slapsie" Maxie Rosenbloom in ten rounds, but he avenged that loss with two wins over Rosenbloom in three weeks, in July 1933.

After defeating Olin for the title, Lewis successfully defended his crown five times before abdicating in 1938. It was just too difficult to maintain the weight limit as a light-heavyweight. He was thus the first native-born black American world light-heavyweight champion and the first to retire from his division undefeated. His bout with Joe Louis on January 25, 1939, was in fact arranged to provide Lewis with a big payday—$17,000. Days later, the truth surfaced that Lewis was half-blind in his right eye before the bout. He never fought again and died in Berkeley, California, on April 18, 1974.

Another who competed with Joe Louis for publicity was Henry "Hammering Hank" Armstrong who was born in Columbus, Mississippi, on December 12, 1912. With the possible exception of George Dixon, Armstrong was the first to be thought of as, pound-for-pound, the best ever. Armstrong began his life as Henry Jackson, to a father who had fifteen children. He saw his mother die of tuberculosis when he was six and an older brother died from a beating he took from attracting the wrong girl. After moving to St. Louis, he worked on a construction gang and read about Kid Chocolate making $75,000 for fighting a half hour in the ring. On the spot, so the story goes, he quit his construction duties and told his grandmother he wanted to be a fighter.

Henry Armstrong's wise grandmother told him, "...son, you can't fight. You ain't no Jack Johnson."[21] But he proceeded anyway and met Harry Armstrong, who became his manager, at the Colored YMCA. With his quick fists and nonstop style, he was soon the featherweight king of St. Louis with no one to fight. So he turned professional in 1931, under the name "Mellody Jackson" and lost his first fight because all he could afford to eat was bread and water. Harry Armstrong had not been told about his diet.

After traveling to California in a box car, Mellody Jackson and Harry Armstrong arranged to sell their management contract to Tom Cox for three dollars. Jackson then decided he wanted to fight as an amateur again so he adopted the name Henry Armstrong. He had by then fought under three different names: Henry Jackson, Henry Armstrong as an amateur, and Mellody Jackson as a professional. But it was probably not the first time it had occurred.

Armstrong tried to make the 1932 Olympic team as a bantamweight but losing the required weight made him so weak that he lost miserably. His contract was then sold by Cox to Wirt "One Shot" Ross for three hundred dollars (a multiple of one-hundred over the three dollar price), as he turned professional for good under the name Henry Armstrong. Immediately, he ran into trouble. Freddie Miller, the feather-

weight champion, would not meet him because of Armstrong's outstanding record. In Mexico for a "fixed" match against a local favorite, Baby Arizmendi, he intentionally lost as agreed and later had his share stolen away, so he fought for nothing.

He fought Arizmendi a second time with an agreement to lose and complied. During a third "fix," Armstrong doublecrossed Arizmendi and crushed him unmercifully. This third bout was watched by the famed entertainer, Al Jolson (who performed in black-face makeup), who, with the actor George Raft, put up $5,000 to buy Armstrong's contract from Ross for Eddie Mead, a local manager. With these connections, he was ready for Madison Square Garden.

When he got his chance, Armstrong overwhelmed the featherweight king, Petey Sarron, in six rounds to capture the title on October 29, 1937. He was awarded *Ring* magazine's Merit Award even though Joe Louis won the heavyweight title that same year. But, as he noted, "...everyone was saving their money to see Joe Louis fight because he's knocking out everybody."[22] Armstrong figured the only way he could get any attention was to win world titles in three weight classes—featherweight, lightweight, and welterweight.

Lou Ambers, the lightweight champion, declined an offer to fight Armstrong but Barney Ross, the Jewish welterweight holder, agreed. After gorging himself with water and high-calorie foods, Armstrong barely made the lower limit for the welterweight class of 147 pounds. Luckily the bout was postponed after the weigh-ins were finished, and when they met on May

31, 1938, Armstrong weighed 133 ½ pounds to Ross' 142. Armstrong won a unanimous fifteen-round decision. Two titles down; one to go.

The lightweight title affair with Ambers was, said Armstrong, "...the bloodiest fight I ever had in my life."[23] The referee, Arthur Donovan, almost stopped it. To solve the problem for himself, Armstrong simply swallowed his own blood from the thirteenth round on. In the fifteenth and final round, he fought in a state of delirium and had to be pulled off of Ambers and carried to his dressing room where he blacked out. When he was revived, he thought he had lost but could remember nothing. He had become the first man in history to hold three world titles at once, and he did not even recall the third one.

Armstrong then abdicated his featherweight crown and lost his lightweight title to Ambers. A try for the middleweight title on March 1, 1940, against Ceferino Garcia failed and on October 4 of that year, he then lost his welterweight crown to Fritzie Zivic. Comebacks failed and two of these included losses to Beau Jack and Sugar Ray Robinson. Though Armstrong's purses totaled over a million dollars, he lost almost all of it to bad advice and bad investments. He now works with the Boy's Clubs in St. Louis and is an ordained minister. That was the way it was for a poor, uneducated child of the Depression.

Between the end of 1940 and the end of 1942, Joe Louis was the only black American world boxing champion. But on December 18, 1942, he was joined by a Georgia-born bootblack, Sidney "Beau Jack" Walker, who won the New York State version of the world lightweight title. As a teenager, Beau Jack worked at the Augusta National Golf Club and was later assisted by Bobby Jones, a club member and winner of golf's Grand Slam titles. Like Henry Armstrong, Beau Jack was raised by his grandmother, who once spanked him for letting another boy take his shoe polish. The next time the adversary tried to nip his polish, Beau Jack fought back and won. "That's the way I want you to be," his grandmother replied approvingly.

Little did his grandmother know what she had started. Beau Jack made his way to Springfield, Massachusetts, to train and eventually wound up in an elimination tournament for Sammy Angott's vacated lightweight title. On December 18, 1942, the five-foot-six-inch boxer's nonstop style won for him the New York State version of the title. Five months later, he lost the title to Bob Montgomery; then regained it on November 19, 1943; then lost it for good to Montgomery on March 3, 1944. He now works at the Konover Hotel in Miami Beach, Florida, and helps to train aspiring fighters.

Bob Montgomery, who twice won the lightweight crown from Beau Jack, was also southern-born in Sumter, South Carolina, on February 10, 1919. After his second title victory he enlisted in the army, and later lost the crown to Ike Williams on August 4, 1947. Montgomery now lives in Philadelphia.

The third and final lightweight champion of the 1940s was Ike Williams of Brunswick, Georgia. After his birth on August 2, 1923, he moved to Trenton, New Jersey, and turned professional at age seventeen. (Black boxers from the South just could not remain at home and hope to succeed in the ring. All the big money fights were up North, especially New York, Chicago, Detroit, Philadelphia, and so on.) He won the National Boxing Association version of the lightweight crown from Juan Zurita in Mexico City on April 18, 1945, on a second-round knockout. Immediately afterwards, bricks, bottles, and cans started flying all over the place and Williams was held up at gunpoint. His championship belt was stolen and he has not seen it since.

In a measure of revenge from Montgomery, Williams won the undisputed world title from him on August 4, 1947, and then lost it to James Carter in 1951. His more long-lasting losses, however, came on the golf course where he came up short in high-stakes games with hustlers. Ike Williams retired in 1955 in modest circumstances.

By the end of the Second World War, it seemed black America could not produce a world champion who could exit the ring gracefully with his earnings safely invested. Still, the professional ranks, at the beginning of the war, had many quality fighters. Some heavyweights, notwithstanding Joe Louis included Roscoe Toles, Turkey Thompson, Harry Bobo, and Lou Brooks. Light-heavyweights around were Jimmy Reeves, Booker Beckwith, Mose Brown, and Lloyd Marshall. Middleweights saw enough of Charley Burley who refused to go to the 1936 Olympics because he disagreed with Adolf Hitler's policies.

Archie Moore, the future world light-heavyweight titleholder, fought for a time as a middleweight in the 1940s, and was joined by Holman Williams. Other welterweights were Jimmy Edgar, Kid Cocoa, and Earl Turner. Willie White and Cleo Shane were lightweights and Davey Crawford fought in the featherweight ranks.

In 1938, one of our black Olympic medalists became involved in a three-way

drama stretching over five years. On October 29, 1937, Henry Armstrong defeated Petey Sarron to win the world featherweight crown. Armstrong then resigned in early 1938, because he could no longer make the weight. In an elimination event to find Armstrong's successor, Joey Archibald won the National Boxing Association (NBA) and New York State version of the title. Archibald later lost his NBA title because he refused to defend it, but New York State let it stand. This set up the possibility of dual champions.

The NBA's new designated champion, Petey Scalzo, lost his title to Richie Lemos on July 1, 1941. Lemos then lost it to the black Olympic silver medalist, Jackie Wilson, on November 18 of that same year. Two months earlier, Albert "Chalky" Wright, another black fighter, won the New York State title over Archibald in eleven rounds. Thus two black champions held the same title at the same time, though Wright's crown was considered more important. Such things happened in boxing's strange world sometimes and it persists to this day. Wilson, who was born in Arkansas in 1909, was five feet five inches, fought seventeen years as a professional, and compiled a 74–41–5 record, including one no-contest and one no-decision.

The Sugar Man

In *The Black Athlete: Emergence and Arrival*, the authors rightfully stated that "If there is any major connecting link through those war years in boxing, it is personified by 'Sugar Ray' Robinson, whom many consider, pound for pound, the best fighter ever."[24] This author agrees. Seldom have such superlatives fit a fighter so well. In

terms of finesse, body control, flair, hand
speed, endurance, athletic ability, and
showmanship, no boxer in history matched
Robinson. He redefined the very image of
the consummate pugilist.

Robinson was born with the name
Walker Smith, Jr. to a very poor family in
Detroit on May 3, 1920. He hung out at the
Brewster Center Gymnasium where Joe
Louis trained in the early 1930s. He even
became a Louis tag-a-long for a time. After
a separation from her husband, his mother
brought him and his two sisters to New York
City in 1932, first to a lower West Side area
known as Hell's Kitchen and then to
Harlem. In Harlem, he became infatuated
with Bill "Bojangles" Robinson, the black
dancer, and performed his routines for
money on downtown streets such as Fifth
Avenue.

He eventually found his way to the
Salem-Crescent Club and its boxing coach,
George Gainford. Initially interested, the
young Smith sold his first donated boxing
outfit and Gainford had second thoughts
about training him. However, "...the
dance-happy kid who loved to play also got
a bang out of the routine of training...he
learned fast."[25]

Smith was taken to various boxing
shows by Gainford and during one such
extravaganza, the promoter needed a last-
minute substitute and Gainford offered
Smith. But there was a problem: Smith
needed an AAU registration card and did
not have one. So Gainford did what thousands of his counterparts would have done;
he faked it. He arranged to use the card of a
recently retired fighter, Ray Robinson, from

Richmond, Virginia. Smith-Robinson fought
as a substitute and won.

He picked up the sobriquet "Sugar" in
Watertown, New York, when a local reporter
witnessed Smith-Robinson in action and
told Gainford, "You got a mighty sweet boy
there."[26] Hence the name Sugar Ray Robinson. Sugar Walker Smith just did not sound
appealing; it did not roll off the tongue.
Sugar Ray Robinson had almost 125 amateur fights—eighty-nine recorded—and registered sixty-nine knockouts, forty-four of
which were in the first round.

As an amateur Robinson won the 1939
Golden Gloves featherweight title and the
1940 lightweight crown, as well as the New
York City-Chicago Intercity title. Then he
turned professional in 1940 under the management of Kurt Horrman, a wealthy heir to
a brewing fortune. Horrman retained Gainford as trainer and arranged for Robinson's
Madison Square Garden debut on October
4, against Joe Echeverria. Robinson won in
a second-round knockout and then proceeded to win another thirty-nine in a row,
twenty-eight by knockout.

Robinson could not hope to match the
lure of Joe Louis but he had his own
personal following during the war. He kept
his reputation clean and his fighting style
was inimitable. He had the endurance of
Beau Jack, the relentlessness of Henry
Armstrong, the finesse was all his own. Few
critics had seen anyone glide across the
canvas like Robinson. All that dancing on
Fifth Avenue had paid off. Finally, as had
happened to just about everyone, he lost.
Jake LaMotta decisioned him in ten rounds
on February 5, 1943, in their second meet-

ing. Undaunted, the Sugar Man began another winning streak of ninety-six bouts without a loss that stretched over eight years. Included in that second string of victories was a win over the aging Henry Armstrong, three of his six world titles, and an army tour that ended in 1946. Save Jack Johnson and Joe Louis, Sugar Ray Robinson influenced his craft more than any other black fighter until the coming of Muhammad Ali.

The Olympians

Though the professionals received most of the ring publicity, there was a group of amateur Olympians who made names for themselves. Ben Pointeau was part of the 1920 Olympic squad but did not win a medal. The 1936 Games in Berlin offered opportunities for five black Americans in four weight classes. They were Arthur Oliver, heavyweight; Willis Johnson, heavyweight alternate; James C. Atkinson, middleweight; Howell King, welterweight alternate; and Jackie Wilson, bantamweight. The highly touted Charley Burley earned a place on the squad but declined.

Jackie Wilson's silver medal was the only prize won by the group. His loss in the finals to Italy's Ulderico Sergo was Wilson's sole defeat as an amateur. By every account, Wilson's demise was a political move because of Italy's partnership with Adolf Hitler. When Wilson met Sergo one year later, he won and left the amateur ranks with a record of fifty wins and one loss. He was also the AAU flyweight winner that same year.

The amateurs as a group had made tremendous advances by the beginning of World War II, and most of them were trained east of the Mississippi River. By 1943, six of the eight national AAU champions were black as were five of the eight national Golden Gloves winners. New York City's Salem-Crescent Club in particular fielded many talented fighters. Boxing was used in the armed forces to toughen the men, and the quality of the instruction and intra-service competition was quite high. The respectability of the sport had never been better. Even the middle-class-oriented NAACP got involved.

In Washington, D.C., in 1945, for instance, the NAACP sued the local AAU affiliate to integrate its boxing tournament. Eugene Meyer, whose paper, the *Washington Post*, sponsored the event, threatened to withdraw his patronage if the AAU did not open up. By a vote of 12 to 4, the AAU Washington, D.C., affiliate changed its previously all-white tournament. The future looked promising for those who wanted to pursue "the sweet science" as a profession.

But a look back could not have provided much encouragement. Yes, the money to be made was more than the average person could earn in several lifetimes. But as Edwin B. Henderson noted in the August 21, 1948, *Afro-American* newspaper, "...professional boxers...theirs is a sad story. For every one who plummets upward to fame and money the road is strewn with punch drunk wrecks."[27] He was right. However, after the war, new generations of young black athletes decided to follow their predecessors into the ring; motivated by the same personal experiences of poverty, a lack of respect for segregated education, and a strong belief that there was just no other way to untold riches. They, too, traveled a "Hard Road to Glory."

Notes

1. Nat Fleischer, *Black Dynamite: The Story of the Negro in the Prize Ring from 1782 to 1938* (New York: *Ring* magazine, 1947) Vol. 5, p. 49.
2. Ibid., p. 50.
3. Ibid., Vol. 5, p. 106.
4. Doug Smith, Monograph, 1985, p. 4.
5. Margery Miller, *Joe Louis: American* (New York: Hill & Wang, 1945), p. 20.
6. Gerald Astor, *And a Credit to His Race: The Hard Life and Times of Joseph Louis Barrow* (New York: Saturday Review Press, 1974), p. 27.
7. Joe Louis, *My Life Story* (New York: Duell, Sloan & Pearce, 1947), p. 27.
8. Ibid., p. 29.
9. Ibid.
10. Gerald Astor, *And a Credit to His Race: The Hard Life and Times of Joseph Louis Barrow*, p. 42.
11. Ibid., p. 60.
12. Ibid., p. 80.
13. Ibid., p. 67.
14. Ibid., p. 97.
15. *California Eagle*, 31 August 1934.
16. Doug Smith, Monograph, 1985, p. 11.
17. Gerald Astor, *And a Credit to His Race: The Hard Life and Times of Joseph Louis Barrow*, p. 169.
18. Doug Smith, Monograph, 1985, p. 15.
19. Gerald Astor, *And a Credit to His Race: The Hard Life and Times of Joseph Louis Barrow*, p. 176.
20. Joe Louis, *My Life Story*, p. 101.
21. Peter Heller, *In This Corner: Forty World Champions Tell Their Stories* (New York: Simon & Schuster, 1973), p. 196.
22. Ibid., p. 211.
23. Ibid., p. 24.
24. Edwin B. Henderson and *Sports*magazine, *The Black Athlete: Emergence and Arrival* (Cornwell Heights: Pennsylvania Publishers Co. Inc., 1968), p. 157.
25. Ibid., p. 179.
26. Ibid., p. 182.
27. *Baltimore Afro-American*, 21 August 1948.

CHAPTER 3

SINCE 1946

Joe Louis' Legacy: The Brown Bomber retired (for the first time) in 1949 after a dozen years as the world heavyweight champion. Although he had tax difficulties with the Federal Government, most everyone, especially black Americans, loved him. To black Americans he was larger than life. To boxing impresarios, he was money in the bank, someone who could be counted on to "fill the house." Memories of the controversial first black heavyweight champion, Jack Johnson, haunted Louis and, with the help of his managers, John Roxborough and Mike Jacobs, he strove to make amends.

There were other black champions during the Louis era, such as Henry Armstrong and Sugar Ray Robinson, but they did not have Louis' following. Louis dutifully served in the Army, and was an inspiration to fighters the world over. Partly because of his reputation, boxing made some key organizational changes in the 1940s. In 1944, the Gillette Company began sponsoring weekly bouts at Madison Square Garden, and in 1949, James Norris founded the International Boxing Club (IBC), in order to stage live televised fights.

The general mood of optimism surrounding the sport after World War II had resulted in part from Louis' image. For blacks, the combination of Louis and Jackie Robinson between 1946 and 1949 formed a major part of their postwar euphoria. These two athletes even contributed to the confidence of those in the Civil Rights Movement.

Though Louis carried boxing through some difficult times, he left it in less than ideal hands. Manager Mike Jacobs' contemporaries were more concerned with profitability than with boxing's traditions, especially the small clubs, which were the life-blood of the sport. A new *modus operandi* was forthcoming.

Among the growing number of black ex-professional fighters, only one, Harry Wills, had managed to retire financially sound. The September 1946, issue of *Ebony* magazine reported that, "out of the million dollars he earned in more than twenty years in the ring, Wills today still has a big piece invested in two big Harlem apartment houses and two country estates . . . and an annual income of more than $25,000."[1] Matters would get worse before they got better.

New Boxing Environment: In 1949, the International Boxing Club (IBC) was founded by James Norris. The IBC virtually controlled the sport for ten years via shrewd agreements among boxers, arenas, and television. It was extremely difficult for any fighter to secure a championship bout without Norris' involvement.

There were 85 million television viewers in the United States in 1950, but Norris was not sure whether white America would watch mixed-race bouts without protest if blacks won most of them. Though the number of sets amounted to less than ten percent of American homes, boxing matches were full of racial symbolism and metaphor. Would southern whites, for instance, boycott Gillette shaving products because of its sponsorship?

Mike Jacobs wrote a thought-provoking article in the May 1950 issue of *Ebony* magazine entitled "Are Negroes Killing Boxing?" His answer was essentially no, and he added that "Negroes are entitled to whatever dominance of boxing or any other sport they achieve."[2] Hence, Jacobs achieved a reputation in the black community somewhat akin to that of Branch Rickey, the Brooklyn Dodgers president who signed Jackie Robinson to a contract as the first black major league baseball player of the modern era.

James Norris also sought to include blacks in the IBC administration. He hired Truman K. Gibson, Jr., to become a matchmaker at Chicago Stadium. Gibson, a lawyer, had helped arrange the Army boxing tours for Joe Louis, and had promoted the Sugar Ray Robinson–Jake LaMotta bout in 1951.

The IBC concentrated on staging bouts on closed-circuit television, the first being between Joe Louis and Lee Savold. This pulled fans away from the small clubs, and total boxing receipts slumped to only $4 million dollars for 1950. By 1954, there were roughly five televised boxing shows per week. A year later, the IBC was under investigation for violation of antitrust laws.

For the next four years, the IBC fought to retain its stranglehold on the sport. However, on January 12, 1959, the United States Supreme Court upheld a lower court ruling that the IBC had indeed violated federal antitrust laws. Two years later, Frank "Blinky" Carbo, an alleged organized-crime figure and Norris associate, was sentenced to twenty-five years in prison for conspiracy and extortion.

Between 1949 and 1953, the IBC promoted thirty-six of forty-four world title bouts. Consequently, black boxers and their managers were forced to operate within IBC confines. The demise of the IBC in 1959 paved the way for more competitor-oriented promotion in the 1960s. From the time of Joe Louis' retirement in 1949 through 1984, black boxers made more money than all other black professional athletes combined. What initially promised to be a vertical monopoly of all weight classes ended up with a concentration of black champions in the middle and upper weight divisions. Theirs is an enviable record in the ring, matched only by the predominance of black professional basketball players in the 1980s.

THE FIFTIES

Featherweights: 119–126 lbs.

Sandy Saddler: He was, pound for pound, one of the hardest punchers in the history of the sport. In 162 official bouts, he scored 103 knockouts (KOs). (Twenty-eight of his first thirty-eight professional bouts were KOs.) He fought the champions of seven countries before securing a title bout. Saddler began his professional career in 1944, and averaged 14 bouts per year through 1951. He was best known for his four bouts with Willie Pep between October 29, 1948, and September 26, 1951. Saddler won the vacant junior lightweight title in 1949, but after one defense, relinquished it. He served in the United States Army in 1952–53, and he retired following an automobile accident in 1956. There would be no more black junior lightweight champions for almost thirty years.

Davey Moore: This Lexington, Kentucky, native was also the 1952 AAU bantamweight champion. His professional career began in 1953. He won the featherweight title from Hogan "Kid" Bassey on August 19, 1959, and defended it four times. He lost his title to Sugar Ramos on March 21, 1963, and died two days later of head injuries suffered in the bout. There have been no black featherweight champions since.

Lightweights: 127–135 lbs.

Ike Williams: This feisty battler won the National Boxing Association (NBA) title from Juan Zurita in 1945, in a second-round KO. He then won the world title two years later from Bob Montgomery. Williams, who admitted to heavy gambling losses in golf games, turned professional in 1940 and, retired four years after losing to James Carter in 1951.

James Carter: A South Carolina native, Carter was the first man to hold the same world title three times. After winning the title from Ike Williams, he lost it to Lauro Salas. He regained it from Salas, lost it to Paddy deMarco, then regained it again from de-Marco. Wallace "Bud" Smith finally ended Carter's career hopes in 1955.

Wallace "Bud" Smith: He turned professional after winning the 1948 National AAU title. Seven years later he won the world title from James Carter in fifteen tough rounds and successfully defended against him four months later. He lost the title to Joe Brown in 1956, after holding it for fourteen months. He retired in 1959, and died in 1973.

Joe "Old Bones" Brown: Born and raised in New Orleans during the Depression, Brown began his career in the military as the all-service lightweight champion. He turned professional after World War II and proved to be a durable fighter. After winning the world title from "Bud" Smith in 1956, he kept it five years and two months—longer than any lightweight title-holder since Benny Leonard in 1917–23.

Brown acquired the nickname "Old Bones" because he won the title at age thirty-one. A very hard puncher, he was feared by many fighters in the welterweight class. His eventual conqueror, Carlos Ortiz, referred to him as "a murderous puncher . . . a good left hooker, terrible body puncher."[3] Perhaps his most interesting bout was against Ralph Dupas in Houston, Texas, in 1958. Dupas, also from New Orleans, sued in his home state to prove he was not white. If Dupas had been listed as black, he would have circumvented Louisiana's rule, at the time, barring interracial sports. Louisiana refused to change his racial classification, so subsequently the fight was held in Houston. Brown won before 11,000 fans.

Eighteen years passed before another black lightweight champion was crowned.

Welterweights: 136–147 lbs.

Sugar Ray Robinson: Sugar Ray (formerly Walker Smith, Jr.) turned professional in 1940 and spent the 1940s as a welterweight. He won the world title from Tommie Bell in fifteen rounds on December 20, 1946. However, Robinson had a problem keeping his weight below the 147-pound limit. After winning the Pennsylvania middleweight title on June 5, 1950, from Robert Villemain, Robinson decided to become a permanent middleweight, and he subsequently relinquished his welterweight title after defeating Charley Fusari on August 9, 1950.

Johnny Bratton: He moved to Chicago from his native Little Rock, Arkansas. He turned professional in 1944 at age seventeen and won the vacant NBA title seven years later over Charley Fusari. He held his crown just two months and four days, losing it to Kid Gavilan.

Johnny Saxton: Saddler had an enviable amateur career, winning thirty-one of thirty-three bouts, the AAU crown, and the Golden Gloves in his hometown of Newark, New Jersey. After winning the world title from Gavilan in fifteen grueling rounds in 1954, he lost it six months later to Tony deMarco by a fourteenth-round KO. Saxton regained the title from Carmen Basilio in 1956 and lost it again six months later.

Virgil Akins: After a short amateur career of fourteen wins in fifteen bouts, this St. Louis, Missouri, fighter won the vacant world title by defeating Vince Martinez in 1958 on a fourth-round KO. He had defeated Isaac Logart in an elimination bout just three months earlier. Akins kept the title exactly six months, losing it to Don Jordon on December 5, 1958. A serious eye injury in 1962 forced him into retirement.

Middleweights: 148–160 lbs.

The story of the middleweight division in the 1950s is the story of Sugar Ray Robinson. He was unquestionably the most colorful boxer of the decade, and many experts have rated him pound for pound as the best ever. Before he had even reached his prime as a middleweight, he was named among such greats as John L. Sullivan, Joe Gans, Henry Armstrong, and Joe Louis. Dan Parker, of the *New York Mirror*, said in his column on February 14, 1951, that Robinson is "the greatest combination of brains, brawn, and boxing skill the modern prize ring has seen."[4]

One of Robinson's antagonists, Carl "Bobo" Olson, said Sugar Ray was "the greatest fighter that ever lived."[5] Another opponent, Paul Pender, added, "He was the greatest puncher that ever lived, with a repertoire of punches that nobody could throw . . . a great left hook, a great right-hand uppercut, a great right-cross."[6]

As early as 1950, Robinson had acquired a reputation as being difficult. He was labeled "boxing's bad boy." A few times he failed to appear for scheduled bouts, claiming misunderstandings with promoters. In 1947, the New York State Athletic Commission suspended him for thirty days for failing to report a bribery attempt. Yet by the black public in particular, he was idolized.

Robinson made constant reference to the sorry state of many ex-fighters. "A broke fighter is a pitiful sight . . . most fighters end up broke . . . I certainly don't intend to finish my career battered and broke."[7] However, he sometimes failed to heed his own advice. Perhaps no fighter believed more in his own invincibility. After all, he had survived life as a ghetto street kid in Detroit's Black Bottom district.

Born Walker Smith, Jr., on May 3, 1921, to Walker and Leila Smith, he learned to box at the Brewster Center two blocks from his home. When he was eleven he moved with his mother and sister to New York City's Hell's Kitchen neighborhood. They later moved to Harlem, where he began boxing in the Police Athletic League program.

His natural skills attracted the attention of George Gainford of the old Salem-Crescent Athletic Club. Gainford encouraged young Smith and showed him how to evade the rules against amateur fighters collecting prize money. When a youngster won a bout, Robinson recalled, "they give you a watch and then buy it back for ten dollars."[8]

He acquired his new name in Kingston, New York, when he was forced by local officials to produce his AAU card. Since he did not have one, he was persuaded by Gainford to use Ray Robinson's card as a substitute. Unknown outside Harlem, he was able to make the switch undetected. (The real Ray

Robinson was born in Richmond, Virginia, on August 25, 1919.) As such, Robinson decided to keep his new name.

Robinson received his nickname from Jack Case, a writer for a Watertown, New York, newspaper, who noted to Gainford after watching him, "That's a real sweet fighter you've got there. As sweet as sugar."[9]

Robinson, who was 5 feet 11½ inches tall, began as a featherweight, winning the Golden Gloves title. He also won all of his eighty-five amateur bouts, sixty-nine by KO, forty of them in the first round. His professional debut came on November 4, 1940, at Madison Square Garden, where Henry Armstrong was the headliner. Robinson moved about the ring effortlessly, partly because of dancing lessons and in part because of natural ability. Harry Wills stressed to him that "Balance son, balance is the fighter's most important asset."[10] Robinson himself freely acknowledged that, "rhythm is everything in boxing."[11]

He spent many hours with Joe Louis at Louis' training camp in Greenwood Lake, New York, and agreed to allow Louis' manager, Mike Jacobs, to arrange some of his bouts. All the time, though, he kept Gainford by his side. Robinson was intensely loyal to his friends. After sixteen months in the Army, from February 1943 to June 1944, he married former Cotton Club (New York City) dancer Edna Mae Holly and resumed his ring career. He was proud of the fact that during the war, he helped to integrate the entertainment shows at Keesler Field in Mississippi.

Robinson won his first world middleweight crown on Valentine's Day 1951 from Jake LaMotta on a thirteen-found TKO. He was thirty years old, and euphoric about his feat. The IBC had been forced to give him a title shot when he won the Neil Award. IBC president Jim Norris wanted Robinson to get rid of Gainford but he refused. To punish Robinson, Norris withheld his title bout as long as possible.

Before a scheduled defense with Randy Turpin in England, Robinson traveled to Paris to train and to entertain with a nightclub act. (During an audience with the French President and his wife, the impulsive Robinson suddenly reached out and kissed Madame Vincent Aurial on the cheek.) As a result of being undertrained, he lost his crown to Turpin on July 10, 1951, in fifteen rounds.

The rematch at the Polo Grounds in front of 61,370 fans on September 12 of that year set a record for gate receipts in a non-heavyweight fight: $767,626.17. Sugar Ray won the title for a second time by a 10-round TKO. (Turpin, who was also black, eventually lost his money and committed suicide.) Following victories over Carl "Bobo" Olson and Rocky Graziano, he tried to win the light-heavyweight title from Joey Maxim.

On an oppressively hot and humid June 25, 1952, Robinson came within six minutes of winning. With the night-time temperature at 104 degrees, he collapsed on his stool at the end of the thirteenth-round. All three judges had him ahead at the time: 10–3; 9–3–1; 7–4–2. Robinson said after the fight, "The heat didn't get me. God willed it that way."[12] He then decided to retire to show business.

After two and a half years of less than spectacular success on the stage, Robinson returned to the ring at age thirty-four. Incredibly, he won the middleweight crown for a third time from Carl "Bobo" Olson on a second-round KO in Chicago. He lost it to Gene Fullmer on January 2, 1957, in fifteen rounds and then astounded the sports world once more with his fourth title victory—a fifth round KO over Fullmer on May 1, 1957. Robinson became the first man to win a world title four times. Following a fifteen-round title defense loss to Carmen Basilio on a split decision, he won a fifth middleweight title on March 25, 1958, over Basilio at Chicago, also in fifteen rounds.

As much as fans marvelled at his prowess at age thirty-seven, they knew he had money troubles. He owed hundreds of thousands of dollars in back taxes by the time of his third title win. Robinson was unabashedly loose with his hard earned purses. "There were nights when I'd go through $500 in handouts when I had it on me."[13]

Joe Glaser, who was brought in to help rearrange his financial matters, eventually foreclosed. The Internal Revenue Service then put liens on his purses. For a time, Robinson earned $500,000 and never saw a dime of it. His wife, Edna Mae, divorced him, his café was closed, and his Cadillac was sold. "Only me was left."[14] "I went through four million dollars, but I have no regrets."[15]

At age forty Robinson was still fighting. He lost twice to Paul Pender in 1960. He retired for good in 1965 and devoted his time to the Sugar Ray Robinson Youth Foundation in Los Angeles. He is most remembered by the public for his bouts against Jake LaMotta, Carl "Bobo" Olson, and Carmen Basilio, but boxing experts remember his unexcelled boxing skills over a quarter of a century.

Robinson's career was summed up this way by Jimmy Jacobs, owner of the world's largest collection of fight films: "Sugar Ray Robinson . . . was probably the greatest fighter of all time—lightweight, welterweight, or heavyweight."[16] Robinson died in Culver City, California, April 12, 1989 at age 62.

Light Heavyweights: 161–175 lbs.

This weight division was also a one-man show during the fifties. Joey Maxim was the champion. Sugar Ray Robinson tried to win the title as a middleweight, but failed because he collapsed at the end of the thirteenth-round. But Archie Moore (formerly Archibald Lee Wright), at age thirty-seven, took Maxim's crown on December 17, 1952.

Moore was one of the cagiest boxers ever to lace on a pair of gloves, but his road to the world title was difficult. He says he was born on December 13, 1913 in Benoit, Mississippi and later moved to St. Louis, Missouri. He learned to box in reform school and turned professional at age twenty-three. After seventeen years of boxing, that included 170 bouts, he finally received a shot at the title.

Moore had been the number-one contender for five years, and five former champions passed up opportunities to fight him. As champion, Moore was the second oldest light heavyweight title holder. (Bob Fitzsimmons was forty-one.) To prepare for Maxim he was forced to lose sixteen pounds.

Since there was little demand for light heavyweight bouts during the early 1950s, Moore fought most of the time as a heavyweight.

Maxim demanded the most one-sided prize money split in memory. He was to be guaranteed $100,000 while Moore was to receive $800 plus expenses. After his fifteen-round win, Moore refused to let his manager lift him in the air in a victory hug. "Turn me loose!" he demanded. "Don't do that. Just slip my robe on my shoulders. Be cool. Don't get excited. There's nothing to be excited about. I could have won this thing twelve years ago. This is nothing new to me. Be cool."[17] He dedicated his victory to Argentine President Juan Peron, a long-time friend and supporter.

During his career his fighting weight varied from 152 to 192 pounds. At one time he was ranked number three among heavyweights. Because of limited competition in the heavyweight ranks, Moore was given a chance to win the world heavyweight title from Rocky Marciano on September 21, 1955, but he was knocked out in the ninth round in a bout shown in 133 theaters and drive-ins in ninety-two cities. The NBA finally lifted Moore's light heavyweight title on October 25, 1960, because of inactivity, though the New

York State Athletic Commission and the European Boxing Union waited another two years to do the same.

The NBA action was not without justification. Fourteen months after his loss to Marciano, Moore fought a second time for the world heavyweight title—this time against the young Floyd Patterson for Marciano's vacated crown on November 30, 1956. The forty-three-year-old Moore lost in a fifth-round knockout at Chicago in front of 14,000 fans. In the three-man elimination contest, Moore received a bye, while Patterson defeated Tommy "Hurricane" Jackson in a split twelve-round decision.

Moore's last light heavyweight title defense was a win in fifteen rounds over Giulio Rinaldi at Madison Square Garden, on June 10, 1961. Now forty-eight years old, he was known as the "Old Mongoose." Less than a year later he fought a ten-round draw with Willie Pastrano in Los Angeles.

Moore's next to last career bout was against a brash, fast-talking, lightning quick young heavyweight named Cassius Clay. Twenty-eight days short of his forty-ninth birthday, November 15, 1962, Moore lost on a knockout in the fourth round in Los Angeles. No fighter in his weight class had lasted as long with his skills intact. One of the best defensive boxers ever, he retired without a loss in his division after winning the title. His three losses were to men who either had won or would eventually win the heavyweight title.

Heavyweights: 191 lbs. and Above

Ezzard Charles: He had a most bizarre history on his way to the world heavyweight title. Born in Lawrenceville, Georgia, in 1921, he later moved to Cincinnati, Ohio. His parents divorced and his father, a janitor, allowed him to be raised by his grandmother. Charles began his boxing career at age fourteen as a featherweight. He eventually won

the Golden Gloves middleweight title twice and was the 1939 AAU National middleweight champion. He turned professional shortly thereafter, but didn't catch the public's eye until 1947 when an opponent, Sam Baroudi, died after their bout.

Though greatly affected by Baroudi's death, Charles now had a reputation as a hard puncher despite his tall, angular frame. Trained by the famed Ray Arcel, Charles fought Jersey Joe Walcott for the vacant NBA title on June 22, 1949, and won in fifteen rounds at Chicago. Charles was twenty-eight and Walcott was thirty-five. Even though Joe Louis had retired, he was still considered by many fight fans to be heavyweight champion. As Louis needed money badly, it was no mere coincidence that he and Charles fought for the title on September 27, 1950, in New York City. Charles won in fifteen rounds and was the second of only three men to defeat Louis during the Brown Bomber's professional career.

With the heavyweight division so muddled at the time, Walcott earned another chance at Charles' title. Charles could not sustain the onslaught from the shorter and more aggressive Walcott, and he lost his title in 1951. Three months after Charles' loss to Walcott, Joe Louis lost to Marciano. The lack of any clear-cup contenders allowed Charles to fight three more times for the world title, but he failed each time. One of the most underrated champions, Charles died of lateral sclerosis in 1965.

"Jersey" Joe Walcott: He was born January 31, 1914, at Merchantville, New Jersey—hence the nickname "Jersey" Joe. He began his professional career during the Depression, preferring to scrounge out a living in the ring rather than selling apples on street corners. As Walcott fought most of his bouts within fifty miles of New York City, he had a local following.

Joe Louis gave Walcott a title shot on December 5, 1947, at Madison Square Garden. Almost everyone who saw this battle— writers and fans alike—agree that Walcott should have been given the decision. He knocked Louis down twice, but back-pedaled in the fourteenth and fifteenth rounds and lost a split decision.

The first knockdown was in round one, and Louis was up at the count of two. The next knockdown was in round four, and Louis was up at the count of seven. It was evident to the 18,194 fans that Louis' best days were behind him. The referee, Ruby Goldstein, gave the fight to Walcott. But judges Marty Monroe and Frank Forbes scored it 9–6 and 8–6–1, respectively, for Louis. In a rematch at Yankee Stadium six months later, on June 25, 1948, Louis knocked out Walcott in the eleventh round in front of 42,657 fans.

Walcott's title victory over Ezzard Charles on July 18, 1951, at the age of thirty-seven was his fifth championship opportunity. He lost his title on a thirteenth-round knockout to Rocky Marciano in Philadelphia on September 23, 1952. Though he eventually won over $1 million dollars in purses, he lost most of it in bad investments. He later became the New Jersey State Athletic Commissioner and was inducted into boxing's Hall of Fame, in 1969.

Floyd Patterson: His life as a boxer was nothing short of a rags-to-riches story with a fairytale ending. Patterson was born on January 4, 1935, to an extremely poor family in Waco, North Carolina. His family later moved to New York City in search of a better life. But the sensitive and emotionally troubled young Patterson was unable to adjust.

Patterson became a delinquent and a truant, who hid out in subway tunnels in order to avoid going to school. He picked fights with anyone who made fun of his dirty and ill-fitting clothes. His mother even once sent him to a detention center to keep him out of

trouble. Finally, arrangements were made to send him to the Wiltwyck School for troubled youngsters. The move proved a fortunate one. There, he learned to box, starting as a middleweight. His brother, Frank, who won the New York Golden Gloves 160-pound title in 1949, became his hero.

Patterson had incredibly fast hands, and as an amateur he developed his famous peek-a-boo defense, saying he could appreciate "the importance of avoiding being hit."[18] Patterson won the Golden Gloves title, and he also earned a berth on the 1952 Olympic Boxing Team as a middleweight. He won the Gold Medal. He also gained the National AAU middleweight title that year.

After Patterson turned professional, his manager, Cus D'Amato, became obsessed with the IBC's intentions toward him. D'Amato, some thought, believed the IBC wanted to take Patterson away from him and to force Patterson to fight for the heavyweight crown. Patterson claims D'Amato wanted him to win Archie Moore's light heavyweight crown before tackling the heavyweight division. In any event, after Rocky Marciano retired in 1955, Patterson (who sustained a broken right hand) defeated Tommy "Hurricane" Jackson in a split twelve-round decision for the right to meet Archie Moore for Marciano's vacated crown. The twenty-one-year-old Patterson needed just five rounds to dispose of Moore, who was twenty-two years his senior. It was a strange contest, pitting the world light heavyweight champion against an opponent who was a natural light heavyweight himself. The $114,257 purse was for Patterson "riches beyond my wildest dreams, but insignificant compared to what was to come."[19]

Patterson's first title defense was significant because it was not promoted by the IBC. He was constantly nagged by critics, who claimed he was not worthy of the title, that he was just a blown-up light heavyweight with quick fists and a big heart. Consequently, these same critics were not surprised when the Swede, Ingemar Johansson took Patterson's crown on June 26, 1959, at Yankee Stadium.

Johansson, a four to one underdog, knocked Patterson down seven times to win by a technical knockout in the third round. The fight had been delayed one day because of rain and only 21,961 fans showed up. A sensitive and giving man, Patterson had attended graduation ceremonies at his old school, P.S. 614, just before the fight. The loss devastated him. "I felt I had let so many people down, all of America."[20]

Six days short of a year later, Patterson became the first heavyweight champion to regain his title, scoring a fifth-round knockout over Johansson at the Polo Grounds. It was the highlight of his career, and it was done without D'Amato's assistance. (D'Amato's license had been revoked on November 24, 1959.) Almost 32,000 fans and a closed circuit audience of half a million paid over $2 million dollars to witness Patterson's comeback. And on March 13, 1961, Patterson defeated Johansson for the second time, at Miami Beach on a sixth-round knockout. It was to be his last shining moment in the ring.

Against the strong objections of D'Amato, who was again advising him, Patterson fought Charles "Sonny" Liston on September 25, 1962. He lost by a knockout two minutes, six seconds into the first round. Liston, an ex-felon, who was generally disliked and, feared, outweighed Patterson by twenty-five pounds, 212 to 187, as well as having a thirteen-inch reach advantage. Their encounter was, in retrospect, the most publicized fight since Jack Dempsey–Gene Tunney.

Nearly 19,000 fans at Chicago's Comiskey Park paid $665,420 and another 600,000 people in closed-circuit theaters paid over $4 million to view the fight. It was the first time the champion had been knocked out in the

first round, and it was the third-fastest knockout in the history of the heavyweight title. Amazingly, Liston had boxed only five official rounds in the past two years.

Patterson felt that his ego and the nation's prestige were on the line, so he tried to slug it out with the much stronger Liston. "When the bell rang, I was like a robot . . . The President of the United States (John F. Kennedy), Ralph Bunche . . . the millions of letters . . . made Liston a bad guy . . . pressure . . . the President . . . said to me 'make sure you keep that championship.' "[21]

In the eyes of white America, this was a fight between a "good nigger" and a "bad nigger." Dr. Charles Larson, president of the United States National Boxing Association, vehemently opposed the bout and said he spoke for millions of Americans: "I will use my personal influence to prevent Liston being matched against Patterson. In my opinion, Patterson is a fine representative of his race, and I believe the Heavyweight champion of the World should be the kind of man our children could look up to . . ."[22]

Less than a year later, on July 22, 1963, Patterson lost for the second time to Liston at Las Vegas, in two minutes and ten seconds of the first round. The bout had originally been scheduled for April 4, but was postponed because Liston had hurt his knee playing golf.

After his bouts with Liston, Patterson faced the "greatest"—Muhammad Ali. On November 22, 1965, Patterson, outweighed by 16 pounds, lost in 12 rounds to Ali at Las Vegas, Nevada. Ali, a recent convert to the religion of Islam, taunted and teased Patterson before and during their bout. "You're nothing but an Uncle Tom Negro, a white man's Negro, a yellow Negro. You quit twice to Liston. Get into the ring and I'll lick you."[23]

No black athlete had ever publicly spoken so disparagingly to another black athlete. Moreover, their bout came amidst an emotional period in black American history, when demonstrations and marches were front page news and Congress was inundated with civil rights bills. Ali, who was racially defiant in public, had a tremendous following among young blacks. Consequently, Patterson had likened his bout with Ali to a "moral crusade."

Almost all viewers of the fight agreed that Ali could have won the match much sooner than round 12. But he purposefully dragged it out, preferring to "punish" Patterson. All through the fight Ali kept up a verbal barrage, saying to Patterson, "Come on, America, come on white America!"[24]

Just before the fight Ali tendered one of his soon to be much noted poems, one specifically derogatory in tone:

"I'm going to put him flat on his back,
so that he will start acting Black,
because when he was champ he didn't do as he
　should,
he tried to force himself into an all-white
　neighborhood."[25]

Floyd Patterson ended his career with his brains intact and money in the bank. He was the first black world champion since Harry Wills to retire financially secure. He was also the first Olympic gold medalist to go on to win a world title. More importantly to him, he was highly respected among his peers.

As the decade of the 1950s came to a close for black athletics, the United States Supreme Court effectively ended the IBC's monopoly; the Internal Revenue Service agreed to forgive all of Joe Louis' debts in 1960. The next ten years were much more contentious. They were to be dominated by the black social revolution, the death of a United States President, and the quickest and most talkative heavyweight champion the world had ever seen.

THE MUHAMMAD ALI ERA

The new occupational and career opportunities that arose for blacks after World War II did not deter a significant number of youngsters from a boxing career. As the 1960s began, there were many political victories yet to be won, and boxers were still the highest-paid athletes in the world. The availability of internationally televised bouts and the three Olympic Games since the war had helped to spread the popularity of the sport. Also, Third World countries began training top-flight fighters in the lower weight classes.

With the IBC now a thing of the past, organized crime tried to control the major contenders. Consequently, Senator Estes Kefauver of Tennessee began a probe of the sport in 1960, and concluded that organized crime did indeed have substantial influence. The NBA, in a move to reflect its more international scope, changed its name to the World Boxing Association (WBA) in 1962, and it was soon joined by a rival sanctioning body, the World Boxing Council (WBC), which seemed much more representative of Third World countries. African-American fighters made their marks in the heavier weight classes of both groups.

Welterweights: 141–147 lbs.

Curtis Cokes: Cokes won the Texas State title in 1965, and the Southern title in December of that year. After winning an elimination tournament to determine the successor to Emile Griffith, he won the world title from Jean Josselin on November 28, 1966. Cokes had previously defeated Manuel Gonzales on August 24, 1966, for the vacant WBA title. But the 5-foot 9-inch, 145-pound fighter from Dallas lost his title to Jose Napoles in thirteen rounds at Los Angeles on April 18, 1969. He failed in another attempt against Napoles two months later. There would be no more black American welterweight champions until Ray Leonard in 1979.

Light Heavyweights: 161–175 lbs.

Harold Johnson: He won the WBA title from Jesse Bowdrey at Miami Beach, Florida, in a ninth-round technical knockout on February 7, 1961, to capture Archie Moore's old title. Moore, however, would still be recognized as champion by the rest of the world for one more year. Johnson then captured the World title from Doug Jones on May 12, 1962, and lost it thirteen months later to Willie Pastrano in a fifteen-round split decision at Las Vegas.

Initially, Pastrano was hesitant about meeting Johnson. "I didn't want to fight Harold Johnson . . . that animal . . . a fighter's fighter . . . greatest defensive boxer I've ever seen . . . a perfectionist."[26] Johnson and his father, Phil, shared the interesting historical note of having both lost to "Jersey" Joe Walcott—Phil in 1936 and Harold in 1950.

Bob Foster: He was perhaps the most powerful punching light heavyweight champion since John Henry Lewis. Born in Albuquerque, New Mexico, on December 15, 1938, he won the title from Dick Tiger in 1968 at Madison Square Garden. The result was never in doubt, as Foster scored a fourth-round knockout. Like Archie Moore, Foster kept the title a long time—nearly six years. He retired undefeated as a light heavyweight.

Although Foster successfully defended his title fourteen times—a record for a light heavyweight champion—his purses were not nearly as lucrative as those for the heavyweights or some welterweights. Foster made an unsuccessful challenge for the world heavyweight title, losing to Joe Frazier in 1970. He lost an NABF title fight to Muhammad Ali in 1972. He later became a sheriff in his native Albuquerque.

Heavyweights: 191 lbs. and Above

Charles "Sonny" Liston: No contender for the heavyweight title was so generally disliked as Liston, not even the Jack Johnson of 1908. Liston's troubled childhood mirrored that of Archie Moore and Floyd Patterson. Born on May 8, 1932, in Pine Bluff, Arkansas, he was one of twenty-five children his father had by two wives. His father later abandoned his families, and Liston moved to St. Louis, Missouri.

When he was eighteen years old, Liston was incarcerated in the Missouri State Penitentiary for robbing a service station. He learned to box there and was released to the custody of Frank Mitchell, the black owner of the St. Louis *Argus* newspaper. Despite winning the 1952 Golden Gloves title and then turning professional, he would never completely erase his image as a street hoodlum.

Liston was arrested again in 1956 for assaulting a policeman and was sentenced to nine months in a workhouse, in addition to having his boxing license revoked. His troubles with the law and his suspected links with organized crime made it nearly impossible for him to secure fights. He was eventually relicensed, after falsifying his prison record.

One year before Liston fought Floyd Patterson for the title, his manager was Joseph "Peppy" Barone, a known friend of Frank "Blinky" Palermo, Frankie Carbo, and Johnny Vitale—all alleged organized crime figures. Liston's police record at the time showed nineteen arrests. In February of 1962, Liston obtained a new manager, Jack Nilon, and secured a shot at the title.

Liston knocked out Patterson in their title bout within two minutes and six seconds of the first round, on September 25, 1962. Joe Louis stated: "Liston is stronger than any man I've seen."[27] Two months later, after defeating Archie Moore, Cassius Clay said to Liston at ringside, "You're next. You must fall in eight [rounds]."[28] To which Liston replied, "You couldn't lick a Popsicle."

Seven months after defeating Patterson for the second time, Liston faced Cassius Clay at

Miami Beach. It was the most discussed heavyweight fight in years, and was replete with racial and social demagoguery. Clay referred to Liston as "a big ugly bear," (a comment only a black man could have gotten away with at the time). Liston had made matters worse with a heartfelt statement he made after returning home from a European tour soon after the bombing of the Birmingham, Alabama, black church and the killing of four little girls: "I'm ashamed to say I'm in America."[29] The white press had a field day.

But Clay's reputation in white America was also in transformation. He had met the black Islamic leader Malcolm X in Detroit in 1962, and Malcolm was now his spiritual advisor. Malcolm stated that ". . . it was Allah's intent for me to help Cassius prove Islam's superiority before the world . . . people everywhere scoffed at Cassius Clay's chances of beating Liston."[30]

As for Clay, he mixed the practical with the spiritual. Against Liston, he planned to copy Sugar Ray Robinson's strategy against Jake LaMotta: hit and run. At the weigh-in Clay seemed out of control. His plan was to psych out Liston, to "mess with his mind." He entered the ring against Liston truly believing he was divinely destined to win. "It is prophesied for me to be successful!"[31] he roared. "I cannot be beaten." Clay even gave up staying in a plush white Miami Beach hotel, preferring to stay at the black-owned Hampton House motel.

A huge thunder storm drenched Miami just two and a half hours before fight time. Consequently, only 8,297 patrons attended the bout. Liston, a seven to one favorite, was guaranteed 40 percent of the live gate, television, radio, and movie rights; Clay got 22.5 percent. The promotion was a financial flop. But in the ring a new era in boxing had begun.

Clay was in constant motion while Liston kept looking for an opening for his lethal right hand. At the start of the seventh round, Liston refused to leave his stool, claiming later that he could not move his left arm.

Alleged ties to organized-crime continued to follow Liston, and many people thought that the fight was fixed, since $50,000 of Clay's purse was paid by Intercontinental Promotions (ICP), in which Liston was a stockholder. Half of Liston's shares in ICP were held in Sam Margolis' name, a known friend of "Blinky" Palermo's. As a result, the sports press made the assumption that Liston owed money to Palermo.

The second fight on May 25, 1965, in Lewiston, Maine, between Liston and Muhammad Ali (Clay changed his name a day after their first fight), was even more controversial than the first one. Coming just three months after Malcolm X's assassination and two months after Ali's failure to pass an Army preinduction mental examination, the fight was over in one minute, fifty-two seconds of the first round. There was even a mixup over the exact time the fight ended.

Ali nailed Liston with what ringsiders say was a phantom right hand and Liston hit the canvas at 1:42. But referee Jersey Joe Walcott somehow miscounted. At one point, *Ring Magazine* publisher Nat Fleischer shouted to Walcott, "Joe, the fight is over!" Walcott finally stopped the bout two minutes and twelve seconds into the round.

Liston was never the same again. In 1969, he was knocked out by Leotis Martin in the ninth round of a NABF title fight. A year later he was dead of a drug overdose in Las Vegas.

Muhammad Ali (formerly Cassius Marcellus Clay, Jr.): When young Cassius Clay, Jr., decided to become a boxer he could not have picked a more difficult period to begin. Born during World War II on January 17, 1942, in Louisville, Kentucky, he had his first boxing lessons in the mid-fifties. At first, the 4-foot, 87-pound novice only wanted to learn to fight in order to keep older and bigger boys from taking his bicycle. His teacher was an Irish-American cop named Joe Martin.

In 1953, nineteen fighters died as the result of injuries suffered in the ring. Consequently, the January 1955 issue of *Ebony* magazine headlined an article titled "Should Boxing Be Abolished?" In addition, boxers continued to find themselves in dire financial straits. (Sam Langford, named one of the ten greatest athletes of the first half-century, died penniless in a Boston nursing home on January 12, 1956.) Why, then, did a young man like Cassius Clay, who was from a comfortable home with a solid nuclear family, choose professional boxing as a career? *Because he was good; in fact, he was very good.*

In 1958, when he was only sixteen, Clay won his hometown's Golden Gloves light heavyweight title and reached the quarter finals of the Golden Gloves Tournament of Champions in Chicago. He stood 6 feet tall and weighed 170 pounds. While in Chicago he heard for the first time about Elijah Muhammad, leader of the Black Nation of Islam.

The year 1960 was an incredible one for Clay. He was graduated from Louisville's Central High School number 376 in a class of 391. In the ring that year he won his sixth Kentucky Golden Gloves title; the Tournament of Champions in Chicago; the National Golden Gloves; the AAU title; and an Olympic Gold Medal—all as a light heavyweight. The year before, he had won the National Golden Gloves and the AAU titles. But he lost in a bid for the United States Pan-American Games Boxing Team.

By the time of the 1960 Olympics in Rome, Clay had already earned a deserved reputation as a loudmouthed, brash, and cocky fighter. He was, in actuality, the most publicly vocal black athlete since Jack Johnson. Neither white nor black Americans knew what to make of him. After defeating Zbiegniew Pietrzykowski in the Olympic finals for his forti-

eth consecutive win, he was asked what he wanted next. "I want money, plenty of it!"[32]

Clay, during his stay in Rome, refused to back down from giving his opinion on weighty issues. In answer to a Soviet reporter's question about the condition of blacks in America, he shot back: "To me, the USA is still the best country in the world, counting yours."[33] But when he returned to Louisville as an Olympic champion he realized that life for him had not changed because of his new fame. "With my gold medal actually hanging around my neck, I couldn't get a cheeseburger served to me in a downtown Louisville restaurant."[34] Clay later threw his Olympic gold medal into the Ohio River, in a gesture of racial defiance of American hypocrisy.

As colorful and controversial as he was, a respected group of white Louisville businessmen with an intent to capitalize on Clay's notoriety, agreed to form a syndicate to sponsor their newly acknowledged hometown hero. The syndicate members were Archibald M. Foster, Patrick Calhoun, Jr., Gordon Davidson, William S. Cutchins, J.D. Stetson Coleman, William Faversham, Jr., James R. Todd, Vertner D. Smith, Sr., George W. Norton IV, William Lee Lyons Brown, E. Gary Sutcliffe, and Robert W. Bingham. The syndicate agreement was arranged by a black lawyer, Alberta Jones, who received $2,500 for her services and was later fired. (Clay had also received management offers from Archie Moore, Rocky Marciano, and Cus D'Amato.)

In return for 50 percent of Clay's earnings in and out of the ring, the syndicate gave him a $10,000 bonus to sign, an $80,000 guarantee over the first two years, $6,000 for the next four years, and all training expenses. The agreement was to last six years, from 1960 to 1966.

Leaving behind an amateur record of 161–6, Clay fought his first professional fight at Freedom Hall in Louisville on October 29, 1960. He collected $2,000 for a six-round decision over Tunney Hunsaker. Immediately after his win, he signed Angelo Dundee as his trainer for $125 per week.

Clay began calling the round in which his opponents would fall, beginning with Alex Miteff on October 7, 1961. He claimed he patterned his showmanship after the wrestler "Gorgeous" George Wagner. By now known by an assortment of nicknames—the Louisville Lip, Cash the Brash, Gaseous Cassius, Mighty Mouth, Clap Trap Clay, and Kentucky Rooster—he correctly named the knockout round in thirteen of seventeen fights. "Humble people I've found don't get very far. If you're a nice guy people trample on you."[35]

After defeating forty-nine-year-old Archie Moore on November 15, 1962, Clay set his sights on the recently crowned heavyweight champion, Charles "Sonny" Liston. Between the Moore and Liston bouts, his boxing skills were questioned and his verbal pronouncements debated. On June 18, 1963, the Englishman Henry Cooper knocked him down in their bout, leading experts to believe he could not take a punch. A month later, he made a phonograph record, "I Am The Greatest." *Ebony* magazine ran an editorial that focused on his value and worth to the black community.

During this period Clay became more and more attracted to Islam. He made frequent trips to Chicago and Detroit to meet with Malcolm X and Elijah Muhammad. A day after winning the world heavyweight title for the first time, he changed his name to Muhammad Ali, which means "worthy of all praise." While the black sports press tolerated this conversion, only a few white sports figures—Howard Cosell, Bud Collins, and Robert Lipsyte, among others—continued to support him.

Ali disdained his appellation as a "Black Muslim." "That is a word made up by the white press. I am a black man who has adopted Islam . . . I love to be black, and I love to be with my people . . ."[36]

Ali's spiritual mentor, Malcolm X, had been forthright about his young disciple. "Clay . . . is the finest Negro athlete I have ever known, the man who will mean more to his people than Jackie Robinson was, because Robinson is the white man's hero. But Cassius is the black man's hero. Do you know why? Because the white press wanted him to lose . . . because he is a Muslim. You noticed nobody cares about the religion of other athletes. But their prejudice against Clay blinded them to his ability."[37]

On February 26, 1964, Ali made a simple announcement. "I believe in the religion of Islam. I believe in Allah and peace . . . I'm not a Christian anymore."[38] His troubles were just beginning.

Ali rolled over his opponents, taunting them in the ring. He railed at Liston in Maine during their second bout, "Get up and fight, you bum!" The state of Massachusetts and the WBA refused to sanction this fight. He married Sonji Roi on August 14, 1964, and divorced her in January 1966, claiming she would not agree to Muslim customs.

In February 1966, Ali was reclassified 1-A by the Selective Service. He immediately issued his negative response in the form of a poem:

Keep asking me, no matter how long
On the war in Viet Nam, I sing this song
I ain't got no quarrel with the Viet Cong.

Nearly three hundred theaters cancelled contracts for Ali's bout with Ernie Terrell. Getting no response from American promoters, Ali fought in Europe, where he was served with a notice for failing to pay all money. His syndicate contract with the Louisville businessmen expired prematurely in October of 1963.

Ali finally secured Houston, Texas, as the site for his fifteen-round bout with Terrell on

February 6, 1967. Before the fight, Terrell had referred to Ali as Clay. In the ring Ali called Terrell "a dog" and kept asking him, "What's my name?" The bout set an indoor attendance record of 37,321. Ali stated afterwards: "I am an astronaut of boxing. Joe Louis and Dempsey were just jet pilots. I'm in a world of my own."[39]

Ali was ordered to report to the Army induction center in Houston on April 28. "For months I've drilled myself for this moment,"[40] he said later, "but I still feel nervous. I hope no one notices my shoulders tremble." Three times Ali refused the call for "Cassius Clay" to step forward and be inducted into the United States Army. The voice of the induction officer noticeably wavered.

After signing an official document stating his refusal on religious grounds Ali walked out of the building to a chorus of cheers from supporters and students from Texas Southern University. Eight days before his induction procedure, he had declared: "I am not going ten thousand miles from here to help murder and kill and burn poor people simply to help continue the domination of white slave masters over the darker people."[41] Without waiting for an indictment, the WBA and the NY SAC stripped Ali of his title.

Ten days later, on May 8, a federal grand jury indicted Ali for failing to submit to the draft. He confided to Sugar Ray Robinson, "I'm afraid, Ray. I'm real afraid."[42] Robinson recalled, "That night . . . His eyes were glistening with tears—tears of torment, tears of indecision."[43] On the phone with his mother the day before, Ali was tearfully told, "G.G. [his mother's nickname for him], do the right thing . . . take the step."[44]

On June 19 and 20, Judge Joe Ingram of the United States District Court for the Southern District of Texas tried the Ali case and sentenced him to five years in jail and a $10,000 fine. Ali posted the bail and was released.

Some prominent black athletes publicly came to Ali's support: Lew Alcindor, the UCLA basketball player; Bill Russell, player/coach of the Boston Celtics; Sid Williams and Walter Beach of the Cleveland Browns; Curtis McClinton of the Kansas City Chiefs; Bobby Mitchell and Jim Shorter of the Washington Redskins; Willie Davis of the Green Bay Packers; and Gale Sayers of the Chicago Bears. The traditional black civil rights leaders, however, were very wary about publicly supporting Ali.

With the assistance of lawyer Hayden Covington, Ali appealed his case first to the Fifth Circuit Court of Appeals and then to the United States Supreme Court. (The Fifth Circuit Court upheld the District Court verdict). Ironically, Covington's sister was married to General Lewis Hershey, the Director of the Selective Service System.

For two years thereafter, boxing was in a state of limbo. Ali, twenty-five years old at the time of his induction refusal, spent twenty-nine months in exile. With the war in Vietnam at its peak, he was sought as an antiwar speaker. "My main livelihood is coming from my appearances at colleges, black and white . . . support for me is high."[45]

On June 28, 1970, the United States Supreme Court, in an 8–0 decision, declared Ali free because of a technical error by the Justice Department. At first, Justice William Brennan was the only one of the Supreme Court's Justices willing to hear the Ali appeal—known as *Clay v. United States*. His case had come before the Court two terms before, but the Court had refused to hear it. But when the Court heard that the FBI had illegally tapped Ali's phone, they changed their minds.

The original vote (with the black Justice Thurgood Marshall abstaining because he had been the federal government's Solicitor General when the case began), was 5–3 against Ali. But Justice John Harlan's clerk convinced him that Ali was genuine in his beliefs and "For all practical purposes, Ali was opposed to all wars."[46]

Subsequently, an additional vote was taken and the Court deadlocked 4 to 4. Justice Potter Stewart proposed that the Court simply set Ali free because of the wiretap. Though Ali thanked Allah and the Court for "recognizing the sincerity of the religious teaching that I've accepted,"[47] in the words of Woodward and Armstrong, "he did not know how close he had come to going to jail."[48]

While most black Americans and antiwar protesters were jubilant over Ali's release, veterans groups and President Richard M. Nixon were incensed. ". . . You know Cassius Clay is Nixon's pet peeve,"[49] Jackie Robinson told Nelson Rockefeller. "Nixon hates his guts."

Now relicensed, Ali trained in Miami before leaving for an exhibition at Morehouse College and a bout with Jerry Quarry in Atlanta. Before leaving Miami he received two packages in the mail: one contained a decapitated black chihuahua dog and the other a hanged doll with a note saying: "To Cassius Clay, From Georgia." Ali meant to use this fight and a win over Oscar Bonavena as tuneups for Joe Frazier, the new WBA titleholder.

The Ali-Frazier bout on March 8, 1971, at the new Madison Square Garden became known as "The Fight." Frazier had come up the hard way, winning both the NYSAC and WBA titles. (In January 1970, three men laid claim to a heavyweight title: Jimmy Ellis, WBA; Frazier, NYSAC; and Ali, recently deposed as WBC champion.) Over 20,000 fans in Madison Square Garden and 1.3 million on closed circuit television saw Frazier defeat Ali in fifteen of the toughest rounds in memory. The fight truly lived up to its billing.

Ali was his old self again. In answer to Frazier's warning that he would come out "smokin'," Ali said, "Well, smokin's bad for the lungs, gives you cancer . . . Maybe this will shock and amaze ya, but I'm gonna retire

that Joe Frazier."[50] When the fight ended, both combatants had to go to the hospital. Frazier would not fight for the next ten months.

After winning the NABF title in 1971, Ali lost to Ken Norton on March 31, 1973. Norton used hypnosis as part of his training for this bout, and he fractured Ali's jaw in the first round. Ali regained the NBAF title from Norton on September 10, 1973, and prepared to defend it against Frazier on January 28, 1974. (George Foreman held the world title as a result of a win against Frazier on January 22, 1973.) Ali defeated Frazier in twelve rounds at Madison Square Garden in a fight witnessed by a 20,746 live gate and a closed-circuit audience of 1.1 million. The total gross receipts were roughly $25 million.

Ali then signed to meet George Foreman for the world title on October 30, 1974, in Kinshasa, Zaire—a bout billed as "The Rumble in the Jungle." Foreman, viewed as the strongest heavyweight since Liston, fell in the eighth round before 62,000 screaming Zaireans. Ali, then age thirty-two, became the second man to regain the heavyweight title. It was also the first heavyweight title fight on the African continent. Don King, a black promoter and an ex-felon, had arranged this $10 million fight with Zaire's President Mobutu.

Ali used what he called his "rope-a-dope" technique to tire out Foreman. He simply leaned back against the ropes and protected his head, allowing the much stronger Foreman to punch and, thereby, burn himself out. Foreman, however, said he followed the instructions of his trainer, Dick Saddler, who advised him to "get it over with quickly."

Ali had his third and final meeting with Frazier on September 30, 1975, in Manila, the Philippines. Dubbed "The Thrilla in Manila" and "Super Fight III," it was hailed by many who saw it as the greatest fight in the history of the sport. The two fighters went at it nonstop for fourteen rounds. With his boxer's body bruised and battered, trainer Eddie

Futch refused to let Frazier come out for round 15. He cut Frazier's gloves off to end the fight. "Sit down, son. It's all over," Futch said. "No one will ever forget what you did here today."[51]

Ali stated it was ". . . The hardest fight I've ever had in my life—the deadliest and the most vicious . . . me and Joe Frazier had rumbled together this night for the last time. And it's over. The dinosaurs met for the last time . . ."[52] In the postbout press conference it was Frazier who said, "I hit him with punches that would bring down walls." Ali spoke of a feeling like being close to death.[53] Frazier was magnanimous in defeat. Brotherly, he said to Ali, "You one bad nigger. We both bad niggers. We don't do no crawlin'."[54]

At age thirty-six, Ali lost his world title to Leon Spinks on Feburary 15, 1978, in a fifteen-round split decision in Las Vegas. Though undertrained and overweight, Ali roared, quoting General Douglas MacArthur, "I shall return." And return he did. On September 15, 1978, before the largest ever indoor boxing audience, 63,350 at the New Orleans Superdome, he regained the WBA version of his title—becoming the first man to win the heavyweight title three times. Spinks, who held the title only seven months, lost a unanimous fifteen-round decision.

Ali retired for the second time (the first time was in early 1970) and then came back to lose to WBC champion Larry Holmes, on October 2, 1980. Holmes "carried" Ali through eleven rounds at Caesar's Palace in Las Vegas. Ali was almost thirty-nine years old.

In his post-retirement years, Ali, who was elected to the Hall of Fame of *Ring Magazine* September 14, 1987, suffered from Parkinson's Syndrome. But his clout as one of the world's most popular personalities didn't diminish. In November 1990, Ali and several others visited Iraq and met with Saddam Hussein, who held numerous foreigners, including U.S. citizens against their will just prior to US intervention in the Persian Gulf conflict. Fifteen hostages were immediately released, including Harry Brill-Edwards, who said of Ali, "He's quiet, but he's better than I expected. His speech is halting but he's sharp . . . he's a tremendous human being."

No one had a greater influence over the sport since Joe Louis. Ironically, Ali's rise to prominence came amid the black social revolution of the 1960s and America's distress over the Vietnam War. This extraordinary athlete was a hero to thousands of young people throughout the world. In retrospect one must agree with Ali's self-assessment: He was The Greatest.

Ernie Terrell: He was one of the tallest heavyweights since Primo Carnera, standing 6-feet 6-inches and 200 pounds. He was born on April 4, 1939, in Chicago, and after turning professional in 1957, fought there almost exclusively until 1962. He won the vacant WBA title over Eddie Machen on March 5, 1965, in Chicago. He then lost in a bid for the world title to Muhammad Ali on February 6, 1967, in fifteen rounds. In the WBA Elimination Tournament in 1967, he lost in twelve rounds to Thad Spencer. He retired four months later.

Terrell's bout with Ali was marked by much name calling. Terrell referred to Ali in the prefight buildup as Cassius Clay, and experts believed Ali deliberately prolonged this fight to punish Terrell. (*See* Muhammad Ali.) After a two-year retirement, Terrell returned to the ring and eventually lost a twelve-rounder to Chuck Wepner on June 23, 1973, for the United States heavyweight title. He retired for good with a 46–9 professional record.

Jimmy Ellis: This Louisville, Kentucky, native's primary claim to fame at the beginning of his professional career was as Muhammad Ali's sparring partner. However, Ellis, who was born on February 24, 1940, soon earned the right through the WBA Elimination Tournament to fight Jerry Quarry for that group's vacant title. He won in fifteen rounds in Oakland, California.

The Elimination Tournament had been held to name a successor to Ali's vacated title. The boxers in the tournament included Floyd Patterson, Oscar Bonavena, Jerry Quarry, Karl Mildenberger, Ernie Terrell, Thad Spencer, Jimmy Ellis, and Joe Frazier. (Frazier later refused to join the group.)

After defeating Floyd Patterson in fifteen rounds in his first title defense, Ellis lost to Joe Frazier in a bid for the vacant world title on February 16, 1970. Ellis, who stood 6-feet 1-inch and weighed 205 pounds, was managed by Angelo Dundee. This clever fighter with a solid left jab retired in 1975 after losses to Muhammad Ali, Ernie Shavers, and Joe Frazier (for the second time).

Joe Frazier: "Smokin' Joe" was born in Gullah country, in Beaufort, South Carolina, on January 12, 1944. He was unquestionably one of the hardest-working fighters in the history of the ring. If Ali's style was "hit and run," Frazier's could be classified as "hit, and hit again." He first fought professionally in Philadelphia after winning an Olympic heavyweight gold medal in 1964.

Copying the syndicate formula used for Muhammad Ali, Frazier was also sponsored by a group of white businessmen. Known as Cloverlay, Inc., these investors capitalized their group at $250 per share. Their return was eventually a whopping 1,350 percent, or $3,350 per share. Frazier got to keep 50 percent of his purses while the other 50 percent was split between Cloverlay and his manager/trainer, Yancey Durham, 35 percent and 15 percent, respectively. They were encouraged to invest because Frazier had won thirty-eight of forty amateur bouts as well as the Golden Gloves title in 1962, 1963 and 1964.

Known as "Billy Boy" as a teenager, Frazier began boxing in a Police Athletic League gymnasium to lose weight. He developed his tremendous upper-body strength while working in a meat packing plant in Philadelphia. His first eleven fights were won by KOs, none of which lasted more than six rounds. After defeating George Chuvalo on July 19, 1967, he refused to join the WBA Elimination Tournament that began less than a month later, on August 5. Instead, Frazier opted to pursue the vacant NYSAC title and won it by defeating Buster Mathis on March 4, 1968, in an eleventh-round knockout.

With Ali in exile, Frazier's path to the world title was easier. He won it against Jimmy Ellis, then the current WBA champion, on February 16, 1970, in a fifth-round KO. His first world-title defense was against the light heavyweight champion, Bob Foster, whom he overwhelmed in a second round knockout. That set the stage for his three meetings with Ali.

In one of the sport's epic battles, Frazier defeated Ali in the first of their three fights. (*See* Muhammad Ali.) Though he won this encounter over fifteen of the most outstanding rounds ever seen, he was so battered in his face, chest, and arms that he could not fight again for ten months. After two successful defenses, he lost his world title via a second-round KO to George Foreman. It was the most embarrassing loss of his career.

Frazier was a three to one favorite over Foreman, but the challenger knocked him down six times in less than six minutes. Using the same "go for broke" style as he employed against Ali, Frazier was never given a chance to even loosen up. Foreman waited for openings to deliver his lethal right hand and simply overpowered Frazier, whom he outweighed by sixteen pounds.

Frazier lost his next two battles with Ali, a twelve-rounder in New York for the NABF title on January 28, 1974, and a fourteenth-round

TKO in Manila, The Philippines, on October 1, 1975. (*See* Muhammad Ali.) His second fight with Foreman was a nontitle affair on June 15, 1976, and he lost in a fifth-round KO. By then Foreman had lost his world title to Ali in Zaire.

Frazier finally retired in 1981 and devoted himself to the career of his son, Marvis, a promising young heavyweight. He was elected to Boxing's Hall of Fame in 1980. His short but brilliant career of 37 professional fights included 27 knockouts, 5 victories by decision, 1 draw, 1 loss by decision, and 3 losses by knockouts. He was one of the most popular fighters since World War II.

THE SEVENTIES

When the decade of the seventies began, it reminded boxing observers of the early fifties. The glamour division—the heavyweight class—was muddled, and three separate fighters claimed the title for three separate sanctioning bodies: Jimmy Ellis for the WBA; Joe Frazier for the NYSAC; and Muhammad Ali, as the deposed and exiled WBC champion.

Additional weight classes had been introduced to boxing during the previous fifteen years. The International Olympic Committee had inserted more weight classes in its program, and American television had encouraged more classes, as there would be more champions to promote. But even though boxing was now more accessible, black American champions continued to be concentrated in the higher-weight classes. In the seventies, there were no black American champions in the following divisions: flyweight, junior featherweight, featherweight, bantamweight, junior lightweight, lightweight, and junior welterweight.

There were other changes, as well. Joe Louis' image had become altered as a result of the black social revolution of the sixties. In his prime, he was the most well-known black man on earth. Unfortunately, for the first ten years following his retirement, he was seen as the victim of bad financial management and of his own spending habits. However, during the sixties, it became standard practice among a new, young, and iconoclastic generation of black historians to lump him among the "Uncle Toms" of the post-war period. Nevertheless, sentiment toward Louis had changed again by the mid-seventies. While he had continued to be a hero to black Americans thirty-five and over, those who had castigated him ten years before were now more realistic. Louis worked as a greeter at the Caesars' Palace Hotel and Casino in Las Vegas and his mental faculties were failing. In essence, he had white America tending to his needs in the end.

In the ring, black boxers finally began assuring their financial futures. Three in particular, George Foreman, Larry Holmes and Sugar Ray Leonard, were among the wealthiest of all black athletes upon their retirements. (But like many other aging athletes intoxicated by the limelight and big dollar payoffs, all three staged comebacks.)

In the seventies black promoters like Don King and Butch Lewis competed against their white counterparts, (e.g., Bob Arum and Jerry Perenchio) to stage the most attractive bouts. Subsequently, for the first time in twenty years, stars in the lower-weight division outdrew the heavyweights.

Welterweights: 141–147 lbs.

Wilfredo Benitez: He was born in the Bronx, New York, on September 12, 1958, and was managed and taught by his father. At 5-feet 10-inches, this 154-pound elusive and talented fighter is more closely identified with the Hispanic community than the black community. He fought nearly six years as a professional before his first loss—to Ray Leonard at Las Vegas on November 30, 1979, via a fifteenth-round TKO.

Benitez first attracted international notice when he won the World Junior Welterweight title in San Juan, Puerto Rico, on March 6, 1976, from Antonio Cervantes. Three years later, he won the WBC welterweight title from Carlos Palomino in San Juan on January 14, 1979, in fifteen rounds. Benitez was very difficult to hit and a master of defense and counterpunching. After losing his welterweight title to Ray Leonard, he won the WBC Junior Middleweight title from Maurice Hope at Las Vegas on May 23, 1981, via a twelfth-round knockout. He lost this crown to Thomas Hearns on December 3, 1982, at New Orleans in fifteen rounds. Benitez was one of only a handful of fighters to win titles in three separate weight divisions.

"Sugar" Ray Charles Leonard: No black fighter was as carefully managed—financially and athletically—as Ray Leonard. Born on May 17, 1956, in Wilmington, North Carolina, this showstopper was named after the blind black singer. His father, Cicero, also a boxer, moved his family to Washington, D.C., in 1960. Young Ray sang in his church's choir and learned to box at the Palmer Park Recreation Center. His lightning quick hands and blazing foot speed helped him to earn a National Golden Gloves 132-pound title in 1972. After winning an Olympic Gold Medal in the 1976 Montreal Games, Leonard became an instant hero and was acclaimed as a "can't miss" future titleholder. Sarge Johnson, the assistant United States Olympic boxing coach, said, "Pound for pound, Leonard is the finest fighter I've seen in thirty years of working with the amateurs."[55] Head Boxing Coach Pat Nappi added, "Sugar Ray is the best amateur I've ever seen, and that includes Muhammad Ali."[56]

Leonard had originally planned to give up boxing after the Olympics to attend college. Less than a week after his win in Montreal, he was sued by his local county officials because the mother of his son, Ray Junior, had filed for welfare payments. He then changed his mind about pursuing a professional boxing career. Like Ali and Frazier before him, he used a syndicate of businessmen to initially back him. Twenty-four sponsors put up $21,000, as Leonard promised repayment within four years at 8 percent interest. He paid them back after his first professional fight. His earnings from this inaugural bout were a record $38,000, which stood until Ed "Too Tall" Jones left the Dallas Cowboys football team to try his hand in the ring. (Jones collected $70,000 for his first professional fight.) With the help of his lawyer, Mike Trainer, he formed Sugar Ray Leonard Enterprises and in 1977 he negotiated a six-fight, $320,000 package deal with ABC Television. In 1979, ABC upped the ante to $1 million for five fights.

Trained by Angelo Dundee and his good friend Janks Morton, Leonard won the NABF title from Pete Ranzany at Las Vegas on August 12, 1979. Three months later he acquired the WBC title via a fifteenth-round knockout of Wilfredo Benitez at Las Vegas on November 30. A showman and a crowd pleaser, Leonard's popularity was nearly unbounded.

Leonard's idolatry from white boxing fans caused slight resentment in the black community. While not oblivious to his standing in black America, he was forthright with an explanation: "Blacks criticize me because I'm so popular with whites."[57] Part of black America's problem with Leonard was that he avoided getting vocally involved in any racial issues. Leonard had earned more than $3 million in his first three years as a professional and many believed the money had simply gone to his head.

In the ring, he was remembered for his championship fights against Benitez, Roberto

Duran, and Thomas "Hit Man" Hearns. After winning the WBC title from Benitez on national television, he lost it in fifteen rounds to Duran in Montreal on June 20, 1980. He had incensed his Panamanian opponent by saying "I'll kill you"[58] before their fight. Their combined ring records listed 98 wins and 1 loss. The fight was so close that the judges' score cards read 148–147, 146–144, and 145–144.

Before their return bout on November 25 of that year, Leonard sought to rile his Latin adversary by incessantly talking about what strategy he would pursue during the fight, just as Ali had tried to do against Sonny Liston. Leonard regained the World title when Duran refused to continue fighting during the eighth round. Duran, baffled by Leonard's ability to hit and run, literally gave up, saying, *"No mas, no mas"* (Spanish for "no more, no more"). From his two bouts with Duran, Leonard had grossed more than $16 million, more than the combined career winnings of Joe Louis, Sugar Ray Robinson, Floyd Patterson, and Archie Moore.

Leonard then stepped up one weight class and captured the world junior middleweight crown from Ayub Kalule in Houston on June 25, 1981, in a ninth-round KO. He followed this with a spectacular fourteenth-round TKO of Thomas Hearns on September 16, 1981, unifying both the WBA and WBC welterweight titles.

Following his bout with Hearns, Leonard underwent surgery for a detached retina and retired after one last bout in 1984 to pursue a career as a television boxing commentator for HBO. Along with Muhammad Ali, he was the most charismatic boxer of the seventies and eighties.

In a totally unexpected turnabout, Leonard came out of retirement three years later (April 6, 1987) to battle unbeaten "Marvelous" Marvin Hagler for the middleweight title. Leonard stunned Hagler, the Boxing Writers' Fighter of the Year in 1983 and 1985, winning

a split decision. Said Hagler: "It was unfair . . . Leonard didn't beat me . . . I felt I fought a very good fight . . . the only thing I didn't do was knock him out."

Leonard continued his comeback in December 1988, defeating Don LaLonde by a TKO in the ninth round. Leonard and Thomas Hearns fought to a draw in June 1989. Six months later, Leonard defeated Roberto Doran in a dull 12 rounder.

In his final bout on February 9, 1991, Leonard, then 34, was thoroughly thrashed by 23-year old Terry Norris, who kept his junior middleweight title. "I knew before I got in the ring, it wasn't there," Leonard said. "I had to find out myself. This signifies it's time to call it quits." And so he did.

Three months later, Leonard admitted that he had used cocaine and abused alcohol from 1983–86. "I stand here ashamed, hurt; I think about my parents, my ex-wife, my kids, people who care for me, my fans who made me what I am."

Light Heavyweights: 161–175 lbs.

Marvin Johnson: Like so many before him, Johnson had a sensational amateur career. In 1972, he won the National Golden Gloves light heavyweight title and an Olympic bronze medal as a middleweight. Born on April 12, 1954, in Indianapolis, Indiana, the left-handed Johnson turned professional in 1973 and won eleven of his first twelve bouts by knockouts.

In 1977, after winning the vacant NABF title by defeating Matthew Saad Muhammad (formerly Matthew Franklin), Johnson won the WBC version of the title from Mate Parlov of Yugoslavia on December 2, 1978, via a tenth-round knockout. After losing his WBC title to Muhammad on April 22, 1979, via an eighth-round knockout, he won the WBA version from Victor Galindez in New Orleans on November 30, 1979, in an eleventh-round KO.

Four months later he lost his WBA title to Eddie Mustafa Muhammad (formerly Eddie Dee Gregory) in Knoxville, Tennessee, via an eleventh-round knockout. Though he held both versions of the title, he kept neither for more than four months.

Matthew Saad Muhammad (formerly Matthew Franklin): Muhammad did not start out as well as his contemporaries. He was born Matthew Franklin on August 5, 1954, in Philadelphia, Pennsylvania. He was also known as Maxwell Antonio Loach. His conversion to Islam produced his current name. He suffered losses in his first and third years as a professional and a draw in his second year, but managed to win the vacant NABF title over Marvin Johnson on July 26, 1977, in a twelfth-round KO.

Almost two years later, he defeated Johnson again for the WBC version of the title. He then blossomed as a light heavyweight, successfully defending the title eight times before losing it to Dwight Muhammad Qawi (Dwight Braxton). Qawi defeated him again in a rematch for the WBC title on August 7, 1982, in Philadelphia, via a sixth-round KO.

Heavyweights: 191 lbs. and Above

George Foreman: He came from humble beginnings, and was one of the most physically imposing boxers ever seen in the ring. He was born on January 22, 1948, in Marshall, Texas, and grew to a height of 6-feet 3-inches and weighed 220 pounds. Foreman had a rough childhood in the streets of Houston, where he snatched purses and engaged in petty larcenies. He publicly claims that he was saved by the Job Corps and football player Jim Brown.

Those who knew Foreman in Houston understood when he later declared, "I got out of that (purse snatchings) right quick because I never wanted to hurt anybody . . . some-

times, I would like to find those people I did that to and give them some money."[59] "We'd end up dropping the purse when a woman would cry: 'Lord Jesus, don't take my money.' It hurt us so we would leave the purse."[60] But he still angered many black Americans by waving a small American flag at the 1968 Summer Olympics, after winning the heavyweight gold medal.

Upon retiring in 1977, Foreman compiled an impressive knockout record—42 in 47 professional fights—a feat that even Joe Louis could not match. On January 22, 1973, he became only the second former Olympic heavyweight gold medalist to win the world title, by defeating Joe Frazier in Kingston, Jamaica, in a second-round knockout. Before this fight, Foreman had been extended to ten rounds only three times.

Foreman defended his title against José Roman and Ken Norton in a combined total of three rounds for both bouts. The Norton victory enabled him to meet Muhammad Ali, who had defeated Joe Frazier two months earlier. Foreman entered the Ali fight in financial trouble and hired President John F. Kennedy's brother-in-law, Sargent Shriver, to assist him.

Foreman was a three to one favorite over Ali, the NABF titleholder, in their bout in Kinshasa, Zaire, on October 30, 1974. In this first-ever heavyweight title fight in Africa, Foreman tired badly after seven rounds and was floored by Ali in the eighth. (*See* Muhammad Ali.) Foreman's feared right hand, which he called his "anywhere punch," never landed on Ali's head. The "Rumble In The Jungle," as this bout was known, attracted 62,000 fans.

Foreman abandoned the ring after a 1977 loss to Jimmy Young. He went home to Marshall, Texas, and became a preacher for the Church of the Lord Jesus Christ.

Foreman's return to the ring was prompted more by dwindling funds than a desire to return to the spotlight. He first attempted to strengthen his bank account by accepting preaching engagements around the country. He soon became humiliated by the meager donations raised in his behalf.

He is quoted in *Sports Illustrated* (7/17/89) as saying, "I made a vow. I said, I'll never do this again. I know how to make money. I went back and put on my boxing trunks."

In 1988, his first year on the comeback trail, Foreman won nine bouts, all by KOs or TKOs. His age (39), television endorsements, and a lucrative HBO deal gave him movie-star appeal. The 19-year old who proudly waved an American flag after winning an Olympic gold medal in 1972 at the Games made famous by black power salutes found greater acceptance as an American hero as a 40-year-old pugilist.

At 42, Foreman's comeback was slowed by a lost to Evander Holyfield in April 19, 1991. Foreman completed his fifth year on the comeback trail 25–1, and 70–3 overall with 66 knockouts.

Leon Spinks: Spinks was the lightest heavyweight champion since Jimmy Ellis, standing 6-feet 1-inch and weighing 205 pounds. Born on July 11, 1953 in St. Louis, Missouri, this ex-Marine won the light heavyweight gold medal at the 1976 Montreal Olympic Games. His brother, Michael, won the Olympic middleweight gold medal.

In Spinks' second year as a professional and in only his eighth fight, he surprised Muhammad Ali in Las Vegas on February 15, 1978, winning the world title in fifteen rounds. Exactly seven months later, he lost it to Ali in New Orleans in fifteen rounds. After losing to Larry Holmes in Detroit for the WBC title on June 12, 1981, he won the vacant NABF Cruiserweight (190 lbs.) title over Jesse Burnett in McAfee, New Jersey, on October 31, 1982, in twelve rounds.

Kenneth Howard Norton: Like Leon Spinks, Norton was an ex-Marine who started

his professional career later than most—at age twenty-four. He was born on August 9, 1943, in Jacksonville, Illinois, and grew to 6-feet 3-inches and weighed 220 pounds. So well proportioned was his physique that he could have had a career as a model, which he sometimes tried.

For the first six years of his career, he never fought outside of Southern California. He then arranged a bout with Muhammad Ali for the NABF title in San Diego, and won in twelve rounds. He underwent hypnosis before this bout in an attempt to correct some bad boxing habits, and broke Ali's jaw in the first round. After losing the NABF title to Ali, six months later, he lost to George Foreman for the World title in a second-round knockout in Caracas, Venezuela, on March 26, 1974. Following another loss to Ali for the world title on September 28, 1976, in New York City in fifteen rounds, he was proclaimed the WBC champion two years later.

Norton became the WBC champion because Leon Spinks, the world champion, refused to defend the WBC portion of the title against an assigned challenger. Norton then lost his WBC crown to Larry Holmes in Las Vegas on June 9, 1978, in fifteen rounds. He retired to a career in movies and sports management, following a first-round KO by Gerry Cooney on May 11, 1981, in New York City.

Larry Holmes: Without a doubt, Holmes was the most underrated and underpublicized heavyweight champion in history. It was Holmes' (or any heavyweight's) misfortune to have come to prominence when Muhammad Ali and welterweight Sugar Ray Leonard were garnering most of the headlines. Born on November 3, 1949, in Cuthberth, Georgia, this 6-foot 3-inch, 220-pound heavyweight turned professional at age twenty-four.

Following a twelve-round win over Earnie Shavers in 1978, Holmes won the WBC title from Ken Norton on June 9 of that year. After seven successful WBC defenses he unified the vacant world title by defeating Muhammad Ali on October 2, 1980, in an eleventh-round knockout at Las Vegas. Ali was thirty-eight years old and only a shadow of his former self, clearly no match for Holmes.

Holmes won 48 consecutive bouts, one short of Rocky Marciano's record. He suffered his first loss in a title bout to Michael Spinks September 21, 1985. Seven months later, Spinks defeated Holmes in a rematch.

Holmes retired after a fourth round knockout loss to "Iron" Mike Tyson on January 22, 1988.

Inspired by George Foreman's popularity and success as an aging warrior, Holmes resumed fighting in 1991. He ended the year 5–0 with three knockouts and with a career record of 53–3 with 37 knockouts.

John Tate: Tate was big for a modern heavyweight, 6-foot 4-inches and 240 pounds. He was born in Marion City, Arkansas, on January 29, 1955, and turned professional at age twenty-two. After only three years of professional fighting, he defeated the South African Gerrie Coetzee on October 20, 1979, in Pretoria, South Africa, for the vacant WBA title. Five months later, he lost it to Mike Weaver in a fifteen-round KO on March 31, 1980, in Knoxville, Tennessee.

THE EIGHTIES

The end of the seventies saw Larry Holmes defeat Muhammad Ali on October 2, 1980. Professional boxing in the eighties was marked mainly by the emergence of "Iron" Mike Tyson, who established himself as one of the game's most vicious punchers. Tyson, a tough kid from the South Bronx (New York), wreaked havoc in and out of the ring. His marriage to actress Robin Givens lasted less than a year. Soon afterwards, he came under the influence of boxing promoter Don King. Tyson fell from grace in 1992 after being convicted by an Indiana jury of raping Desiree Washington, a black beauty queen contestant. He received a six-year prison term.

Boxing continued to expand in the 80s, characterized by the creation of additional weight classes and a dramatic increase in the size of purses. Gone was much of the racial turmoil that had distinguished the beginning of the previous decade, and there were no relevant Supreme Court cases looming or waiting to be heard. There were no marches in the streets by black students and the Vietnam war had been over for half a decade. The U.S.-led boycott of the 1980 Moscow Summer Olympics hardly made a difference in boxing. There were so many international amateur competitions for aspiring American fighters that, despite the forfeiture of a possible medal, their talent could still be showcased.

The influence of organized crime was hinted at only to the extent that the gambling palaces in Las Vegas went out of their way to stage the most attractive bouts. Two of the most successful and well-known promoters were black—Don King and Butch Lewis. Surprisingly, the biggest gate attraction was a welterweight, not a heavyweight. That had not been the case since Joe Louis retired and Sugar Ray Robinson, a middleweight, claimed the fight world's adulation.

Though 1980 began with black world champions in the heavyweight, light heavyweight, and welterweight divisions, within four years other black champions in six additional weight classes would join them.

Bantamweights: 113–118 lbs.

Jeff Chandler: He was the first black American bantamweight champion since Harold Dade won the title in 1947. Born on September 3, 1956, in Philadelphia, Pennsylvania, this 5-foot 7-inch, 120-pounder was undefeated as a professional for seven years. He won the WBA world title from Julian Solis on November 14, 1980, and, after nine successful defenses, he lost it to Richard Sandoval via a fifteenth-round knockout on April 7, 1984.

Junior Featherweights: 119–122 lbs.

Leo Randolph: Born on February 27, 1958, in Tacoma, Washington, Randolph went on to win an Olympic gold medal as a flyweight in 1976. Randolph, 5-feet 5-inches and 122 pounds, had a very short career—19-bouts in three years. He won the WBA title from Ricardo Cardona in a fifteenth-round KO on May 4, 1980. He lost it three months later to Sergio Palma by a KO in the fifth round.

Junior Lightweights: 127–130 lbs.

Roger Lee Mayweather: He won the WBC title on January 19, 1983, in an eighth-round KO over Samuel Serrano in San Juan, Puerto Rico. It was only his fifteenth professional fight. After two defenses, he lost his title to Rocky Lockridge in a stunning first round KO. Mayweather won the WBC welterweight title March 24, 1988, defeating Maurico Aceves in a third-round knockout. In April 1990, he won the WBA title, defeating Ildemor Paison in a 12-round decision. Mayweather was born on April 24, 1961, in Grand Rapids, Michigan.

Ricky "Rocky" Lockridge: He took longer to become a contender than Mayweather. After winning the New Jersey and USBA titles, he met Eusebio Pedroza for the WBA title and lost in fifteen rounds of October 4, 1980. Ten months after losing a second WBA title bout to Pedroza in fifteen rounds, he defeated Mayweather for the WBC title on February 26, 1984, in a first-round knockout. He won the IBF lightweight title August 9, 1987, defeating

Barry Michael in the ninth round on a TKO and successfully defended his title four times.

Lightweights: 131–135 lbs.

James Hilmer Kenty: Within three years of his professional debut, Kenty won the WBC title from Ernesto Espana in Detroit, Michigan, on March 2, 1980, by a ninth-round knockout. Born July 30, 1955, and managed by the shrewd Emanuel Steward, Kenty defended his title three times before falling to Sean O'Grady, in fifteen rounds on April 12, 1981. He has had only two losses in eight years.

Pernell "Sweet Pea" Whitaker: He defeated Fred Pendleton in an IBF title bout February 3, 1990. The Norfolk based boxer was 20–1, with 13 knockouts through 1992.

Junior Welterweights: 136–140 lbs.

This weight class has been one of the best for black Americans in the eighties. Few experts expected this much success.

Saoul Mamby: Mamby was born on June 4, 1947, in the Bronx, New York, and bar mitzvahed into the Jewish faith at age thirteen. He had been fighting professionally for nine years before he lost his first chance at the WBC title in 1977. He finally won it two and a half years later against Sang-Hyun Kim of Korea on February 23, 1980, by a fourteenth-round KO. He lost it to Leroy Haley in 1982. He was unsuccessful at regaining it from Haley in 1983. He also lost a second try at regaining the title from Bill Costello in 1984, in a twelve-round decision.

Aaron Pryor: It is astonishing that Pryor managed the self-discipline to fight at all. Born on October 20, 1955, in Cincinnati, Ohio, he stated, "I was a kid nobody paid any attention to. Some nights I just said to hell with it and slept in a doorway."[61]

Though Pryor won the WBA title from Antonio Cervantes in Cincinnati, by a fourth-round KO in 1980, he is best known for his two bouts with the Nicaraguan, Alexis Arguello. Both wins were knockouts, the first in round fourteen and the second in round ten. Pryor's style was nonstop hitting, and reminded observers of a smaller Joe Frazier. Pryor, who earned more than $4 million in his career, abdicated his WBA title after the second Alexis Arguello fight.

Leroy Haley: He was one of the least-known champions. Fighting almost exclusively out of Las Vegas, this 5-foot 6¾-inch, 140-pound native of Garland County, Arkansas, won the WBC title from Saoul Mamby on June 26, 1982, in fifteen rounds. He lost it to Bruce Curry less than a year later.

Bruce Curry: The brother of welterweight Donald Curry, Bruce was born March 29, 1956, in Marlin, Texas. After winning the NABF title, he won the WBC title from Leroy Haley on May 20, 1983, in twelve rounds. He lost it to Bill Costello by a tenth-round knockout in 1984.

John T. "Bump City" Bumphus: This stringbean of a fighter had an enviable amateur career, winning the 1977 AAU featherweight title, the 1979 Golden Gloves lightweight title, and the 1980 National AAU light welterweight title. In his fifth year as a professional, he won the vacant WBA title from Lorenzo Garcia in fifteen rounds, on January 22, 1984. He lost it to Gene Hatcher five months later by an eleventh-round knockout.

William Donald "Bill" Costello: After five years as a professional, Costello defeated Bruce Curry for the WBC title on January 29, 1984, at Beaumont, Texas, by a tenth-round

KO. He was undefeated as of the end of 1984. He was born in Kingston, New York, on April 10, 1956.

Meldrick Taylor: This Philadelphian won the IBF junior welterweight crown, beating James McGirt in the 12th round on a TKO. He was 29–1 with 15 knockouts through 1992.

Welterweights: 141–147 lbs.

Ray Charles "Sugar Ray" Leonard: (*See* 1970s, Welterweights.)

Thomas "Hit Man" Hearns: Few fighters in the late seventies or eighties have been as exciting as Hearns. Standing 6-foot 1-inch and weighing 145 pounds, Hearns was one of the most feared right hands in the history of the division. His first seventeen bouts were won by KOs, as were thirty of his first thirty-two. Managed by Emanuel Steward, Hearns had trouble booking fights, such was his reputation.

Born on October 18, 1958, in Memphis, Tennessee, Hearns moved to Detroit where he won the WBA title from Pipino Cuevas on August 2, 1980, in a second-round knockout. In one of the most exciting title bouts of the eighties, he lost to Ray Leonard in a bid to unify the world title at Las Vegas on September 16, 1981, in a fourteenth-round TKO. Earlier in the fight Hearns had rocked Leonard with right hands, but Leonard recovered enough to stop the taller Hearns in the fourteenth.

Hearns also captured the WBC version of the junior middleweight title from Wilfredo Benitez at New Orleans on December 3, 1982, in fifteen rounds. He later stepped up one weight class because of a lack of competition. On June 15, 1984, he unified the world junior middleweight title by defeating WBA champion Roberto Duran, in a second-round knockout. He thus became one of the few fighters to lose in a chance for a world title in one division and later win a world title in a heavier weight class. Hearns took the WBC light heavyweight crown March 7, 1987, defeating Virgil Hill in a 12-round decision. At 34, Hearns completed 1991 with a 50–3–1 record with 40 knockouts.

Donald "Cobra" Curry: Born September 7, 1961, at Forth Worth, Texas, this 5-foot 10-inch, 147 pounder won the 1979 National AAU title before turning professional. After winning the NABF and USBA titles, he won the vacant WBA version on February 13, 1983, by defeating Jun-Sok Hwang in fifteen rounds. The brother of Bruce Curry, former WBC junior welterweight champion, Donald lost an IBF junior middleweight title bout to Michael Nunn, October 18, 1990, and a WBC junior middleweight title bout to Terry Norris, June 1, 1991. Curry completed 1991 with a 33–5 record.

Milton "Iceman" McCrory: Along with Thomas Hearns, McCrory gave Detroit a powerful boxing twosome in the eighties. Managed by Emanuel Steward, McCrory won the vacant WBC title when he defeated Colin Jones on August 13, 1983, in twelve rounds. McCrory suffered his first loss December 12, 1985, to Donald Curry in a second round knockout. He was 35–4–1 with 25 knockouts at the end of 1991.

Mark Breland: This Brooklyn-based fighter won the WBA welterweight crown, defeating Harold Volbrecht in a 7-round TKO, February 6, 1987. He successfully defended his title six times and was 30–3–1 with 22 knockouts through 1991.

Junior Middleweights: 148–154 lbs.

Ray Charles "Sugar Ray" Leonard: (*See* 1970s, Welterweights.)

Davey Moore: Though another Davey Moore died as a result of ring injuries in 1963, this Davey Moore was born in the Bronx, New York, on June 9, 1959. He had two losses in sixteen fights by the end of 1984. In only his ninth professional fight, Moore won the WBA title from Tadashi Mihara in Tokyo, Japan, on February 2, 1982, via a sixth-round knockout. He lost the title after three defenses to Roberto Duran on June 16, 1983, by an eighth-round KO.

Thomas "Hit Man" Hearns: (*See* 1980s, Welterweights.)

Mark Medal: Medal won the IBF title by defeating Earl Hargrove on March 11, 1984, in a fifth-round knockout.

Middleweights: 155–160 lbs.

"Marvelous" Marvin Hagler: This left-hander, who was born on May 23, 1954, in Newark, New Jersey, was the 1973 National AAU middleweight champion. Fighting out of Brockton, Massachusetts, he paid his ring dues before defeating Alan Minter for the world title on September 27, 1980, in London, England. It was his fifty-fourth professional fight. He had drawn with Vito Antuofermo for the world title ten months earlier in Las Vegas in fifteen rounds.

There were racial overtones to the Minter bout. During the prefight buildup, Minter was quoted as saying, "I don't intend losing my title to a black guy."[62] After Hagler's third-round knockout of Minter, fans threw bottles at the ring and the new champion needed a police escort to leave the stadium.

Hagler had a nonstop, aggressive style. His bald pate was his trademark. In his day, he was arguably the best known boxer in the world. He was devastated by the 1987 split decision loss to Sugar Ray Leonard, who bolted out of retirement to defeat one of the ring's most feared punchers. Hagler's ego seemed more bruised than his body.

"This is the greatest accomplishment of my life," beamed Leonard.

Said Hagler: "A split decision should go to the champion."

The loss sapped Hagler's will to fight.

Light Heavyweights: 161–175 lbs.

Eddie Mustafa Muhammad (nee Eddie Dee Gregory): He was born April 30, 1952, in Brooklyn, New York, and won the WBA title from Marvin Johnson on March 31, 1980, by an eleventh-round knockout. After two defenses he lost his title to Michael Spinks in fifteen rounds. His first chance to fight for the title came in a losing fifteen-round effort against Victor Galindez in 1977.

Michael Spinks: He is the brother of the former heavyweight champion Leon Spinks. Born July 13, 1956, in St. Louis, Missouri, he won an Olympic gold medal as a middleweight in 1976. In his fifth year as a professional, he won the WBA title from Eddie Mustafa Muhammad on July 18, 1981. On March 18, 1983, he unified the vacant world title by defeating Dwight Muhammad Qawi in fifteen rounds at Atlantic City. He became the first light heavyweight champ to win the heavyweight title, upsetting previously unbeaten Larry Holmes on September 21, 1985. Spinks defeated Holmes in a rematch seven months later. Spinks stay in the big time was cut short by Mike Tyson on June 27, 1988, in a first round knockout.

Dwight Muhammad Qawi (formerly Dwight Braxton): He did not impress his managers until his third year as a professional. Standing only 5-feet 6¾-inches and weighing 174 pounds, most experts thought he was too short for the likes of Michael Spinks and Eddie Muhammad. He won the WBC title from Matthew Saad Muhammad in Atlantic City, New Jersey, on December 19, 1981, via a tenth-round knockout. He lost his opportunity for the vacant world title against Michael Spinks, losing a fifteen-round decision on March 18, 1983. Qawi lost his cruiserweight title to Robert Daniels on November 28, 1989, finishing the year with a 32–7 record.

HEAVYWEIGHTS: 191 LBS. AND ABOVE

The Rise And Fall of "Iron" Mike Tyson

The seemingly invisible "Iron" Mike Tyson lost his heavyweight crown to Buster Douglas in a stunning 10th-round knockout in Tokyo on February 11, 1990.

But a penetrating, verbal barrage—delivered two years later in an Indianapolis courtroom by a 108-pound black beauty contestant—proved far more damaging to the career of one of the more devastating punchers in boxing history.

A wobbly Tyson went down for the count in Tokyo, his face and ego badly bruised by Douglas' relentless attack. But the impact of Douglas' punches paled in comparison to 18-year-old Desiree Washington's courtroom assault. Washington, a petite, softspoken college student from Rhode Island, convinced the jury that Tyson raped her in an Indianapolis hotel during a Miss Black America Pageant.

The six-year jail sentence jolted Tyson like nothing he'd ever felt.

Upon learning that the Indiana Supreme Court refused his request to be freed on bail pending an appeal, Tyson was an emotional knockout victim.

"Today for the first time in my life, I was trying to cry. I couldn't. It's terrible not to be able to cry, especially when you know that you didn't do anything wrong" (*The New York Daily News*, April 25, 1992).

Since his early bouts with crime on New York City's tough streets, Tyson frequently flirted with danger and succumbed to temptations.

He was rescued from hard times by Cus D'Amato when he was 13. D'Amato and his companion, Camille Ewald, brought him into their Catskills, New York, home and became the parents he never really had.

It took D'Amato only two months to decide that he was raising a future heavyweight champion.

Tyson became the youngest man (20 years old) to win the (WBC) heavyweight title, defeating Trevor Berbick on November 22, 1986. D'Amato also trained Floyd Patterson, previously the youngest heavyweight.

A year later, Tyson defeated Larry Holmes by a knockout in the fourth round. Afterwards, Holmes called Tyson a "great champion." Tyson returned the compliment (*Sports Illustrated*, December 27, 1987).

But as he watched Tyson bounce from one problem to another, Holmes accurately predicted that the man called "Iron" Mike would end up dead or in jail.

Immaturity and poor judgment proved too deadly a combination for Tyson to overcome. After D'Amato and manager Jimmy Jacobs died, Tyson was managed by Bill Cayton.

That arrangement was altered somewhat when Tyson married actress Robin Givens. Givens and her mother, Ruth Roper, got Cayton to agree to—among other things—reduce his cut of deals from the standard 33 percent to 25 percent.

Said Tyson: "For anyone to get 33 percent of my outside money is totally absurd."

Tyson had no problems with the amount when Jacobs got 33 percent.

Tyson's marriage soured after Givens, in a nationally televised interview, described Tyson as a manic depressive and suggested that he had been physically and verbally abusive.

Tyson's marriage to Givens ended in divorce in less than a year. Then Don King came courting.

Tyson broke his pact with Cayton and King became his promoter and friend.

Tyson was baptized in Cleveland, with King and the Reverend Jesse Jackson present among a crowd of 700. "I felt so clean, so pure and reborn," Tyson said. "I think religion is going to change my life. Baptism is an unbelievable experience."

After losing to Douglas, Tyson won four consecutive fights and was set to face Evander Holyfield in a title bout when a rib injury forced a postponement. He was 41–1 when the prison sentence suspended his career, at least for three years.

Michael Dwayne Weaver: He was born on June 14, 1952, in Gatesville, Texas, and has a very erratic career as a professional. But with the lack of a dominating talent in the division during the early seventies, and with three separate sanctioning bodies, he was able to work his way through the ranks. After winning the California, the vacant NABF and USBA titles, he was knocked out by Larry Holmes as he challenged for the WBC title. Weaver managed to win the WBA title from John Tate at Knoxville, Tennessee, on March 31, 1980, in a fifteenth-round knockout.

Afterwards, he traveled to racially troubled Bophuthatswana, South Africa, to defeat Gerrie Coetzee and retain his WBA title. He later lost his crown to Michael Dokes in 1982, on a first-round knockout. His main vulnerability seemed to be a susceptibility to a knockout punch. Weaver was knocked out by Lennox Lewis in a 1991 bout and ended the year with a 35–16–1 record.

Michael "Dynamite" Dokes: Born on August 10, 1958 in Akron, Ohio, Dokes stands 6-

feet 3-inches and weighs 227 pounds. He turned professional at age eighteen. He did not lose a bout in his first seven years, and he won the WBA title from Mike Weaver on December 10, 1982, in a first-round knockout. He lost the title via a tenth-round knockout to Gerrie Coetzee, on September 23, 1983. Dokes finished 1992 with a 44–3–2 record.

Tim "Terrible Tim" Witherspoon: Born December 27, 1957, in Philadelphia, Pennsylvania, Witherspoon was given a WBC title bout with Larry Holmes on May 20, 1983. He lost in twelve rounds, but when Holmes vacated his title Witherspoon won it with a twelve-round victory over Greg Page on March 9, 1984. Five months later, he lost the WBC title to Pinklon Thomas in twelve rounds.

Pinklon "Pinky" Thomas, Jr: He was born in Pontiac, Michigan, on February 10, 1958, and was a drug addict at age thirteen. Though he dropped out of school in the tenth grade, this 6-foot 3-inch, 216-pound heavyweight returned to get his G.E.D. Diploma. Training in Joe Frazier's gymnasium in Philadelphia, he had only three amateur fights before turning professional. In his last bout of 1984, on August 31, he won the WBC title from Tim Witherspoon in twelve rounds. Thomas, a very powerful puncher, compiled a stellar knockout record—twenty in twenty-six fights. He finished 1991 with a 30–6–1 record.

Gregory Edward Page: Born on October 25, 1958, in Louisville, Kentucky, he is 6-feet 3-inches and weighs 240 pounds. He simply overpowered his amateur competition in winning the 1977 and 1978 National AAU titles, and the 1978 National Golden Gloves title. Fifteen of his first sixteen professional bouts were won by knockouts. After winning the USBA title, he lost to Tim Witherspoon in twelve rounds for the vacant WBC title in

1984. However, he won the WBA title from Gerrie Coetzee on December 1, 1984, in an eighth-round knockout. The title fight with Coetzee took place in South Africa.

Page was under tremendous pressure not to fight in that racially torn country. However, he was managed by Don King, who owned the promotional rights to this title bout, and King reportedly sold his promotional rights for $1 million to a South African promoter who staged the fight.

James "Buster" Douglas: He shocked the boxing world with a stunning performance against Mike Tyson. However, Douglas ballooned to nearly 250 pounds when defending his title against Evander Holyfield on October 25, 1990. Holyfield flattened Douglas with a 3rd round knockout, but Douglas floated into oblivion supported, no doubt, by a $19-million purse.

Riddick Bowe: This Brooklyn-born basher captured the heavyweight title by defeating Evander Holyfield in a Las Vegas bout in December 1992. He quickly signed a six-fight deal with HBO that could pay him more than $100 million.

EPILOGUE

The boxer was black America's—and indeed all America's—first athletic hero. The sport itself has ancient beginnings and is considered the ultimate contest in individual competition. Black fighters have been a part of boxing history in its entirety and black Americans were part of that first generation of scientific pugilists.

Bill Richmond and Tom Molineaux were the first recorded black American athletes in recognized international sports. Exactly one hundred years after Molineaux's illegal defeat in 1810, Jack Johnson won a racial psychological victory in defeating Jim Jeffries, a "white hope" sent to put him in his place. Though he lost his title in exile in 1915, his mastery of "the sweet science" was unquestioned.

Johnson's successor as the next black heavyweight champion was Joe Louis, who became a near deity to many blacks while other black champions in the lower weight classes continued to succeed. No group of black athletes in any sport had as much influence on the morale of black America and the psyche of white America as did the boxers. Always the wealthiest of athletes, only a few managed to survive their ring careers financially secure.

At the end of 1984, black Americans held world titles in seventeen weight divisions, from bantamweight to heavyweight. It is an outstanding record, matched only by the predominance of the black athlete in professional basketball. Perhaps the day will soon come when young black men will view the sport as just another alternative among occupational opportunities. But until that day the ranks of the black American prizefighters will continue to be from that sector which feels there is no other way to survive in a society where boxers (and other professional athletes) have a greater earning potential than most college graduates.

Notes

1. *Ebony*, September 1946, 25.
2. Mike Jacobs, "Are Negroes Killing Boxing?", *Ebony*, May 1950, 29.
3. Peter Heller, *In This Corner: Forty World Champions Tell Their Stories* (New York: Simon & Schuster, 1973), 369.
4. Bert Randolph Sugar and *Ring Magazine, The Great Fights* (New York: Rutledge Press, 1981), 119.
5. Heller, *In This Corner: Forty World Champions Tell Their Stories*, 322.
6. Ibid., 378.
7. *Ebony*, November 1950, 77, 79.
8. Dave Anderson, *Sugar Ray Robinson* (New York: New American Library, 1970), 33.
9. Ibid., 47.
10. Ibid., 43.
11. Ibid., 62.
12. Sugar and *Ring Magazine, The Great Fights*, 130.
13. Anderson, *Sugar Ray Robinson*, 182.
14. Ibid., 253.
15. Ibid., 278.
16. Ibid., 177.
17. Heller, *In This Corner: Forty World Champions Tell Their Stories*, 314.
18. Floyd Patterson and Milton Gross, *Victory Over Myself* (New York: Bernard Geis Associates and Random House, 1962), 45.
19. Ibid., 141.
20. Heller, *In This Corner: Forty World Champions Tell Their Stories*, 344.
21. Ibid., 345.
22. John Cottrell, *Man Of Destiny: The Story of Muhammad Ali* (London: Frederick Muller Press, 1967), 73.
23. Ibid., 210.
24. Ibid., 243.
25. Ibid., 239.
26. Heller, *In This Corner: Forty World Champions Tell Their Stories*, 394.
27. Cottrell, *Man Of Destiny: The Story of Muhammad Ali*, 115.
28. Ibid., 89.
29. Ibid., 120.
30. Ibid., 173.
31. Ibid.
32. Ibid., 30.
33. Benjamin G. Rader, *American Sports* (Englewood Cliffs, N.J.: Prentice Hall, Inc., 1983), 330.
34. *Newsweek*, 15 July 1968, 57.
35. Cottrell, *Man Of Destiny: The Story of Muhammad Ali*, 39.
36. Ibid., 158.
37. Ibid.

38. Ibid., 157.
39. Ibid., 319.
40. Muhammad Ali, *The Greatest: My Own Story* (New York: Random House, 1975), 171.
41. Cottrell, *Man Of Destiny: The Story of Muhammad Ali*, 335.
42. Anderson, *Sugar Ray Robinson*, 265.
43. Ibid., 266.
44. Ali, *The Greatest: My Own Story*, 159.
45. Ibid., 177.
46. Bob Woodward and Scott Armstrong, *The Brethren* (New York: Simon & Schuster, 1979), 137.
47. Ibid., 138.
48. Ibid., 139.
49. Ali, *The Greatest: My Own Story*, 286.
50. Harry Carpenter, *Boxing: An Illustrated History*, 146.
51. Sugar and *Ring Magazine, The Great Fights*, 182.
52. Ali, *The Greatest: My Own Story*, 414.
53. Carpenter, *Boxing: An Illustrated History*, 158.
54. Ibid., 415.
55. Alan Goldstein, *A Fistful of Sugar* (New York: Coward, McCann and Geoghegan, 1981), 67.
56. Ibid.
57. *Ebony*, July 1982, 34.
58. Ibid., 35.
59. *Ebony*, April 1973, 39.
60. Ibid., 40.
61. *Sports Illustrated*, 9 September 1985, 28.
62. Carpenter, *Boxing: An Illustrated History*, 164.

REFERENCE
SECTION

AFRICAN-AMERICAN WORLD BOXING CHAMPIONS

Weight Class	Name	Year
Heavyweight	Johnson, Jack	1908-15
Welterweight	Walcott, Joe (Barbadian)	1901-04
Welterweight	Brown, Aaron (aka The Dixie Kid)	1904-05
Lightweight	Gans, Joe	1902-08
Featherweight	Dixon, George (Canadian)	1892–1900

AFRICAN-AMERICAN WORLD BOXING CHAMPIONSHIP MATCHES, THROUGH 1919

Weight Class	Name	Ht.	Wgt.	Opponent	Result		Date	Site
Heavyweight	Johnson, Jack	6'1	195	Tommy Burns	KO	14	12/26/08	Sydney, Australia
Welterweight	Walcott, Joe ("Barbados")	5'1	145	Jim Rube Ferns	KO	5	12/18/01	Fort Erie, Ontario
	Walcott, Joe ("Barbados")			Joe Gans	D	20	9/30/03	San Francisco
	Brown, Aaron ("Dixie Kid")	5'8	145	Joe Walcott	WF	20	4/30/04	San Francisco
Lightweight	Gans, Joe	5'6	131-37	Frank Erne	KO	1	5/12/02	Ft. Erie, Ontario
	Gans, Joe			Battling Nelson	WF	42	9/03/06	Goldfield, Colo.
Featherweight	Dixon, George (Canadian)	5'3	105-22	Fred Johnson	KO	14	6/27/92	Coney Island, NY
	Dave Sullivan				WD	10	11/11/98	New York

JACK JOHNSON
(John Arthur Johnson)
(The Galveston Giant)

Born, March 31, 1878, Galveston, Texas. Weight, 195 lbs. Height, 6 ft. 1¼ in. Managed by Morris Hart, Johnny Connors, Alec McLean, Sam Fitzpatrick, Abe Arends, George Little, Tom Flanagan, Sig Hart.

1897
–Jim Rocks, Galveston .... KO   4
–Sam Smith, Galveston .... W   10

1898
–Reddy Bremer, Galveston .... KO   3
–Jim Cole, Galveston .... W   4
–Henry Smith, Galveston .... D   15

1899
Feb. 11–Jim McCormick, Galveston .... NC   7
Mar. 17–Jim McCormick, Galveston .... WF   7
May   6–John (Klondike)Haynes, Chicago .... KO by   5
Dec. 16–Pat Smith, Galveston .... D   12

79

1900

-Josh Mills, Memphis .... W 12

1901

Feb. 25–Joe Choynski, Galveston .... KO by 3
Mar. 7–John Lee, Galveston .... W 15
Apr. 12–Charley Brooks, Galveston .... KO 2
May 6–Jim McCormick, Galveston .... KO 2
May 28–Jim McCormick, Galveston .... KO 7
June 12–Horace Miles, Galveston............. KO 3
June 20–George Lawler, Galveston.............. KO 10
June 28–John (Klondike) Haynes, Galveston .... D 20
-Willie McNeal .... KO 15
Nov. 4–Hank Griffin, Bakersfield .... L 20
Dec. 27–Hank Griffin, Oakland................. D 15

1902

Jan. 17–Frank Childs, Chicago................. D 6
Feb. 7–Dan Murphy, Waterbury .... KO 10
Feb. 22–Ed Johnson, Galveston .... KO 4
Mar. 7–Joe Kennedy, Oakland .... KO 4
Apr. 6–Bob White......................... W 15
May 1–Jim Scanlan....................... KO 7
May 16–Jack Jeffries, Los Angeles .... KO 5
May 28–John (Klondike) Haynes, Memphis .... KO 13
June 4–Billy Stift, Denver .... D 10
June 20–Hank Griffin, Los Angeles............. D 20
Sept. 3–Mexican Pete Everett, Victor, Colo......... W 20
Oct. 21–Frank Childs, Los Angeles .... W 12
Oct. 31–George Gardner, San Francisco........... W 20
Dec. 5–Fred Russell, Los Angeles .... WF 8

1903

Feb. 3–Denver Ed Martin, Los Angeles .... W 20
(Won Negro Heavyweight Title)
Feb. 27–Sam McVey, Los Angeles .... W 20
(Retained Negro Heavyweight Title)
Apr. 16–Sandy Ferguson, Boston................ W 10
May 11–Joe Butler, Philadelphia .... KO 3
July 31–Sandy Ferguson, Philadelphia .... ND 6
Oct. 27–Sam McVey, Los Angeles .... W 20
(Retained Negro Heavyweight Title)
Dec. 11–Sandy Ferguson, Colma, Calif .... W 20

1904

Feb. 16–Black Bill, Philadelphia................ ND 6

Apr. 22–Sam McVey, San Francisco .... KO 20
(Retained Negro Heavyweight Title)
June 2–Frank Childs, Chicago .... W 6
Oct. 18–Denver Ed Martin, Los Angeles.......... KO 2
(Retained Negro Heavyweight Title)

1905

Mar. 28–Marvin Hart, San Francisco .... L 20
Apr. 25–Jim Jeffords, Philadelphia............. KO 4
May 3–Black Bill, Philadelphia................. KO 4
May 9–Walter Johnson, Philadelphia........... KO 3
May 19–Joe Jeannette, Philadelphia .... ND 6
June 26–Jack Monroe, Philadelphia .... ND 6
July 13–Morris Harris, Philadelphia............. KO 3
July 13–Black Bill, Philadelphia................ ND 6
July 18–Sandy Ferguson, Chelsea, Mass .... WF 7
July 24–Joe Grim, Philadelphia .... ND 6
Nov. 25–Joe Jeannette, Philadelphia .... LF 2
Dec. 1–Young Peter Jackson, Baltimore .... W 12
Dec. 2–Joe Jeannette, Philadelphia .... ND 6

1906

Jan. 16–Joe Jeannette, New York .... ND 3
Mar. 14–Joe Jeannette, Baltimore .... W 15
Apr. 19–Black Bill, Wilkes-Barre .... KO 7
Apr. 26–Sam Langford, Chelsea, Mass. .... W 15
June 18–Charlie Haghey, Gloucester, Mass....... KO 2
Sept. 3–Billy Dunning, Millinocket, Me. .... D 10
Sept. 20–Joe Jeannette, Philadelphia .... ND 6
Nov. 8–Jim Jeffords, Lancaster, Pa............. W 6
Nov. 26–Joe Jeannette, Portland, Me............. D 10
Dec. 9–Joe Jeannette, New York .... W 3

1907

Feb. 19–Peter Felix, Sydney................... KO 1
Mar 4–Jim Lang, Melbourne .... KO 9
July 17–Bob Fitzsimmons, Philadelphia .... KO 2
Aug. 28–Kid Cutler, Reading, Pa. .... KO 1
Sept. 12–Sailor Burke, Bridgeport .... W 6
Nov. 2–Fireman Jim Flynn, San Francisco .... KO 11

1908

Jan. 3–Joe Jeannette, New York................ D 3
June 11–Al McNamara, Plymouth, England .... W 4
July 31–Ben Taylor, Plymouth, England .... KO 8
Dec. 26–Tommy Burns, Sydney................. KO 14
(Won World Heavyweight Title)

1909

Mar.	10–Victor McLaglen, Vancouver, B.C. . . . . ND	6
	(Retained World Heavyweight Title)	
Apr.	–Frank Moran, Pittsburgh. . . . . Exh.	4
May	19–Phila. Jack O'Brien, Philadelphia. . . . . ND	6
	(Retained World Heavyweight Title)	
June	30–Tony Ross, Pittsburgh. . . . . ND	6
	(Retained World Heavyweight Title)	
Sept.	9–Al Kaufman, San Francisco . . . . ND	10
	(Retained World Heavyweight Title)	
Oct.	16–Stanley Ketchel, Colma, Calif. . . . . KO	12
	(Retained World Heavyweight Title)	

1910

July	4–James J. Jeffries, Reno . . . . KO	15
	(Retained World Heavyweight Title)	

1911

(Inactive)

1912

July	4–Fireman Jim Flynn, Las Vegas, N.M. . . . . . . KO	9
	(Retained World Heavyweight Title)	

1913

Dec.	19–Battling Jim Johnson, Paris, France. . . . . D	10
	(Retained World Heavyweight Title)	

1914

June	27–Frank Moran, Paris, France . . . . W	20
	(Retained World Heavyweight Title)	
Dec.	–Enrique Wilkinson, Buenos Aires. . . . . Exh. KO	
Dec.	15–Jack Murray, Buenos Aires . . . . Exh. KO	3

1915

Jan.	–Vasco Guiralechea, Buenos Aires. . . . . Exh. KO	
Apr.	3–Sam McVey, Havana, Cuba . . . . Exh.	6
Apr.	5–Jess Willard, Havana, Cuba. . . . . KO by	26
	(Lost World Heavyweight Title)	

1916

Mar.	10–Frank Crozier, Madrid, Spain . . . . W	10
July	10–Arthur Craven, Barcelona, Spain . . . . KO	1

1917

(Inactive)

1918

Apr.	3–Blink McCloskey, Madrid, Spain . . . . W	4

1919

Feb.	12–Bill Flint, Madrid, Spain . . . . KO	2
Apr.	7–Tom Cowler, Mexico City . . . . D	10
June	2–Tom Cowler, Mexico City . . . . KO	12
July	4–Paul Sampson, Mexico City. . . . . KO	6
Aug.	10–Marty Cutler, Mexico City. . . . . KO	4
Sept.	28–Capt. Bob Roper, Mexico City. . . . . W	10

1920

Apr.	18–Bob Wilson, Mexicali . . . . KO	3
May	17–George Roberts, Tijuana. . . . . KO	3
Nov.	25–Frank Owens, Leavenworth. . . . . KO	6
Nov.	25–Topeka Jack Johnson, Leavenworth . . . . W	5
Nov.	30–George Owens, Leavenworth . . . . KO	6

1921

Apr.	15–Jack Townsend, Leavenworth . . . . KO	6
May	28–John Allen, Leavenworth . . . . Exh.	2
May	28–Joe Boykin, Leavenworth . . . . KO	5

1922

(Inactive)

1923

May	6–Farmer Lodge, Havana, Cuba. . . . . KO	4
May	20–Jack Thompson, Havana, Cuba . . . . ND	15
Oct.	1–Battling Siki, Quebec. . . . . Exh.	6

1924

Feb.	22–Homer Smith, Montreal . . . . W	10

1925

(Inactive)

1926

May	2–Pat Lester, Nogales, Mexico . . . . W	15
May	30–Bob Lawson, Juarez, Mexico. . . . . WF	8

1927

(Inactive)

1928

Apr.	16–Bearcat Wright, Topeka, Kansas . . . . KO by	5
May	15–Bill Hartwell, Kansas City, KS . . . . KO by	7

TB	KO	WD	WF	D	LD	LF	KO BY	ND	NC
112	45	29	4	12	2	1	5	14	0

Died, June 10, 1946, Raleigh, N.C.
Elected to Boxing Hall of Fame, 1954.

Reference Section

JOE WALCOTT

Born, March 13, 1873, Barbados, West Indies. Nationality, West Indian. Weight, 145 lbs. Height, 5 ft. 1½ in. Managed by Tom O'Rourke. Came to America in 1887 and lived in Boston. Boxed and wrestled as amateur 1887-1889

1890

Feb.	29–Tom Powers, So. Boston	KO 2

1891

Jan.	30–J. Barrett, Providence	KO 1
Mar.	26–Alex. Clark, Cambridge	W 2
Dec.	12–G.V. Meakin, Boston	W 4
Dec.	12–Teddy Kelly, Boston	L 3
Dec.	23–Alex. Clark, Boston	W 3

1892

Mar.	28–T. Warren, Boston	W 4
May	17–Tom Powers, Boston	W 3
Aug.	4–Frank Carey, Walpole	D 3
Aug.	29–J.J. Leahy, Cambridge	KO 3
Oct.	22–Fred Morris, Philadelphia	D 4
Oct.	22–Joe Larg, Philadelphia	W 3
Oct.	29–Andy Watson, Philadelphia	D 4
Nov.	4–Harry Tracey, Boston	D 5
Nov.	11–Charley Jones, Philadelphia	W 3
Nov.	12–Jack Lymon, Philadelphia	KO 1
Dec.	5–Sam Boden	D 4
Dec.	5–Jack Connors, New York	KO 1
Dec.	8–Billy Harris, New York	KO 2

1893

June	5–Paddy McGuiggan, Newark	W 10
June	17–Mike Harris, New York	L 4
Aug.	22–Jack Hall, New York	KO 1
Dec.	22–Harry Tracey, Boston	WF 1
Dec.	28–Danny Russell	KO 2

1894

Jan.	11–Tommy West, So. Boston	KO 3
Feb.	26–Mike Welsh, Boston	KO 2
Apr.	19–Tom Tracey, Boston	KO 16
June	22–Mike Harris, Boston	KO 6
July	6–Dick O'Brien, Boston	KO 12
Oct.	15–Austin Gibbons, New York	KO 4
Nov.	1–Frank Carpenter, Chicago	KO 3
Nov.	3–Frank Neill, Chicago	W 8
Nov.	3–Shorty Ahern, Chicago	KO 8
Nov.	14–George Thomas, Louisville	KO 1
Nov.	15–Billy Green, Louisville	KO 2

1895

Mar.	1–Billy Smith, Boston	D 15
Apr.	3–Mick Dunn, Coney Island	W 8
Aug.	28–O'Brien, Boston	KO 1
Dec.	2–Geo. Lavigne, Maspeth	L 15

1896

Jan.	30–Jim Jackson, New York	W 4
Mar.	16–Scott Collins, L.I.C.	KO 7
May	10–Scaldy Bill Quinn, Woburn	W 20
Oct.	12–Scaldy Bill Quinn, Maspeth	W 17
Dec.	9–*Tommy West, New York	D 19

*Timer's error ended bout in 19th round. Referee Charley White called it a draw.

1897

Mar.	3–Tommy West, New York	L 20
Apr.	20–Jim Watts, New York	D 4
June	14–Tom Tracey, Philadelphia	D 6
Sept.	16–George Green, San Francisco	W 18
Oct.	29–Kid Lavigne, San Francisco	L 12
	(World Lightweight Title)	
Dec.	27–Tom Tracey, Chicago	D 6

1898

Apr.	4–Mysterious Billy Smith, Bridgeport	D 25
	(Welterweight Title Bout)	
Apr.	22–Tommy West, Philadelphia	ND 6
Apr.	28–Kid McPartland, Detroit	D 8
Dec.	6–Mysterious Billy Smith, N.Y.	L 20
	(Welterweight Title Bout)	

1899

Feb.	4–Australian Jimmy Ryan, Cincinnati	KO 14
Mar.	16–Billy Edwards, New York	KO 13
Apr.	8–Jim Judge, Toronto	KO 11
Apr.	25–Dan Creedon, New York	KO 1
May	8–Charley Johnson, Athens	W 11
May	19–Dick O'Brien, New York	KO 14
May	30–Jim Watts, Louisville	KO 8
June	12–Harry Fisher, Baltimore	W 11
June	23–Dan Creedon, New York	W 20
Nov.	25–Dan Creedon, Chicago	W 6
Nov.	29–Dan Creedon, Utica	W 20
Dec.	5–Bobby Dobbs, New York	KO 6

1900

Feb.	23–Joe Choynski, New York	KO 7
Mar.	16–Andy Walsh, New York	W 20

Apr. 10–Dick Moore, Baltimore . . . . KO 4
May 4–Mysterious Billy Smith, N.Y. . . . . W 25
May 11–Jack Bonner, Philadelphia . . . . ND 6
Aug. 27–*Tommy West, New York . . . . KO by 11
Sept. 24–Mysterious Billy Smith, Hartford . . . . WF 10
Dec. 13–Billy Hanrahan, Hartford . . . . KO 12
*Walcott quit at end of 11th round.

1901

Jan. 17–Kid Carter, Harford . . . . LF 10
Mar. 21–Chas. McKeever, Waterbury . . . . KO 6
July 26–Jack Bonner, Bridgeport . . . . W 15
Sept. 27–George Gardner, San Fran. . . . . W 20
Oct. 15–Kid Carter, San Fran. . . . . KO by 7
Nov. 28–Young Jackson, Baltimore . . . . W 20
Dec. 18–Jim Rube Ferns, Fort Erie . . . . KO 5
(Won Welterweight Title)

1902

Jan. 13–Young Peter, Jackson, Phila. . . . . ND 6
Feb. 14–Jimmy Handler, Philadelphia . . . . KO 2
Mar. 13–Young Peter, Jackson, Balti. . . . . D 10
Mar. 15–Billy Stift, Chicago . . . . W 6
Apr. 4–Fred Russell, Chicago . . . . D 6
Apr. 11–Phil. Jack O'Brien, Phila. . . . . ND 6
Apr. 25–George Gardner, San Fran. . . . . L 20
June 23–*Tommy West, London . . . . W 15
Oct. 7–George Cole, Philadelphia . . . . ND 4
Oct. 9–Frank Childs, Chicago . . . . L 3
*Title bout.

1903

Mar. 9–Mike Donovan, Pittsburgh . . . . W 10
Mar. 11–Charley Haghey, Boston . . . . KO 5
Mar. 18–George Cole, Pittsburgh . . . . KO 4
Apr. 2–Billy Woods, Los Angeles . . . . D 20
Apr. 15–Mike Donovan, Boston . . . . W 10
Apr. 20–Phil. Jack O'Brien, Boston . . . . D 10
May 28–Mysterious Billy Smith, Portland . . . . W 4
June 18–Young Peter Jackson, Portland . . . . D 20
July 3–Mose La Fontise, Butte . . . . KO 3
Aug. 13–Tom Carey, Boston . . . . KO 8
Sept. 11–Joe Grimm, Philadelphia . . . . ND 6
Sept. 21–Tom Carey, Boston . . . . KO 5
Oct. 13–Kid Carter, Boston . . . . W 15
Nov. 3–Kid Carter, Boston . . . . W 15
Nov. 10–Sandy Ferguson, Boston . . . . L 15
Dec. 29–Larry Temple, Boston . . . . D 15

1904

Jan. 18–Chas. Haghey, New Bedford . . . . KO 3
Feb. 26–Black Bill, Philadelphia . . . . ND 6
Apr. 30–Dixie Kid, San Francisco . . . . LF 20
(Lost welterweight title)
May 12–Dixie Kid, San Francisco . . . . D 20
(Welterweight title bout)
May 23–Sandy Ferguson, Portland . . . . D 10
June 10–Young Peter Jackson, Baltimore . . . . KO by 4
June 24–Mike Donovan, Baltimore . . . . W 5
July 1–Larry Temple, Baltimore . . . . D 10
Sept. 5–Sam Langford, Manchester . . . . D 15
Sept. 10–Dave Holly, Philadelphia . . . . ND 6
Sept. 30–Joe Gans, San Francisco . . . . D 20
(World Welterweight Title)
(Dixie Kid outgrew class; Walcott claimed title)

1906

July 10–Jack Dougherty, Chelsea . . . . KO 8
Sept. 30–Billy Rhodes, Kansas City . . . . D 20
Oct. 16–Honey Mellody, Chelsea . . . . L 15
(Lost welterweight title)
Nov. 29–Honey Mellody, Chelsea . . . . L 12

1907

Jan. 15–Mike Donovan, Providence . . . . L 10
June 18–Mike Donovan, Brazil, Ind. . . . . D 10
Oct. 17–Billy Payne, Rockland, Me. . . . . KO 6
Oct. 25–Mike Donovan, Providence . . . . D 15
Dec. 26–George Cole, Philadelphia . . . . ND 6

1908

Jan. 7–Jimmy Gardner, Boston . . . . L 12
Jan. 14–George Cole, Troy, N.Y. . . . . ND 6
Jan. 15–Mike Donovan, Montreal . . . . D 10
Mar. 3–Mike Donovan, Canadagua, N.Y. . . . . D 10
Apr. 3–Charlie Hitte, Schenectady . . . . L 6
June 11–Charles Kemp, Springfield, O. . . . . KO 5
June 16–Mike Lansing, Rochester, N.Y. . . . . W 6
June 18–Russell Van Horne, Columbus . . . . W 6
June 29–Billy Hurley, Schenectady . . . . ND 6
July 5–Jack Robinson, New York . . . . ND 6
Sept. 8–Bartley Connelly, Portland, Me. . . . . L 6
Nov. 17–Larry Temple, Boston . . . . KO by 10
Nov. 18–Jack Robinson, Easton, Pa. . . . . W 10

1909

May 10–Ed Smith, Columbus, O. . . . . ND 6
Sept. 6–Tom Sawyer, Portland, Me. . . . . ND 6
Dec. 3–Young Jack Johnson, Haverhill, Mass. . . . . . . D 6

1910

Mar.   7–Jimmy Potts, Minneapolis . . . . D   10
Apr.   25–Bill McKinnon, Brockton, Mass. . . . . LF   6
May   13–Kyle Whitney, Brockton L   6

1911

Oct.   17–Bob Lee, Boston . . . . KO   2
Nov.   2–Tom Sawyer, Lowell, Mass. L   3
Nov.   13–Henry Hall, Eastport, Me. . . . . ND   6

TB	KO	WD	WF	D	LD	LF	KO BY	ND	NC
150	34	45	2	30	17	3	4	15	0

Killed in automobile accident near Massillon, Ohio, October, 1935.

Elected to Boxing Hall of Fame 1955.

DIXIE KID
(Aaron L. Brown)
Born Dec. 23, 1883, Fulton, Mo. Weight, 145 lbs. Height 5 ft. 8 in.

1899

Knockouts: Tony Rivers, 1; Dan Ranger, 3: Clyde Burnham, 8. Draw: Kid Williams, 20; Billy Woods, 10.

1900

Knockouts: Mike McCure, 2; Tim Leonard, 1; Black Sharkey, 4; Bobby Dobbs, 4; Frank Dougherty, 2; Jack Dean, 10.

1901

Knockouts: Fresno Pete, 4; John Phillips, 2; Kid Ruggles, 6.

1902

Knockouts: Ben Hart, 4: Young McConnell, 4; Medal Dukelow, 1; Henry Lewis, 11; Guy Boros, 1; Medal Dukelow, 6. Won: Chas. Thurston, 20.

1903

Knockouts: Fred Mueller, 8; Soldier Green, 6; Eddie Cain, 2; Chas. Thurston, 1; Al Neil, 20; Mose La Fontise, 10.

1904

Apr.   30–Joe Walcott, San Francisco . . . . WF   20
(Won Welterweight Title)
May   12–Joe Walcott, San Francisco . . . . D   20
(Title Bout)
Sept. 21–Joe Grim, Saginaw . . . . W   10

Oct.   3–Joe Grim, Mt. Clemens, Mich. . . . . W   6
(Dixie Kid outgrew class and gave up title)
Nov.   12–Philadelphia Jack O'Brien Philadelphia . . . . . ND   6
Knockouts: Al Neil, 1; John Salomon, 11; Joe Mills, 9; John Dancer, 4; Chas. Thurston, 20; Young Peter Jackson, Draw, 15. No decisions: Dave Holly, 6; Larry Temple, 6; Dave Holly, 6.

1905

Jan.   2–Larry Temple, Baltimore . . . . D   15
Won: Joe Grim, 6, No decision: Geo. Cole, 6.

1908

Knockout: Fighting Ghost, 2. No decision: Cub White, 6; Fighting Ghost, 6; Geo. Cole, 6; Tommy Coleman, 6.

1909

Knockouts: Sailor Cunningham, 5; Bert Whirlwind, 3; Kid Williams, 4; Yg. Sam Langford, 1; Battling Johnson, 6; Sam Bolen, 6; Mike McDonough, 10; Al Grey, 8; Fighting Ghost 8, twice.

1910

Jan.   3–Chris Williams, Memphis . . . . KO   3
Jan.   10–Sam Langford, Memphis . . . . KO by   3
Jan.   26–Jack Ferrole, N.Y.C. . . . . KO   9
Mar.   2–Jack Fitzgerald, N.Y.C. . . . . ND   10
Mar.   14–Bill Hurley, Troy, N.Y. . . . . KO   4
Mar.   15–Kyle Whitney, Boston L   8
Mar.   21–Kid Henry, Troy, N.Y. . . . . N.D.   8
Apr.   2–George Cole, N.Y.C. . . . . KO   4
Apr.   5–Bill Hurley, Glen Falls, N.Y.C. . . . . ND   10
May   5–Jimmy Clabby, N.Y.C. . . . . ND   10
May   12–Fighting Kennedy, N.Y.C. . . . . KO   8
July   16–Fighting Kennedy, N.Y.C. . . . . ND   10
Aug.   1–Frank Mantell, N.Y.C. . . . . ND   10
Sept. 9–Willie Lewis, N.Y.C. . . . . ND   10
Sept. 19–Fighting Dick Nelson, N.Y.C. . . . . ND   10
Aug.   19–Billy West, N.Y.C. . . . . KO   4
Oct.   2–Dennis Tighe, N.Y.C. . . . . ND   10
Nov.   17–Willie Lewis, N.Y.C. . . . . ND   10
Nov.   24–Frank Mantell, Waterbury . . . . NC   5

1911

Jan.   17–Mike Twin Sullivan, Buffalo . . . . ND   10
Jan.   29–Joe Gaynor, N.Y.C. . . . . KO   3
Feb.   10–Bob Moha, Buffalo . . . . ND   10
Feb.   13–Kid Wilson, Harrison, N.J. . . . . ND   10
Feb.   17–Bill Hurley, Glens Fls., N.Y. . . . . W   8
Apr.   29–*Willie Lewis, Paris, France L   20

May   20–Young Laughrey, Paris, Fr. . . . . WF 10
June   14–Fred Stuber, Reims, Fr. . . . . KO   3
July   3–Blink McCloskey, London. . . . . LF   3
July   10–Harry Duncan, Dublin, Ire. . . . . ND   6
Aug.   29–Georges Carpentier, Tourville . . . . KO   5
Sept. 22–Seaman Brown, Plymouth, England . . . . KO   6
Nov.   9–Johnny Summers, Liverpool, England. . . . . KO   2
   *Referee's decision was reversed by jury of Parisian sports-
men in favor of Dixie.

1912

Jan.   18–Harry Lewis, Liverpool . . . . KO by 8
May   5–Dan Flynn, Glasgow, Scot. L   10
June   1–Jack Morris, London, England L   10
Oct.   4–Marcel Thomas, Paris, France L   15
Oct.   12–Johnny Mathieson, Birmingham, England L   20
Nov.   18–Johnny Mathieson, London . . . . D   10
Dec.   8–Bob Retson, London. . . . . KO   3
Dec.   20–Arthur Harman, London . . . . KO   9
Dec.   21–Arthur Evernden, Liverpool. . . . . KO   7

1913

Jan.   1–Arthur Harman, London . . . . KO   9
Jan.   2–Arthur Evernden, Liverpool. . . . . KO   9
Jan.   13–Johny Mathieson, Birmingham
Feb.   13–Jack Morris, Liverpool . . . . KO   4
Mar.   1–Seaman Hulls, Plymouth . . . . KO   3
Mar.   17–Louis Verger, London. . . . . W   20
Mar.   26–Johnny Mathieson, Leicester, England . . . . . LF 12
Apr.   10–Jerry Thomson, Liverpool L   1
Sept. 22–Private Harris, London L   10
Oct.   11–Jack Goldswain, London . . . . KO   4
Oct.   27–Albert Scanlon, London . . . . W   20
Nov.   2–"Bat." Dick Nelson, London . . . . KO   5
Nov.   29–Demlen, Paris L   15
Dec.   –Dick Nelson, London . . . . W   20
Dec.   22–Fireman Anderson, London . . . . W   10

1914

Jan.   1–Bandsman Blake, London L   20
Jan.   12–Fireman Anderson, Birkenhead . . . . KO   2
Jan.   28–Con. Pluyette, Yarmouth. . . . . W   4
Feb.   28–Tom Stokes, London . . . . W   10
Mar.   3–Fred Drummond, London . . . . KO   5
Mar.   9–Jim Rideout, Acton. . . . . KO   8
Mar.   16–Bill Bristowe, London L   20
Mar.   28–Dick Nelson, London L   20

Mar.   30–Bill Bristowe, London. . . . . KO   2
Dec.   7–Nicol Simpson, London L   20
Dec.   14–Dick Nelson, London . . . . W   20

TB	KO	WD	WF	D	LD	LF	KO BY	ND	NC
126	63	13	2	6	13	2	3	23	1

Died, October 3, 1935, Los Angeles, Calif.
Elected to Boxing Hall of Fame, 1975

JOE GANS
(Joseph Gaines)
(The Old Master)

Born, November 25, 1874, Baltimore, Md. Weight,
131-137 lbs. Height, 5 ft. 6¼ in. Managed by Al Herford.

1891-1894

–Dave Armstrong, Baltimore . . . . KO 12
–Arthur Coates, Baltimore . . . . KO 22
–Tommy Harden, Baltimore. . . . . KO   7
–George Evans, Baltimore . . . . KO   3
–Dave Armstrong, Baltimore . . . . KO   3
–Jack Daly, Pittsburgh . . . . KO 11
–Dave Horn, Baltimore. . . . . KO   2
–Bud Brown, Baltimore . . . . KO 10
–John Ball, Baltimore. . . . . KO   6
–Jack McDonald, Newark . . . . KO   7
–Dave Horn, Baltimore. . . . . KO 11
–Johnny Van Heest, Baltimore . . . . KO   9

1895

Feb.   6–Fred Sweigert, Baltimore . . . . W   10
Mar.   7–Sol English, Baltimore . . . . W   10
Mar.   16–Howard Wilson, Washington . . . . W   10
Apr.   2–Walter Edgerton, Baltimore . . . . KO   7
Apr.   25–Walter Edgerton, Baltimore . . . . KO   6
May   4–Frank Peabody, Baltimore . . . . KO   3
May   20–Benny Peterson, Baltimore . . . . KO 17
July   15–George Siddons, Baltimore . . . . D   20
Oct.   21–Joe Elliott, Baltimore . . . . KO   6
Nov.   18–Young Griffo, Baltimore . . . . D   10
Nov.   28–George Siddons, Baltimore . . . . KO   7

1896

Jan.   11–Benny Peterson, Philadelphia . . . . KO   3
Jan.   17–Joe Elliott, Baltimore, Md. . . . . KO   7
Jan.   28–Howard Wilson, Baltimore . . . . KO   8
Feb.   22–Jimmy Kennard, Boston . . . . KO   5
June   8–Jimmy Watson, Paterson. . . . . KO   9

1896 (Cont'd.)

June	29–Tommy Butler, Brooklyn	W	12
Aug.	20–Jack Williams, Baltimore	KO	2
Aug.	31–Danny McBride, Baltimore	D	20
Sept.	28–Jack Ball, Philadelphia	W	4
Oct.	6–Dal Hawkins, New York	L	15
Oct.	19–Jack Williams, Baltimore	KO	2
Nov.	12–Jerry Marshall, Baltimore	W	20
Dec.	14–Charles Rochette, San Francisco	KO	12

1897

Apr.	3–Howard Wilson, New York	KO	9
May	19–Mike Leonard, San Francisco	W	10
Aug.	30–Isadore Strauss, Baltimore	KO	5
Sept.	21–Young Griffo, Philadelphia	D	15
Sept.	27–Bobby Dobbs, Brooklyn	L	20
Nov.	6–Jack Daly, Philadelphia	ND-W	6
Nov.	29–Stanton Abbott, Baltimore	KO	5

1898

Jan.	3–Billy Young, Baltimore	KO	2
Jan.	17–Frank Garrard, Cleveland	W	15
Mar.	11–Tom Shortell, Baltimore	ND-W	6
Apr.	11–Young Starlight, Baltimore	KO	3
Apr.	11–Young Smyrna, Baltimore	Exh.	4
May	11–Steve Crosby, Louisville	W	6
June	3–Kid Roberson, Chicago	W	6
Aug.	8–Billy Ernst, Coney Island	KO	11
Aug.	26–Young Smyrna, Baltimore	KO	15
Aug.	31–Tom Jackson, Easton	KO	3
Sept.	26–Herman Miller, Baltimore	KO	4
Nov.	4–Kid McPartland, New York	W	25
Dec.	27–Jack Daly, New York	W	25

1899

Jan.	13–Young Smyrna, Baltimore	KO	2
Jan.	28–Martin Judge, Toronto	W	20
Feb.	6–Billy Ernst, Buffalo	WF	10
Apr.	14–George McFadden, New York	KO by	23
July	24–Jack Dobbs, Ocean City	KO	4
July	28–George McFadden, New York	D	25
Sept.	1–Eugene Bezenah, New York	KO	10
Sept.	15–Martin Judge, Baltimore	W	12
Oct.	3–Spider Kelly, New York	W	25
Oct.	11–Martin Judge, Baltimore	W	20
Oct.	31–George McFadden, New York	W	25
Nov.	24–Steve Crosby, Chicago	W	6
Dec.	11–Kid Ashe, Cincinnati	W	15
Dec.	22–Kid McPartland, Chicago	D	6

1900

Feb.	9–Spike Sullivan, New York	KO	14
Mar.	23–Frank Erne, New York	KO by	12
	(For World Lightweight Title)		
Apr.	2–Chicago Jack Daly, Phila.	KO	5
May	25–Dal Hawkins, New York	KO	2
June	26–Barney Furey, Cincinnati	KO	9
July	10–Young Griffo, New York	KO	8
July	12–Whitey Lester, Baltimore	KO	4
Aug.	31–Dal Hawkins, New York	KO	3
Sept.	7–George McFadden, Phila.	ND-D	6
Oct.	2–George McFadden, Denver	D	10
Oct.	6–Joe Young, Denver Colo.	W	10
Oct.	16–Otto Sieloff, Denver	KO	9
Oct.	19–Spider Kelly Denver	KO	8
Nov.	16–Kid Parker, Denver	KO	4
Dec.	13–Terry McGovern, Chicago	KO by	2

1901

Feb.	15–Jack Daly, Baltimore, Md.	WF	6
Apr.	1–Martin Flaherty, Baltimore	KO	4
May	31–Bobby Dobbs, Baltimore	KO	7
July	15–Harry Berger, Baltimore	ND-W	6
July	15–Jack Donahue, Baltimore	KO	2
July	15–Kid Thomas, Baltimore	ND-D	6
Aug.	23–Steve Crosby, Louisville	D	20
Sept.	20–Steve Crosby, Baltimore	W	12
Sept.	30–Joe Handler, Trenton	KO	1
Oct.	4–Dan McConnell, Baltimore	KO	3
Nov.	15–Jack Hanlon, Baltimore	KO	2
Nov.	22–Billy Moore, Baltimore	KO	3
Dec.	13–Bobby Dobbs, Baltimore	KO	14
Dec.	30–Joe Youngs, Philadelphia	KO	4

1902

Jan.	3–Tom Broderick, Baltimore	KO	6
Jan.	6–Eddie Connolly, Philadelphia	KO	5
Feb.	17–George McFadden, Philadelphia	ND-W	6
Mar.	7–Jack Ryan, Allentown, Pa.	KO	3
Mar.	27–Jack Bennett, Baltimore, Md.	KO	5
May	12–Frank Erne, Fort Erie, Ontario	KO	1
	(Won World Lightweight Title)		
June	27–George McFadden, San Francisco	KO	3
	(Retained World Lightweight Title)		
July	24–Ruge Turner, Oakland, Calif.	KO	15
	(Retained World Lightweight Title)		
Sept.	17–Gus Gardner, Baltimore, Md.	KO	5
	(Retained World Lightweight Title)		

Sept. 22–Jack Bennett, Philadelphia . . . . KO   2
Oct. 13–Kid McPartland, Fort Erie . . . . KO   5
    (Retained World Lightweight Title)
Oct. 14–Dave Holly, Lancaster, Pa. . . . . ND-W 10
Nov. 14–Charley Seiger, Baltimore . . . . KO 14
Dec. 19–Howard Wilson, Providence . . . . KO   3
Dec. 31–Charley Seiger, Boston . . . . W 10

1903
Jan.   1–Gud Gardner, New Britain . . . . WF 11
    (Retained World Lightweight Title)
Mar. 11–Steve Crosby, Hot Springs . . . . KO 11
    (Retained World Lightweight Title)
Mar. 23–Jack Bennett, Allegheny . . . . KO   5
May   13–Tom Tracy, Portland, Ore. . . . . KO   9
May   29–Willie Fitzgerald, San Fran. . . . . KO 10
    (Retained World Lightweight Title)
July   4–Buddy King, Butte, Montana . . . . KO   4
    (Retained World Lightweight Title)
Oct. 19–Joe Grim, Philadelphia . . . . ND-W   6
Oct. 20–Ed Kennedy, Philadelphia . . . . ND-W   6
Oct. 23–Dave Holly, Philadelphia. . . . . ND-L   6
Nov.   2–Jack Blackburn, Philadelphia . . . . ND-D   6
Dec.   7–Dave Holly, Philadelphia . . . . ND-W   6
Dec.   8–San Langford, Boston, Mass. . . . . L 15

1904
Jan. 12–Willie Fitzgerald, Detroit . . . . W 10
Jan. 19–Clarence Connors, Mt. Clemens . . . . KO   2
Jan. 22–Joe Grim, Baltimore, Md. . . . . W 10
Feb.   2–Mike Ward, Detroit, Mich. . . . . W 10
Mar. 25–Jack Blackburn, Baltimore . . . . W 15
Mar. 28–Gus Gardner, Saginaw . . . . W 10
Apr. 21–Sam Bolen, Baltimore . . . . W 15
May   27–Jewey Cooks, Baltimore . . . . KO   8
June   3–Kid Griffo, Baltimore . . . . KO   7
June 13–Sammy Smith, Philadelphia . . . . KO   4
June 27–Dave Holly, Philadelphia . . . . ND-D   6
Sept. 30–Joe Walcott, San Francisco . . . . D 20
Oct. 31–Jimmy Britt, San Francisco . . . . WF   5
    (Retained World Lightweight Title)
Nov.   –Relinquished World Lightweight Title.

1905
Mar. 27–Rufe Turner, Philadelphia . . . . ND-W   6
Sept. 16–Mike (Twin) Sullivan, Baltimore . . . . D 15

1906
Jan. 19–Mike (Twin) Sullivan, San Fran. . . . . KO 15
    (Won Vacant World Welterweight Title)
Mar. 17–Mike (Twin) Sullivan, Los Angeles . . . . KO 10
May   18–Willie Lewis, New York . . . . ND-W   6
June 15–Harry Lewis, Philadelphia . . . . ND-W   6
June 29–Jack Blackburn, Philadelphia . . . . ND-D   6
July 23–Dave Holly, Seattle, Wash. . . . . W 20
Sept. 3–Battling Nelson, Goldfield . . . . WF 42
    (Regained World Lightweight Title)

1907
Jan.   1–Kid Herman, Tonopah, Nev. . . . . KO   8
    (Retained World Lightweight Title)
Sept. 9–Jimmy Britt, San Francisco . . . . KO   6
    (Retained World Lightweight Title)
Sept. 27–George Memsic, Los Angeles . . . . W 20
    (Retained World Lightweight Title)

1908
Jan.   3–Bart Blackburn, Baltimore . . . . KO   3
Apr.   1–Spike Robson, Philadelphia . . . . KO   3
May   14–Rudy Unholz, San Francisco . . . . KO 11
    (Retained World Lightweight Title)
July   4–Battling Nelson, Colma . . . . KO by 17
    (Lost World Lightweight Title)
Sept. 9–Battling Nelson, Colma . . . . KO by 21
    (For World Lightweight Title)

1909
Mar. 12–Jabez White, New York . . . . ND-W 10

TB	KO	WD	WF	D	LD	LF	KO BY	ND	NC
156	85	42	5	15	4	0	5	0	0

    Died, August 10, 1910, Baltimore, MD.
    Elected to Boxing Hall of Fame, 1954.

GEORGE DIXON
(Little Chocolate)
    Born, July 29, 1870, Halifax, Nova Scotia, Canada. Weight, 105-122 lbs. Height, 5 ft. 3½ in. managed by Tom O'Rourke.

1886
Nov.   1–Young Johnson, Halifax . . . . KO   3

1887
Sept. 21–Elias Hamilton, Boston . . . . W   8
    –Young Mack, Boston . . . . KO   3

1888

Jan.	2 –Jack Lyman, Boston	KO 5
Jan.	20 –Charley Parton, Boston	KO 6
Feb.	17 –Barney Finnegan, Boston	KO 7
Mar.	10 –Ned Morris, Boston	KO 3
Mar.	21 –Paddy Kelly, Boston	D 15
Apr.	27 –Tommy Doherty, Boston	D 8
May	10 –Tommy Kelly, Boston	NC 9
June	13 –Jimmy Brackett, Boston	KO 5
June	21 –Hank Brennen, Boston	NC 14
Dec.	14 –Hank Brennan, Boston	NC 9
Dec.	28 –Hank Brennan, Boston	D 15

1889

Jan.	27 –Paddy Kelly, Boston	W 10
	–Frank Maguire, Putnam, Conn.	D 10
May	–Billy James, Haverhill, Mass.............	KO 3
Oct.	14 –Hank Brennan, Boston	NC 26
Dec.	11 –Mike Sullvan, New Bedford.............	W 6
Dec.	27 –Eugene Hornbacher, New York	KO 2

1890

Jan.	7 –Joe Murphy, Providence	Exh. 4
Feb.	7 –Cal McCarthy, Boston	NC 70
	(For American Bantamweight Title)	
Mar.	1 –Paddy Kearney, Paterson	Exh. 4
Mar.	3 –Joe Farrell, Jersey City	Exh. KO 2
Mar.	5 –Jack Carey, Hoboken...............	Exh. KO 3
Mar.	31 –Matt McCarthy, Philadelphia	Exh. KO 3
May	3 –Sailed for England on the *Catalonia*.	
May	12 –Arrived in Liverpool.	
June	27 –Nunc Wallace, London	KO 18
Oct.	23 –Johnny Murphy, Providence............	KO 40
Nov.	5 –J. Allan, Baltimore	Exh. KO 2
Nov.	7 –Virginia Rosebud, Baltimore	Exh. KO 3
Nov.	11 –Lee Andrews, Washington	Exh. KO 4
Nov.	13 –W. Dyson, Washington, D.C.	Exh. KO 2
Dec.	3 –Nick Collins, New York..............	Exh. 4

1891

Mar.	31 –Cal McCarthy, Troy, New York	KO 22
	(Won American Bantamweight Title)	
Apr.	20 –Martin Flaherty, Chicago	W 6
May	19 –Bobby Burns, Providence	Exh. 4
July	28 –Abe Willis, San Francisco	KO 5
Sept	26 –Jimmy Hagen, Philadelphia	Exh. 4
Sept.	28 –Marcellus Baker, Montreal	Exh. 3
Oct.	1 –Dan Coakley, Montreal	Exh. 3

Oct.	2 –Jack Fitzpatrick, Montreal	Exh. 4
Nov.	3 –Eugene Hornbacher, New York	Exh. 4
Nov.	5 –Nick Collins, New York...............	Exh. 4
Nov.	6 –Frank Wall, New York	Exh. KO 2
Nov.	12 –Billy Ross	Exh. 4
Dec.	17 –Lee Damro, Washington, D.C...........	Exh. 4

1892

Jan.	–Tom Warren, Philadelphia	Exh. KO 3
Jan.	11 –Elwood McCloskey, Philadelphia	Exh. 4
Jan.	16 –Young, Philadelphia	Exh. 4
Feb.	4 –Watson, Paterson	Exh. KO 1
May	6 –Billy Russell, New York	Exh. KO 2
June	27 –Fred Johnson, Coney Island	KO 14
	(Won Vacant World Featherweight Title)	
Sept.	6 –Jack Skelley, New Orleans	KO 8
	(Retained World Featherweight Title)	
Oct.	29 –Walter Edgerton, Philadelphia	D 4
Nov.	11 –Walter Edgerton, Philadelphia	D 4

1893

Jan.	25 –Eddie Eckhardt, Brooklyn..............	Exh. 4
Mar.	20 –George Siddons, Coney Island	D 12
Mar.	22 –Eddie Boerum, New York	Exh. KO 4
Apr.	16 –Mike Gillespie, Cincinnati..............	Exh. 4
Apr.	28 –Bill Young, Washington, D.C.............	Exh. 4
June	17 –Jerry Barnett, New York	Exh. 4
June	30 –Walter Edgerton, Philadelphia..........	W 4
Aug.	7 –Eddie Pierce, Coney Island	KO 3
	(Retained World Featherweight Title)	
Aug.	22 –Billy Plimmer, New York	L 4
Sept.	25 –Solly Smith, Coney Island	KO 7
	(Retained World Featherweight Title)	
Nov.	16 –Jack Downey, New York..............	Exh. KO 2
Nov.	21 –P.J. Hennessy, Lawrence............	Exh. KO 4
Dec.	15 –Billy Murphy, Paterson	Exh. 3

1894

Jan.	4 –Robert Heeny, Huntington..........	Exh. KO 2
Jan.	16 –Paddy Lemmons, Cleveland	Exh. KO 1
Mar.	4 –Ed Doyle, New York	Exh. KO 1
Mar.	22 –Walter Edgerton, Philadelphia..........	Exh. 3
June	29 –Young Griffo, Boston	D 20
Oct.	25 –Joe Flynn, Wilmington, Del............	Exh. 4

1895

Jan.	19 –Young Griffo, Coney Island	D 25
Jan.	28 –Walter Sanford, Dayton	Exh. KO 2

Mar.	6–John Conroy, New York .... Exh. KO	2
Mar.	7–Sam Bolen, New York .... Exh.	6
May	8–C. Slusher, Louisville .... Exh.	4
May	–Charlestown, St. Louis .... Exh. KO	2
May	–Frede, St. Louis .... Exh. KO	2
July	31–Tommy Connelly, Boston .... KO	4
Aug.	27–Johnny Griffin, Boston .... W	25
	(Retained World Featherweight Title)	
Oct.	28–Young Griffo, New York .... D	10
Dec.	5–Frank Erne, New York .... D	10

1896

Jan.	30–Pedlar Palmer, New York .... D	6
Mar.	17–Jerry Marshall, Boston .... KO	7
June	16–Martin Flaherty, Boston .... D	20
Sept.	25–Tommy White, New York .... D	20
Nov.	27–Frank Erne, New York L	20

1897

Jan.	22–Billy Murphy, New York .... KO	6
Feb.	15–Jack Downey, New York .... D	20
Mar.	24–Frank Erne, New York .... W	25
Apr.	26–Johnny Griffin, New York .... W	20
June	21–Walter Edgerton, Philadelphia .... ND	6
July	23–Dal Hawkins, San Francisco .... D	20
Oct.	4–Solly Smith, San Francisco L	20
	(Lost World Featherweight Title)	

1898

Mar.	31–Tommy White, Syracuse .... D	20
June	6–Eddie Santry, New York .... W	20
	(Advertised for World Featherweight Title)	
July	1–Ben Jordan, New York L	25
	(Advertised for World Featherweight Title)	
	(Jordan won recognition as champion in Great Britain.)	
Aug.	29–Jimmy Dunn, Fall River, Mass. .... ND-	6
Sept.	5–Joe Bernstein, Philadelphia .... ND-	6
Nov.	11–Dave Sullivan, New York .... W disq.	10
	(Regained World Featherweight Title)	
Nov.	29–Oscar Gardner, New York .... W	25
	(Retained World Featherweight Title)	

1899

Jan.	17–Young Pluto, New York .... KO	10
	(Retained World Featherweight Title)	
May	15–Kid Broad, Buffalo .... W	20
	(Retained World Featherweight Title)	

June	2–Joe Bernstein, New York .... W	25
	(Retained World Featherweight Title)	
July	3–Sam Bolen, Louisville .... KO	3
July	11–Tommy White, Denver .... W	20
	(Retained World Featherweight Title)	
July	14–Eddie Santry, Chicago .... W	6
Aug.	11–Eddie Santry, New York .... D	20
	(Retained World Featherweight Title)	
Oct.	13–Tim Callahan, Philadelphia .... ND-	6
Nov.	2–Will Curley, New York .... W	25
	(Retained World Featherweight Title)	
Nov.	21–Eddie Lenny, New York .... W	25
	(Retained World Featherweight Title)	

1900

Jan.	9–Terry McGovern, New York .... KO by	8
	(Lost World Featherweight Title)	
Feb.	21–Terry McGovern, New York .... Exh.	3
June	4–Tim Callahan, Philadelphia .... ND-	6
June	12–Benny Yanger, Chicago .... D	6
June	23–Terry McGovern, Chicago L	6
July	31–Tommy Sullivan, Coney Island .... KO by	7

1901

Feb.	8–Harry Lyons, Baltimore .... D	20
Aug.	16–Young Corbett, Denver L	10
Aug.	24–Abe Attell, Denver .... D	10
Sept.	26–Benny Yanger, St. Louis L	15
Oct.	20–Abe Attell, Cripple Creek .... D	20
Oct.	28–Abe Attell, St. Louis L	15
Dec.	19–Austin Rice, New London L	20

1902

Jan	17–Joe Tipman, Baltimore .... D	20
Jan.	24–Eddie Lenny, Baltimore .... KO by	9
Feb.	13–Chic Tucker, New Britain .... W	20
May	16–Billy Ryan, Ottawa .... D	15
May	27–Dan Dougherty, Philadelphia .... ND-	6
June	6–Eddie Lenny, Chester, Pa. .... D	6
June	10–Biz Mackey, Findlay, Ohio .... KO by	5
June	30–Tim Callahan, Philadelphia .... ND-	6
Sept.	8–Pedlar Palmer, Glasgow L	15
Sept.	29–Will Curley, Gateshead .... D	15

1903

Jan.	24–Jem Driscoll, London .... D	6
	–Dave Wallace, Birmingham .... D	6

1903 (Cont'd.)

Mar. 7–Fred Delaney, Woolwich	L 6
Apr. 6–Jack Pearson, Liverpool	KO 8
Apr. 16–George Phalin, Liverpool	D 15
Apr. 25–Spike Robson, Newcastle	L 20
May 2–Ben Jordan, London	L 6
May –Harry Paul	D 6
May 16–Spike Robson, Newcastle	L 20
May 25–George Phalin, Birmingham	D 15
June 27–Pedlar Palmer, London	L 8
Aug. 1–Digger Stanley, London	W 6
Aug. 29–Harry Ware, London	W 6
Sept. 13–Charlie Lampey, London	D 6
Sept. 24–Billy Barrett, Liverpool	D 10
Sept. 29–Charlie Lampey, London	D 6
Oct. 10–Jim Williams, London	KO 4
Oct. 12–Digger Stanley, London	L 6
Nov. 7–Harry Slough, West Hartlepool	Exh. 3
Nov. 9–Pedlar Palmer, Newcastle	W 20
Dec. 7–Cockney Cohen, Newcastle	W 15
Dec. 20–Dai Morgan, Newcastle	D 15

1904

Jan. 16–Cockney Cohen, Newcastle	W 20

Feb. 23–Harry Mansfield, Newcastle	D 20
Mar. 7–Cockney Cohen, Leeds	L 15
Mar. 19–Spike Robson, Newcastle	KO 11
Apr. 7–Billy Barrett, London	KO 12
Apr. 9–George Moore, London	D 6
Apr. 21–Tommy Burns, Liverpool	L 20
Aug. 22–Charlie Arrowsmith, New Brighton	Exh. 3
Oct. 17–Owen Moran, London	L 6
Nov. 24–Boss Edwards, London	D 15

1905

Jan. 6–Johnny Hughes, Ashford	D 8
Apr. 6–Jack Foy, London	D 15
Sept. 20–Tommy Murphy, Philadelphia	KO by 2
Dec. 28–Frankie Howe, New York	Exh. 3

1906

Jan. 4–Harry Shea, New York	KO 3
May 21–Billy Ryan, Gloucester	D 12
Dec. 10–Monk the Newsboy, Providence	L 15

TB	KO	WD	WF	D	LD	LF	KO BY	ND	NC
130	27	22	1	42	20	1	5	7	5

Died, January 6, 1909, New York City, N.Y.
Elected to Boxing Hall of Fame, 1956.

MOLINEAUX AND RICHMOND BOXING RECORDS

Thomas Molineaux 5'8", 185 lbs.
Born: Georgetown, D.C., 1784. Died:
Galway, Ireland, Aug. 4, 1818.

1810	July 14	Defeated Tom Blake	8 rounds
	Dec. 10	Lost to Tom Cribb	33 rounds
181!	May 21	Defeated Jim Rimmer	21 rounds
	Sept. 28	Lost to Tom Cribb	11 rounds
1813	April 2	Defeated Jack Carter	25 rounds
1814	May 27	Defeated Bill Fuller	2 rounds
1815	March 10	Lost to George Cooper	14 rounds

Bill Richmond 5'9", 175 lbs.
Born: Richmond, Staten Island, New York Aug. 5, 1793.
Died: London, Dec. 28, 1829.

1805	May 11	Defeated Youssep	6 rounds
	July 8	Defeated Jack Holmes	26 rounds
	Oct. 8	Lost to Tom Cribb	1 hr. 30 minutes
1809	April 11	Defeated Isaac Wood	23 rounds
	April 14	Defeated Jack Carter	25 minutes
	Aug. 9	Defeated George Maddox	52 minutes
1810	May 1	Defeated Young Powers	15 minutes
1814	April 7	Defeated Jack Davis	13 rounds
1815	Aug. 11	Defeated Tom Shelton	23 rounds

AFRICAN-AMERICAN WORLD BOXING CHAMPIONS

Weight Class	Name	Year
heavyweight	Louis, Joe	1937–49
light-heavyweight	Lewis, John Henry	1935–38
middleweight	Flowers, Tiger	1926
middleweight	Jones, Gorilla	1931–32
welterweight	Thompson, Cecil (aka Young Jack)	1930–31
welterweight	Armstrong, Henry	1938–40
lightweight	Armstrong, Henry	1938–39
lightweight	Walker, Sidney (aka Beau Jack)	1942–43, 1943–44 (New York)
lightweight	Montgomery, Bob	1943, 1944–47 (New York)
featherweight	Armstrong, Henry	1937–38
featherweight	Wilson, Jackie	1941–43 (NBA)

JOE LOUIS

(Joseph Louis Barrow)
(The Brown Bomber)

Born, May 13, 1914, Lafayette, Alabama. Weight, 188-218 lbs. Height, 6 ft. 1¾ in. Managed by Julian Black and John Roxborough; later by Marshall Miles.
1934 National AAU Light Heavyweight Champion

1934

July	4–Jack Kracken, Chicago	KO	1
July	12–Willie Davies, Chicago	KO	3
July	30–Larry Udell, Chicago	KO	2
Aug.	13–Jack Kranz, Chicago	W	8
Aug.	27–Buck Everett, Chicago	KO	2
Sept.	11–Alex Borchuk, Detroit	KO	4
Sept.	26–Adolph Wiater, Chicago	W	10
Oct.	24–Art Sykes, Chicago	KO	8
Oct.	31–Jack O'Dowd, Detroit	KO	2
Nov.	14–Stanley Poreda, Chicago	KO	1
Nov.	30–Charley Massera, Chicago	KO	3
Dec.	14–Lee Ramage, Chicago	KO	8

1935

Jan.	4–Patsy Perroni, Detroit	W	10
Jan.	11–Hans Birkie, Pittsburgh	KO	10
Feb.	21–Lee Ramage, Los Angeles	KO	2
Mar.	8–Donald (Reds) Barry, San Francisco	KO	3
Mar.	29–Natie Brown, Detroit	W	10
Apr.	12–Roy Lazer, Chicago	KO	3
Apr.	22–Biff Bennett, Dayton	Exh. KO	1
Apr.	25–Roscoe Toles, Flint	Exh. KO	6
May	3–Willie Davis, Peoria	Exh. KO	2
May	7–Gene Stanton, Kalamazoo	Exh. KO	3
June	25–Primo Carnera, New York	KO	6
Aug.	7–King Levinsky, Chicago	KO	1
Sept.	24–Max Baer, New York	KO	4
Dec.	14–Paulino Uzcudun, New York	KO	4

1936

Jan.	17–Charley Retzlaff, Chicago	KO	1
June	19–Max Schmeling, New York	KO by	12
Aug.	18–Jack Sharkey, New York	KO	3
Sept.	22–Al Ettore, Philadelphia	KO	5
Oct.	9–Jorge Brescia, New York	KO	3
Oct.	14–Willie Davies, South Bend	Exh. KO	3
Oct.	14–K.O. Brown, South Bend	Exh. KO	3
Nov.	20–Paul Williams, New Orleans	Exh. KO	2
Nov.	20–Tom Jones, New Orleans	Exh. KO	3
Dec.	14–Eddie Simms, Cleveland	KO	1

1937

Jan.	11–Stanley Ketchell, Buffalo	Exh. KO	2
Jan.	29–Bob Pastor, New York	W	10
Feb.	17–Natie Brown, Kansas City	KO	4
June	22–James J. Braddock, Chicago	KO	8
	(Won World Heavyweight Title)		
Aug.	30–Tommy Farr, New York	W	15
	(Retained World Heavyweight Title)		

1938

Feb.	23–Nathan Mann, New York	KO	3
	(Retained World Heavyweight Title)		
Apr.	1–Harry Thomas, Chicago	KO	5
	(Retained World Heavyweight Title)		
June	22–Max Schmeling, New York	KO	1
	(Retained World Heavyweight Title)		

1939

Jan.	25–John Henry Lewis, New York	KO	1
	(Retained World Heavyweight Title)		
Apr.	17–Jack Roper, Los Angeles	KO	1
	Retained World Heavyweight Title)		
June	28–Tony Galento, New York	KO	4
	(Retained World Heavyweight Title)		
Sept.	20–Bob Pastor, Detroit	KO	11
	(Retained World Heavyweight Title)		

1940

Feb.	9–Arturo Godoy, New York	W	15
	(Retained World Heavyweight Title)		
Mar.	29–Johnny Paychek, New York	KO	2
	(Retained World Heavyweight Title)		
June	20–Arturo Godoy, New York	KO	8
	(Retained World Heavyweight Title)		
Dec.	16–Al McCoy, Boston	KO	6
	(Retained World Heavyweight Title)		

1941

Jan.	31–Red Burman, New York	KO	5
	(Retained World Heavyweight Title)		
Feb.	17–Gus Dorazio, Philadelphia	KO	2
	(Retained World Heavyweight Title)		
Mar.	21–Abe Simon, Detroit	KO	13
	(Retained World Heavyweight Title)		
Apr.	8–Tony Musto, St. Louis	KO	9
	(Retained World Heavyweight Title)		
May	23–Buddy Baer, Washington, D.C.	W disq.	7
	(Retained World Heavyweight Title)		

June 18–Billy Conn, New York . . . . KO 13
(Retained World Heavyweight Title)
July 11–Jim Robinson, Minneapolis . . . . Exh. KO 1
Sept. 29–Lou Nova, New York . . . . KO 6
(Retained World Heavyweight Title)
Nov. 25–George Giambastiani, Los Angeles . . . . . . Exh. 4

1942

Jan. 9–Buddy Baer, New York . . . . KO 1
(Retained World Heavyweight Title)
Mar. 27–Abe Simon, New York . . . . KO 6
(Retained World Heavyweight Title)
June 5–George Nicholson, Fort Hamilton . . . . Exh.
3

1943
(Inactive)

1944

Nov. 3–Johnny Demson, Detroit . . . . Exh. KO 2
Nov. 6–Charley Crump, Baltimore . . . . Exh. 3
Nov. 9–Dee Amos, Hartford. . . . . Exh. 3
Nov. 13–Jimmy Bell, Washington, D.C. . . . . Exh. 3
Nov. 14–Johnny Davis, Buffalo . . . . Exh. KO 1
Nov. 15–Dee Amos, Elizabeth . . . . Exh. 3
Nov. 17–Dee Amos, Camden . . . . Exh. 3
Nov. 24–Dan Merritt, Chicago . . . . Exh. 3

1945

Nov. 15–Sugar Lip Anderson, San
Francisco . . . . Exh. 2
Nov. 15–Big Boy Brown, San Francisco. . . . . Exh. 2
Nov. 29–Big Boy Brown, Sacramento . . . . Exh. 2
Nov. 29–Bobby Lee, Sacramento . . . . Exh. 2
Dec. 10–Bob Frazier, Victoria . . . . Exh. 3
Dec. 11–Big Boy Brown, Portland . . . . Exh. 2
Dec. 11–Dave Johnson, Portland . . . . Exh. 2
Dec. 12–Big Boy Brown, Eugene . . . . Exh. 3
Dec. 13–Big Boy Brown, Vancouver . . . . Exh. 3

1946

June 19–Billy Conn, New York . . . . KO 8
(Retained World Heavyweight Title)
Sept. 18–Tami Mauriello, New York. . . . . KO 1
(Retained World Heavyweight Title)
Nov. 11–Cleo Everett, Honolulu. . . . . Exh. 4
Nov. 11–Wayne Powell, Honolulu . . . . Exh. 2
Nov. 25–Perk Daniels, Mexicali . . . . Exh. 4

1947

Feb. 7–Arturo Godoy, Mexico City . . . . Exh. 10
Dec. 5–Jersey Joe Walcott, New York . . . . W 15
(Retained World Heavyweight Title)

1948

June 25–Jersey Joe Walcott, New York . . . . KO 11
(Retained World Heavyweight Title)

1949

Mar. 1–Announced retirement.

1950

Sept. 27–Ezzard Charles, New York . . . . L 15
(For World Heavyweight Title)
Nov. 29–Cesar Brion, New York. . . . . W 10

1951

Jan. 3–Freddie Beshore, Detroit . . . . KO 4
Feb. 7–Omelio Agramonte, Miami . . . . W 10
Feb. 23–Andy Walker, San Francisco. . . . . KO 10
May 2–Omelio Agramonte, Detroit. . . . . W 10
June 15–Lee Savold, New York. . . . . KO 6
Aug. 1–Cesar Brion, San Francisco . . . . W 10
Aug. 15–Jimmy Bivins, Baltimore . . . . W 10
Oct. 26–Rocky Marciano, New York . . . . KO by 8

TB	KO	WD	WF	D	LD	LF	KOBO	ND	NC
66	49	13	1	0	1	0	2	0	0

Elected to Boxing Hall of Fame, 1954.
Died, April 12, 1981, Las Veas, Nevada.

JOHN HENRY LEWIS

Born, May 1, 1914, Los Angeles, Calif. Weight, 174 lbs. Height, 5 ft. 11 in. Managed by Ernie Lira, Larry White, Frank Schuler, Gus Greenlee.

1930

–Roy Gunn. . . . . KO 3
–Kid Val Don . . . . KO 3
–Sammy Bass . . . . : . KO 1
–Ray Imm . . . . KO 4
–Jake Henderson. . . . . KO 4
–Young Tiger Flowers. . . . . KO 6

1931

Jan. 30–Palmleaf Wright, Phoenix . . . . KO 2
Feb. 6–Bob Richardson, Phoenix . . . . KO 2

Mar. 11–Sam Terrain, Prescott.................. KO 4
May 15–Tony Cadena, Phoenix.................. KO 1
May 29–Evans Fortune, Phoenix .... KO 3
July 1–Lloyd Phelps, Mesa .... W 8
Sept. 14–Joe Arcienega, Phoenix............... KO 5
Nov. 27–The School Boy, Phoenix.............. KO 3

1932

Career totals to March, 1932: 20 bouts, 18 kayoes, two wins on points.

Apr. 22–Yale Okun, San Francisco .... W 10
July 13–Peitro Georgi, San Francisco............ KO 1
July 29–Jimmy Hanna, San Francisco .... KO 6
Sept. 21–James J. Braddock, San Francisco......... W 10
Oct. 5–Fred Lenhart, San Francisco .... KO 4
Oct. 26–Lou Scozza, San Francisco .... W 10
Nov. 16–Maxie Rosenbloom, San Francisco .... L 10
Dec. 9–Tuffy Dial, Phoenix .... KO 4

1933

Feb. 7–Terris Hill, San Francisco .... KO 4
Apr. 7–Emmett Rocco, San Francisco .... KO 7
May 15–Tom Patrick, San Francisco .... W 10
June 10–Fred Lenhart, San Francisco .... D 10
July 10–Maxie Rosenbloom, San Francisco .... W 10
July 31–Maxie Rosenbloom, San Francisco .... W 10
Oct. 31–Frank Rowsey, Los Angeles............. W 10

1934

Feb. 9–Bobby Brown, Tucson .... KO 1
June 6–Sandy Casanova, Ft. Hauchuca........... KO 3
July 12–Bobby Brown, Tucson .... KO 3
Sept. 3–Tony Poloni, Reno.................... KO 1
Sept. 12–Norman Conrad, Oakland .... W 10
Sept. 20–Young Firpo, Portland .... D 10
Oct. 3–Red Barry, San Francisco .... D 10
Oct. 17–Pietro Georgi, Oakland .... KO 2
Oct. 31–Earl Wise, Oakland .... KO 3
Nov. 16–James J. Braddock, New York .... L 10
Nov. 23–Yale Okun, New York .... KO 3
Dec. 14–Tony Shucco, New York .... W 10

1935

Jan. 29–Don Petrin, Pittsburgh .... KO 7
Feb. 25–Frank Wojack, Syracuse .... KO 3
Mar. 4–Terry Mitchell, Syracuse .... KO 6
Mar. 13–Emilio Martinez, Denver .... W 10
Apr. 12–Bob Olin, San Francisco................ W 10
May 10–Frank Rowsey, San Francisco............ W 10

June 3–Tommy Patrick, Pittsburgh .... KO 1
June 24–Izzy Singer, Paterson .... KO 1
July 8–Lou Poster, Cleveland.................. KO 5
July 17–Maxie Rosenbloom, Oakland .... L 10
July 24–Abe Feldman, New York .... L 10
Oct. 31–Bob Olin, St. Louis .... W 15
(Won World Light Heavyweight Title)
Nov. 29–Maxie Rosenbloom, San Francisco......... L 10
Dec. 11–Georgie Simpson, Oakland .... KO 2
Dec. 19–Coleman Johns, Phoenix .... KO 2
Dec. 20–Dutch Weimer, Tucson .... W 10

1936

Jan. 10–Tiger Jack Fox, Spokane .... KO 3
Jan. 17–Al Stillman, St. Louis .... KO 4
Jan. 29–Emilio Martinez, Denver .... L 10
Jan. 31–Cyclone Lynch, Walsenburg .... KO 1
Mar. 6–Eddie Simms, St. Louis .... W 10
Mar. 13–Jock McAvoy, New York................ W 15
(Retained World Light Heavyweight Title)
Apr. 7–George Nichols, Buffalo .... D 10
Apr. 22–Izzy Singer, Chicago .... W 10
May 27–Charlie Massera, Pittsburgh .... W 10
May 29–Bob Godwin, New York .... KO 1
June 8–John Anderson, New York............... W 10
June 12–Dutch Weimer, York .... KO 5
June 17–Tony Shucco, St. Louis .... KO 8
June 22–Jimmy Merriott, Peoria................ KO 3
July 10–Max Marek, Chicago.................. W 10
July 30–Al Gainer, Pittsburgh .... W 12
Aug. 12–George Nichols, St. Louis .... W 10
Sept. 17–Tiger Hairston, Charleston .... KO 1
Oct. 2–Red Burman, Chicago .... KO 2
Nov. 9–Len Harvey, London .... W 15
(Retained World Light Heavyweight Title)

1937

Jan. 4–Al Ettore, Philadelphia .... D 10
Jan. 11–Art Sykes, Pittsburgh .... KO 6
Jan. 28–Chester Palutis, Scranton .... KO 7
Feb. 8–Al Ettore, Philadelphia .... W 15
Mar. 15–Hans Birkie, Philadelphia .... W 10
Apr. 2–Donald (Reds) Barry, St. Louis .... KO 5
Apr. 9–Babe Davis, Indianapolis............... KO 3
Apr. 13–Harold Murphy, Omaha................ KO 4
Apr. 19–Pret Farrar, Des Moines .... KO 6
May 4–Emilio Martinez, St. Louis .... W 10

May   14–Patsy Perroni, New York . . . . W 10
May   21–Jack Kranz, Kansas City . . . . KO 3
June 3–Bob Olin, St. Louis . . . . KO 8
        (Retained World Light Heavyweight Title)
June 15–Al Ettore, Philadelphia . . . . W 10
June 28–Willie Reddish, Washington . . . . W 10
Aug. 19–Italo Colonello, Pittsburgh . . . . W 12
Oct. 15–Isadore Gastanga, Detroit . . . . L 10
Nov. 26–Salvadore Ruggierello, Minneapolis . . . . KO 4
Dec. 12–Isadore Gastanaga, St. Louis. . . . . KO 9
Dec. 17–Johnny Risko, Cleveland . . . . W 10

1938

Jan.   10–Leonard Neblitt, Nashville . . . . KO 8
Jan.   18–Marty Gallagher, St. Louis . . . . KO 3
Jan.   31–Emil Scholz, Pittsburgh . . . . W 10
Feb.   11–Fred Lenhart, St. Louis . . . . KO 10
Mar.   25–Bud Mignault, St. Paul . . . . W 10
Apr.   4–Bob Tow, Philadelphia . . . . W 10
Apr.   25–Emilio Martinez, Minneapolis . . . . KO 4
        (Retained World Light Heavyweight Title)
May   5–Domenic Ceccarelli, Baltimore . . . . W 10
May   19–Elmer Ray, Atlanta . . . . KO 12
Aug.   25–Domenic Ceccarelli, Nutley . . . . KO 3
Sept. 15–Jimmy Adamick, Philadelphia . . . . W 10
Oct.   28–Al Gainer, New Haven . . . . W 15
        (Retained World Light Heavyweight Title)

1939

Jan.   25–Joe Louis, New York . . . . KO by 1
        (For World Heavyweight Title)
June   –
Announced retirement.

TB	KO	WD	WF	D	LD	LF	KOBO	ND	NC
116	64	39	0	5	7	0	1	0	0

Died, April 18, 1974, Berkeley, Calif.

THEODORE (TIGER) FLOWERS

(The Georgia Deacon)
Born, August 5, 1895, Camille, Georgia. Weight, 160 lbs.
Height, 5ft. 10 in. Southpaw. Managed by Walk Miller.

1918

Knockouts: Billy Hooper, 11; Kid Fox, 2; Batt Hazel, 8. Won:
Batt Henry Williams, 20; Rufus Cameron, 10; Batt Mims, 15.

1919

Knockout: Rough House Baker, 3. Won: Batt Mims, 10; Bill
Hooper, 20.

1920

Knockouts: Tiger Moore, 2; Kid Palmer, 3. Won: Sailor
Darden, 15; Batt Mims, 10.

1921

Knockouts: Kid Brown, 8; Batt Troupe, 3; Kid Brown, 2;
Whitey Black, 1; Kid Williams, 3; Gorilla Jones, 4; Jim Barry, 5;
Mexican Kid Brown, 1. Won: Billy Hooper, 10; Batt Mims, 10;
Batt Mims, 10; Batt Gahee, 10; Batt Gahee, 8; Whitey Black, 8;
Jim Barry, 15. Knockout by: Panama Joe Gans, 5.

1922

Knockouts: Jack Ray, 2; Kid Brown, 2; Kid Paddy, 1; Kid
Davis, 1; Eddie Palmer, 10. Won: Billy Britton, 15; Battling
Gahee, 8; Frankie Murphy, 15; Andy Kid Palmer, 15; Frankie
Carbone, 10; (foul) Eddie Palmer, 8. Knocked out by: Kid
Norfolk, 3; Sam Langford, 2; Lee Anderson, 7; Jamaica Kid, 2.
Draw: Battling Norfolk, 8.

1923

Feb.   21–Bob Lawson, Nashville . . . . W 8
Feb.   28–Batt Mims, Nashville . . . . W 8
Mar.   10–Evansville Jack Ray, Nashville . . . . KO 3
Apr.   20–Jamaica Kid, Toledo . . . . ND 12
May   8–Kid Norfolk, Springfield . . . . KO by 1
May   15–Tom King, Juarez, Mexico . . . . W 15
May   25–Panama Joe Gans, Toledo . . . . ND 12
July   3–Tut Jackson, Atlanta . . . . W 12
July   30–Whitey Black, Detroit . . . . ND 10
Sept.   3–Jamaica Kid, Atlanta . . . . W 12
Sept. 16–Jim Flynn, Mexico City . . . . W 5
Nov.   7–George Robinson, Atlanta . . . . D 12
Dec.   6–Rufus Cameron, Albany . . . . KO 4

1924

Jan.   23–Herbert Moore, Nashville . . . . KO 1
Jan.   30–Sam Goodrich, San Antonio . . . . W 12
Feb.   18–Bob Lawson, Toledo . . . . KO 10
Feb.   25–Battling Gahee, Barberton . . . . W 12
Mar.   3–Jamaica Kid, Fremont . . . . ND 10
Mar.   19–Bob Lawson, Nashville . . . . KO 5
Mar.   29–Lee Anderson, N.Y.C. . . . . W 12
Apr.   9–Dave Thorton, Nashville . . . . KO 2
Apr.   19–Jimmy Darcy, N.Y.C. . . . . W 10
Apr.   29–Geo. Robinson, Atlanta . . . . W 10
May   3–Ted Jamieson, N.Y.C. . . . . W 12

May   14–Willie Walker, N.Y.C. .... KO   7
June 14–Joe Lohman, N.Y.C. .... W   12
June 20–Batt. Gahee, Fremont .... ND   10
June 27–Jamaica Kid, Grand Rapids .... WF   3
July   3–Lee Anderson, Atlanta .... WF   6
July 22–Jamaica Kid, Covington................ WF   3
Aug.   2–Jack Townsend, N.Y.C. .... KO   11
Aug. 12–Oscar Mortimer, San Antonio .... KO   3
Aug. 21–Harry Greb. Fremont .... ND   10
Sept. 1–Tut Jackson, Martins Ferry .... ND   10
Sept. 15–Jamaica Kid, Columbus .... W   12
Sept. 22–Lee Anderson, Columbus .... W   12
Sept. 28–Battling Gahee, Zanesville........... KO   4
Sept. 29–Tut Jackson, Canton .... KO   1
Oct. 11–Jamaica Kid, N.Y.C. .... KO   7
Oct. 21–Cleve Hawkins, Atlanta .... KO   3
Oct. 23–Joe Lohman, Hamilton .... WF   4
Nov.   1–George Robinson, N.Y.C. .... W   12
Nov. 10–*Jerry Hayes, Philadelphia .... KO   2
Nov. 10–*Hughie Clemons, Philadelphia .... KO   2
Nov. 27–Clem Johnson, Canton .... ND   12
Dec.   1–Battling Gahee, Columbus............. KO   2
Dec.   9–Johnny Wilson, N.Y.C. .... KO   3
Dec. 15–Jack Townsend, Philadelphia .... KO   5
Dec. 26–Frankie Schoell, Buffalo .... D   6

*Both in same night.

1925

Jan.   1–Joe Lohman, Brooklyn .... KO   3
Jan.   5–Billy Britton, Boston................. KO   4
Jan.   7–Dan Dowd, Providence .... KO   6
Jan. 16–Jack Delaney, N.Y.C. .... KO by   2
Jan. 28–Tommy Robson, Boston .... KO   8
Feb.   2–Ted Moore, Newark .... ND   12
Feb.   5–Jamaica Kid, Dayton .... KO   10
Feb. 14–Jackie Clarke, N.Y.C. .... KO   5
Feb. 16–Lou Bogash, Boston .... LF   3
Mar.   4–Jack Delaney, N.Y.C. .... KO by   4
Mar. 16–Sailor Darden, Toledo .... W   12
Mar. 20–Lou Bogash, Boston................... W   10
Apr. 29–Sailor Darden, Savannah .... KO   5
May   18–Pal Reed, Boston..................... W   10
May   26–Lou Bogash, Bridgeport .... W   12
June   4–Jock Malone, E. Chicago.............. ND   10
June   8–Lee Anderson, Phildalephia .... W   10
July 24–Lou Bogash, Aurora .... ND   10
July 20–Pat McCarthy, Boston................. W   10
Aug. 28–Jock Malone, Boston .... W   10
Sept. 7–*Ted Moore, Cleveland .... NC   6

Oct. 23–Jock Malone, St. Paul................ ND   10
Oct. 28–Chuck Wiggins, E. Chicago .... ND   10
Dec. 10–Frank Moody, Boston.................. W   10
Dec. 23–Mike McTigue, N.Y.C. L   10
*Referee stopped fight.

1926

Feb. 26–Harry Greb, N.Y.C. .... W   15
(Won World Middleweight Title)
Apr. 16–Panama Joe Gans, Wilkes-Barre .... W   10
June 18–Young Bob Fitzsimmons, Jersey City ...... ND   10
June 28–Ray Neuman, Boston .... W   10
July 11–Lee Anderson, Juarez, Mexico .... KO   2
July 24–Eddie Huffman, Los Angeles........... W   10
Aug. 10–Batt. McCreary, Atlanta .... WF   2
Aug. 19–*Harry Greb, N.Y.C. .... W   15
Sept. 16–Happy Hunter, Memphis .... KO   3
Oct. 15–Maxie Rosenbloom, Boston .... LF   9
Nov. 22–Eddie Huffman, Chicago .... W   10
Dec.   3–Mickey Walker, Chicago............... L   10
(Lost World Middleweight Title)
*Title bout.

1927

Jan.   7–Tut Jackson, Grand Rapids .... KO   2
Jan. 22–Leo Lomski, Los Angeles L   10
Feb. 18–Lou Bogash, Boston................... W   10
Mar. 29–Soldier Geo. Jones, Atlanta.......... KO   1
Apr. 29–Chuck Wiggins, Buffalo............... W   10
May   13–Chuck Wiggins, Grand Rapids .... W   10
May   27–Eddie Huffman, Boston .... W   10
June 16–Bob Sage, Detroit .... W   10
July   3–Maxie Rosenbloom, Chicago .... D   10
July 28–Bing Conley, Norwalk .... W   10
Aug.   3–Chuck Wiggins, Cleveland .... D   10
Aug. 11–Harry Dillon, Portland .... W   10
Aug. 16–Jock Malone, Seattle .... W   6
Sept. 1–Joe Anderson, N.Y.C. .... W   10
Sept. 30–Pete Latzo, Wilkes-Barre .... W   10
Oct. 17–Joe Lohman, Canton .... W   10
Nov.   9–Maxie Rosenbloom, Detroit............ D   10
Nov. 12–Leo Gates, N.Y.C. .... KO   4

TB	KO	WD	WF	D	LD	LF	KOBO	ND	NC
149	49	61	5	6	3	2	8	14	1

Died, November 16, 1927, New York City, N.Y.,
following an operation.
Elected to Boxing Hall of Fame, 1971.

WILLIAM (GORILLA) JONES

Born, May 4, 1910, Memphis, Tenn. Weight, 147-160 lbs.
Height, 5 ft. 6 in. Managed by Suey Welch.

1928

Jan.	27–George Moore, Akron	KO	5
Feb.	23–Black Fitz, Barberton	KO	3
Mar.	1–Sailor Maxwell, Canton	KO	4
Mar.	29–K.O. Kelly, Akron	W	10
Apr.	10–Joe Feldman, Cleveland	KO	1
Apr.	27–Ben Spively, Marietta	KO	4
May	4–Alvin Spence, Cleveland	KO	1
May	17–Young Saylor, Marietta	ND	10
May	29–Allan Beatty, McKeesport	KO	10
June	1–Bobby Brown, Cleveland	L	10
June	18–Mickey Fedor, Akron	KO	5
July	18–Jim Williams, Akron	KO	3
July	25–Bobby Brown, Cleveland	KO	3
Aug.	14–Billy Algers, Akron	W	10
Aug.	29–Sammy Baker, Cleveland	ND	10
Sept.	13–Tommy Freeman, Cleveland	ND	10
Sept.	18–Bobby LaSalle, Cleveland	W	10
Oct.	2–Billy Leonard, Akron	KO	1
Oct.	11–Heavy Andrews, Erie	W	10
Oct.	19–Bucky Lawless, Erie	ND	10
Oct.	25–Bucky Lawless, Erie	W	10
Nov.	2–Jimmy Finley, Akron	W	10
Nov.	16–Pal Silvers, New York	W	8
Dec.	28–Tony Vaccarelli, New York	D	10

1929

Jan.	8–Arturo Shackels, Cleveland	KO	1
Jan.	14–Arturo Shackels, Buffalo	W	10
Feb.	15–Jack Murphy, Erie	KO	4
Feb.	18–Bucky Lawless, Buffalo	L	10
Feb.	25–Nick Testo, Holyoke	LF	5
Mar.	11–Joe Zelinsky, Springfield	KO	1
Apr.	2–George Fifield, Akron	KO	1
Apr.	9–Tommy Freeman, Cleveland	D	12
May	3–Al Mello, New York	W	10
May	17–Izzy Grove, New York	KO	6
June	3–Al Mello, Boston	KO	6
June	14–Jack Palmer, Chicago	KO	5
June	25–Jack McVey, Boston	W	10
July	16–Bucky Lawless, Cleveland	L	12
Aug.	1–Battling Groves, Memphis	KO	3
Aug.	12–Pete Meyers, San Francisco	KO	5

Aug.	20–Fred Mahan, Los Angeles	KO	6
Oct.	9–Jack Horner, Akron	KO	2
Oct.	21–Jackie Fields, San Francisco	L	10
Nov.	8–Jack Sparr, San Diego	KO	4
Dec.	4–Nick Testo, Akron	KO	6
Dec.	13–Jackie Fields, Boston	NC	7

1930

Jan.	1–Billy Angelo, Philadelphia	W	10
Jan.	17–Floyd Hybert, Holyoke	KO	3
Jan.	27–Izzy Grove, New York	KO	6
Feb.	7–Eddie Roberts, San Francisco	D	10
Feb.	14–Wesley Ketchell, San Francisco	W	10
Mar.	14–Meyer Grace, Akron	KO	4
Mar.	17–Jock Malone, St. Paul	ND	10
Apr.	14–Gene Cardi, Wheeling	KO	7
Apr.	22–Roy (Tiger) Williams, Dayton	L	12
May	12–Bucky Lawless, Holyoke	L	10
May	26–Vincent Forgione, Pittsburgh	W	10
June	2–Henry Goldberg, W. Springfield	W	10
June	25–Vincent Forgione, Cleveland	W	10
July	18–Bucky Lawless, San Francisco	KO	9
Aug.	8–Manuel Quintero, San Francisco	D	10
Aug.	15–Ham Jenkins, Denver	W	10
Sept.	4–Harry Smith, Long Island City	NC	9
Sept.	15–Cowboy Jack Willis, Canton	W	10
Oct.	23–Harry Smith, New York	L	10
Nov.	10–Abe Lichtenstein, Rochester	W	10
Nov.	28–Jackie Brady, Erie	L	10
Dec.	26–Clyde Chastain, Akron	KO	4

1931

Jan.	13–Johnny Burns, Oakland	KO	7
Jan.	28–Chick Devlin, San Francisco	D	10
Jan.	30–Mike Hector, Stockton	W	10
Feb.	6–Frank Rowsey, San Francisco	KO	8
Feb.	17–Herman Ratzleff, Portland	W	10
Mar.	11–Bud Gorman, Oakland	W	10
Apr.	14–Paul Pirrone, Cleveland	W	10
Apr.	28–Ham Jenkins, Kansas City	W	10
May	25–Bucky Lawless, Chicago	L	10
Aug.	25–Tiger Thomas, Milwaukee	W	10
Sept.	17–Clyde Chastain, Milwaukee	KO	6
Oct.	21–Johnny Roberts, Akron	KO	3
Nov.	3–George Nichols, Milwaukee	W	10
Nov.	19–Frankie O'Brien, Milwaukee	W	10
Dec.	11–Henry Firpo, Milwaukee	W	10

1932

Jan.	25–Oddone Piazza, Milwaukee .... KO	6
	(Won Vacant World Middleweight Title)	
Mar.	14–Frankie O'Brien, Holyoke .... L disq.	8
Mar.	31–Chuck Burns, Akron .... KO	3
Apr.	7–Bud Saltis, Green Bay .... W	10
Apr.	26–Young Terry, Trenton .... W	12
	(Retained World Middleweight Title)	
June	11–Marcel Thil, Paris................. L disq.	11
	(Lost World Middleweight Title)	
Aug.	9–Jack December, Cleveland .... KO	2
Aug.	29–Kid Leonard, Davenport .... W	10
Oct.	3–Johnny Peppe, Atlantic City............. W	8
Nov.	24–Jackie Purvis, Akron................... KO	3
Dec.	1–Willie Oster, Davenport .... W	10
Dec.	5–Manny Davis, Manche................. WF	6
Dec.	26–Tommy Freeman, Pittsburgh .... D	10

1933

Jan.	13–Young Stuhley, Clinton .... KO	4
Jan.	30–Sammy Slaughter, Cleveland .... KO	7
	(Won Vacant NBA American Middleweight Title)	
Feb.	21–Kid Baker, Indianapolis................. W	10
Feb.	28–Willie Oster, Toledo .... KO	3
Apr.	19–Ben Jeby, Cleveland .... NC	6
June	30–Babe Marino, San Francisco .... KO	10
July	18–Wesley Ketchell, Los Angeles .... W	10
July	28–Vearl Whitehead, Los Angeles. .... L disq.	10
Aug.	8–Vearl Whitehead, Lost Angeles .... D	10
Aug.	25–Harold Hoxwood, Salt Lake City .... D	10
Sept.	3–Manuel Victoria, Tijuana................ KO	7
Sept.	15–Johnny Romero, San Diego .... KO	3
Sept.	21–Billy Papke, Pasadena................. KO	8
Oct.	6–Mike Payan, San Diego................. W	10
Oct.	12–Lou Bertman, Phoenix .... KO	2
Oct.	27–Ed Murdock, San Diego .... KO	10
Dec.	5–Frank Remus, Seattle................. KO	6

1934

Jan.	16–Tony Poloni, Los Angeles .... W	10
Feb.	9–Max Maxwell, San Diego................. D	10
Feb.	23–Dutch Weimer, San Diego L	10
May	22–Freddie Steele, Seattle................. D	10
June	19–Emilio Martinez, Denver L	10
Aug.	21–Oscar Rankin, Los Angeles L	10

1935

Sept.	17–Freddie Steele, Seattle................. L	10

1936

Jan.	1–Tait Littman, Milwaukee .... KO	1
Jan.	27–Tait Littman, Milwaukee .... KO	10
Aug.	5–Art Taylor, Phoenix.................... D	10
Dec.	4–Mickey Bottone, Milwaukee............. KO	1

1937

Jan.	1–Freddie Steele, Milwaukee L	10
	(For NBA-New York World Middleweight Title)	
Jan.	29–Frankie Battaglia, Milwaukee............. D	10
Apr.	13–Battling Nelson, Omaha .... KO	4
July	–Frankie Misko, Sioux City.............. KO	5
Aug.	9–Tommy Freeman, Council Bluffs .... W	10
Oct.	27–Andy Miller, Sioux City................ W	8
Nov.	23–Alabama Kid, Springfield L	10
Dec.	15–Bob Turner, Akron .... W	10

1938

Jan.	12–Frankie Hughes, Akron................. W	10
Jan.	19–Tiger Carsonia, Louisville .... KO	2
Feb.	16–Johnny Davis, Akron................... KO	8
Feb.	23–Jack Moran, Akron.................... W	10
Apr.	4–King Wyatt, Fort Wayne................ D	10
May	10–Babe Risko, Akron L	10

1939

Jan.	24–Angelo Puglisi, Seattle................. W	10

1940

May	29–Vern Earling, Kellogg L	10

TB	KO	WD	WF	D	LD	LF	KOBO	ND	NC
140	55	42	1	13	17	4	0	5	3

Died, January 4, 1982, Los Angeles Calif.

HENRY ARMSTRONG
(Henry Jackson)
(Homicide Hank)
Born, December 12, 1912, Columbus, Miss. Weight, 124-146
lbs. Height, 5 ft. 5½ in. Managed by Wirt Ross, Eddie Mead.

1931

July	27–Al Iovino, North Braddock........... KO by	3
Aug.	–Sammy Burns, Millville................. W	6

1932

Aug.	30–Eddie Trujillo, Los Angeles L	4

Sept.	27–Al Greenfield, Los Angeles	L	4
	–Max Tarley	W	4
	–Young Bud Taylor	KO	2
	–Vince Trujillo	KO	2
Dec.	13–Gene Espinosa, Los Angeles	W	4

1933

	–Mickey Ryan	W	6
	–Georgie Dundee	W	6
	–Steve Harky	W	6
Mar.	21–Paul Wangley, Los Angeles	KO	4
	–Young Corpus	W	6
	–Johnny Granone	KO	5
May	31–Max Tarley, Los Angeles	KO	3
July	11–Baby Manuel, Los Angeles	L	6
Aug.	8–Bobby Calmes, Los Angeles	KO	5
Aug.	30–Hoyt Jones, Los Angeles	D	4
Sept.	5–Perfecto Lopez, Los Angeles	D	4
Oct.	11–Perfecto Lopez, Los Angeles	D	4
Nov.	3–Kid Moro, Pismo Beach	W	10
Nov.	23–Kid Moro, Stockton	D	10
Dec.	14–Gene Espinosa, Sacramento	KO	7
Dec.	–Kid Moro, Watsonville	D	10

1934

Jan.	26–Baby Manuel, Sacramento	W	10
Feb.	13–Benny Pelz, Los Angeles	W	6
Mar.	17–Young Danny, Los Angeles	KO	1
May	22–Johnny DeFoe, Los Angeles	KO	6
June	5–Vincente Torres, Los Angeles	W	4
June	14–Davy Abad, Sacramento	W	10
July	17–Perfecto Lopez, Los Angeles	W	6
Aug.	28–Perfecto Lopez, Los Angeles	KO	5
	–Mark Diaz	W	8
	–Tully Corvo	KO	7
Nov.	3–Baby Arizmendi, Mexico City	L	10
Dec.	2–Joe Gonde, Mexico City	KO	7
Dec.	15–Ventura Arana, Mexico City	KO	5

1935

Jan.	2–Baby Arizmendi, Mexico City	L	12
	(For Vacant Calif.-Mexican World Featherweight Title)		
Mar.	19–Sal Hernandez, Los Angeles	KO	2
Mar.	31–Davy Abad, Mexico City	L	10
Apr.	16–Frankie Covelli, Los Angeles	W	8
May	28–Davy Abad, LosAngeles	W	10
June	25–Varias Milling, Los Angeles	W	10
Sept.	18–Perfecto Lopez, San Francisco	D	8

Oct.	21–Lester Marston, Oakland	KO	7
Nov.	12–Leo Lomelli, Oakland	KO	6
Nov.	27–Midget Wolgast, Oakland	W	10
Dec.	6–Alton Black, Reno	KO	8

1936

Jan.	1–Joe Conde, Mexico City	L	10
Feb.	26–Ritchie Fontaine, Oakland	L	10
Mar.	31–Ritchie Fontaine, Los Angeles	W	10
Apr.	17–Alton Black, Reno	KO	8
May	19–Pancho Leyvas, Los Angeles	KO	4
June	22–Johnny DeFoe, Butte	W	10
Aug.	4–Baby Arizmendi, Los Angeles	W	10
	(Won Calif.-Mexican World Featherweight Title)		
Aug.	28–Juan Zurita, Los Angeles	KO	4
Sept.	3–Buzz Brown, Portland	W	10
Sept.	8–Dommy Ganzon, Sacramento	KO	1
Oct.	27–Mike Belloise, Los Angeles	W	10
Nov.	2–Gene Espinosa, Los Angeles	KO	1
Nov.	17–Joey Alcanter, St. Louis	KO	6
Dec.	3–Tony Chavez, St. Louis	LF	8

1937

Jan.	1–Baby Casanova, Mexico City	KO	3
Jan.	19–Tony Chavez, Los Angeles	KO	10
Feb.	2–Moon Mullins, Los Angeles	KO	2
Feb.	19–Varias Milling, San Diego	KO	4
Mar.	2–Joe Rivers, Los Angeles	KO	4
Mar.	12–Mike Belloise, New York	KO	4
Mar.	19–Aldo Spoldi, New York	W	10
Apr.	6–Pete De Grasse, Los Angeles	KO	10
May	4–Frankie Klick, Los Angeles	KO	4
May	28–Wally Hally, Los Angeles	KO	4
June	9–Mark Diaz, Pasadena	KO	4
June	15–Jackie Carter, Los Angeles	KO	4
July	8–Alf Blatch, New York	KO	3
July	19–Lew Massey, Brooklyn	KO	4
July	27–Benny Bass, Philadelphia	KO	4
Aug.	13–Eddie Brink, New York	KO	3
Aug.	16–Johnny Cabello, Washington, D.C.	KO	2
Aug.	31–Orville Drouillard, Detroit	KO	5
Sept.	9–Charley Burns, Pittsburgh	KO	4
Sept.	16–Johnny DeFoe, New York	KO	4
Sept.	21–Bobby Dean, Youngston	KO	1
Oct.	18–Joe Marcienti, Philadelphia	KO	3
Oct.	29–Petey Sarron, New York	KO	6
	(Won World Featherweight Title)		
Nov.	19–Billy Beauhuld, New York	KO	5

Nov. 23–Joey Brown, Buffalo . . . . KO 2
Dec. 6–Tony Chavez, Cleveland . . . . KO 1
Dec. 12–Johnny Jones, New Orleans . . . . KO 2

1938

Jan. 12–Enrico Venturi, New York . . . . KO 6
Jan. 21–Frankie Castillo, Phoenix . . . . KO 3
Jan. 22–Tommy Brown, Tucson . . . . KO 2
Feb. 1–Chalky Wright, Los Angeles . . . . KO 3
Feb. 9–Al Citrino, San Francisco . . . . KO 4
Feb. 25–Everett Rightmire, Chicago . . . . KO 4
Feb. 28–Charley Burns, Minneapolis . . . . KO 2
Mar. 15–Baby Arizmendi, Los Angeles . . . . W 10
Mar. 25–Eddie Zivic, Detroit . . . . KO 4
Mar. 30–Lew Feldman, New York . . . . KO 5
May 31–Barney Ross, Long Island City . . . . W 15
(Won World Welterweight Title)
Aug. 17–Lou Ambers, New York . . . . W 15
(Won World Lightweight Title)
–Relinquished world featherweight title.
Nov. 25–Ceferino Garcia, New York . . . . W 15
(Retained World Welterweight Title)
Dec. 5–Al Manfredo, Cleveland . . . . KO 3

1939

Jan. 10–Baby Arizmendi, Los Angeles . . . . W 10
(Retained World Welterweight Title)
Mar. 4–Bobby Pacho, Havana, Cuba . . . . KO 4
(Retained World Welterweight Title)
Mar. 16–Lew Feldman, St. Louis . . . . KO 1
(Retained World Welterweight Title)
Mar. 31–Davey Day, New York . . . . KO 12
(Retained World Welterweight Title)
May 25–Ernie Roderick, London . . . . W 15
(Retained World Welterweight Title)
Aug. 22–Lou Ambers, New York . . . . L 15
(Lost World Lightweight Title)
Oct. 9–Al Manfredo, Des Moines . . . . KO 4
(Retained World Welterweight Title)
Oct. 13–Howard Scott, Minneapolis . . . . KO 2
(Retained World Welterweight Title)
Oct. 20–Ritchie Fontaine, Seattle . . . . KO 3
(Retained World Welterweight Title)
Oct. 24–Jimmy Garrison, Los Angeles . . . . W 10
(Retained World Welterweight Title)
Oct. 30–Bobby Pacho, Denver . . . . KO 4
(Retained World Welterweight Title)
Dec. 11–Jimmy Garrison, Cleveland . . . . KO 7
(Retained World Welterweight Title)

1940

Jan. 4–Joe Ghnouly, St. Louis . . . . KO 5
(Retained World Welterweight Title)
Jan. 24–Pedro Montanez, New York . . . . KO 9
(Retained World Welterweight Title)
Mar. 1–Ceferino Garcia, Los Angeles . . . . D 10
(For World Middleweight Title)
Apr. 26–Paul Junior, Boston . . . . KO 7
(Retained World Welterweight Title)
May 24–Ralph Zanelli, Boston . . . . KO 5
(Retained World Welterweight Title)
June 21–Paul Junior, Portland . . . . KO 3
(Retained World Welterweight Title)
July 17–Lew Jenkins, New York . . . . KO 6
Sept. 23–Phil Furr, Washington, D.C. . . . . KO 4
(Retained World Welterweight Title)
Oct. 4–Fritzie Zivic, New York . . . . L 15
(Lost World Welterweight Title)

1941

Jan. 17–Fritzie Zivic, New York . . . . KO by 12
(For World Welterweight Title)
Oct. 1–Knocked out two opponents in two rounds each
in exhibition bouts in Oklahoma City.
Oct. 12–Knocked out two opponents in two rounds each
in exhibition bouts.

1942

June 1–Johnny Taylor, San Jose . . . . KO 4
June 24–Sheik Rangel, Oakland . . . . W 10
July 3–Reuben Shank, Denver . . . . L 10
July 20–Joe Ybarra, Sacramento . . . . KO 3
Aug. 3–Aldo Spoldi, San Francisco . . . . KO 7
Aug. 13–Jackie Burke, Ogden, ... W 10
Aug. 26–Rudolfo Ramirez, Oakland . . . . KO 8
Sept. 4–Leo Rodak, San Francisco . . . . KO 8
Sept. 7–Johnny Taylor, Pittman . . . . KO 3
Sept. 30–Earl Turner, Oakland . . . . KO 4
Oct. 13–Juan Zurita, Los Angeles . . . . KO 2
Oct. 26–Fritzie Zivic, San Francisco . . . . W 10
Dec. 4–Lew Jenkins, Portland . . . . KO
Dec. 14–Saverio Turiello, San Francisco . . . . KO

1943

Jan. 5–Jimmy McDaniels, Los Angeles . . . . W
Mar. 2–Willie Joyce, Los Angeles L
Mar. 8–Tippy Larkin, San Francisco . . . . KO
Mar. 22–Al Tribuani, Philadelphia . . . . W

Apr. 2–Beau Jack, New York L
Apr. 30–Saverio Turiello, Washington, D.C. . . . . KO
May 7–Tommy Jessup, Boston . . . . KO
May 24–Maxie Shapiro, Philadelphia . . . . KO
June 11–Sammy Angott, New York . . . . W
July 24–Willie Joyce, Hollywood . . . . W
Aug. 6–Jimmy Garrison, Portland . . . . W
Aug. 14–Joey Silva, Spokane, Wash. . . . . W
Aug. 27–Ray Robinson, New York L

1944

Jan. 14–Aldo Spoldi, Portland . . . . KO
Jan. 26–Saverio Turiello, Kansas City . . . . KO
Feb. 7–Lew Hanbury, Washington, D.C. . . . . KO
Feb. 23–Jimmy Garrison, Kansas City . . . . KO
Feb. 29–Jackie Byrd, Des Moines . . . . KO
Mar. 14–Johnny Jones, Miami . . . . KO
Mar. 20–Frankie Wills, Washington, D.C. . . . . W
Mar. 24–Ralph Zanelli, Boston . . . . W
Apr. 25–John Thomas, Los Angeles . . . . W
May 16–Ralph Zanelli, Boston . . . . W
May 22–Aaron Perry, Washington, D.C. . . . . KO
June 2–Willie Joyce, Chicago L
June 15–Al (Bummy) Davis, New York . . . . KO
June 21–Nick Latsios, Washington, D.C. . . . . W
July 4–John Thomas, Los Angeles L
July 14–Slugger White, Hollywood . . . . D
Aug. 21–Willie Joyce, San Francisco . . . . W
Sept. 15–Aldo Spoldi, St. Louis . . . . KO
Nov. 4–Mike Belloise, Portland . . . . KO

1945

Jan. 17–Chester Slider, Oakland . . . . D
Feb. 6–Genaro Rojo, Los Angeles . . . . W
Feb. 14–Chester Slider, Oakland L

TB	KO	WD	WF	D	LD	LF	KOBO	ND	NC
174	98	47	0	9	17	1	2	0	0

Elected to Boxing Hall of Fame, 1954.

YOUNG JACK THOMPSON

(Cecil Lewis Thompson)
Born, 1904, Los Angeles, Calif. Weight, 145 lbs. Height, 5 ft. 8 in. Managed by Clyde Hudkins, Ray Alvis.

1922

Nov. 20–Bud Kelly, San Francisco . . . . KO 2

1923

Feb. 13–Billy Springfield, San Francisco . . . . KO by 2
Dec. 6–Joe Powell, San Jose. . . . . KO 2
Dec. 20–Manny (Kid) Robinson, San Jose . . . . W 4

1924

Jan. 4–Kid Martin, San Francisco . . . . KO 2
Apr. 24–Leo Spencer, San Meteo . . . . L 4
May 15–Joe Powell, San Jose . . . . L 5
May 29–Pete Francis, San Jose . . . . D 4
June 24–Angelo Papas, San Meteo . . . . D 4
Aug. 7–Henry Faligano, San Jose . . . . D 4
Aug. 19–Min Minnick, San Jose . . . . L 4
Sept. 22–Min Minnick, San Jose . . . . D 4

1925

Jan. 21–Eddie Cortez, Los Angeles . . . . KO 1
Feb. 4–Joe Martinez, Los Angeles . . . . KO 6
Feb. 18–Eddie Sylvester, Los Angeles . . . . KO 3
Mar. 11–Charley Burns, Los Angeles . . . . W 10
Mar. 13–Joe Carter, San Diego . . . . KO 1
Mar. 20–Kid Bello, San Diego . . . . D 6
Apr. 3–Battling Ward, San Diego . . . . W 6
Apr. 13–Battling Ward, Los Angeles . . . . KO 4
May 1–Charley Feraci, San Dlego . . . . L 10
July 24–Young Harry Wills, San Dlego . . . . D 10
 7–Harry Scott, Oakland . . . . L 6

1926

Jan. 14–Tarzan Lopez, Pasadena . . . . KO 3
Jan. 22–Baby Pete, San Diego . . . . W 6
Feb. 10–Bobby Ertle, Oakland . . . . KO 1
Mar. 9–Joe Layman, Vernon . . . . D 6
Mar. 31–Young Sam Langford, Los Angeles L
 –Billy Sprinfield . . . . D 6
May 18–Young Corbett III, Fresno . . . . L 6
May 21–Ad Ruiz, San Diego . . . . W 6
May 28–Buddy Bairie, San Diego . . . . W
June 18–Billy McCann, San Diego . . . . KO 8
July 24–Harry Whybrow, Los Angeles . . . . KO 2
Sept. 28–Jack Silver, Los Angeles . . . . KO 8
Oct. 15–Billy Adams, San Francisco . . . . KO 5
Nov. 5–Billy Alger, San Francisco . . . . W 10
Nov. 14–Ted Makagon, San Francisco . . . . D 10
Nov. 23–Russ Whalen, Los Angeles . . . . L 10

1927

Feb. 11–Tommy Cello, San Francisco . . . . D 10

Feb. 18–Harry (Kid) Brown, San Francisco .... KO 5
Mar. 4–King Tut, San Francisco .... W 10
Mar. 11–Harry (Kid) Brown, San Francisco .... W 10
Apr. 8–Irineo Flores, San Francisco .... KO 2
June 24–Young Corbett III, San Freancisco .... D 10
July 22–Charley Feraci, San Francisco .... KO 5
       –Frankie Turner .... KO 8
       –Charley Pitts .... KO 4

1928

Jan. 17–Johnny Adams, Los Angeles .... KO 4
Jan. 27–Don Fraser, San Francisco .... KO 3
Feb. 13–Young Corbett III, San Francisco .... L 10
Mar. 16–Johnny O'Donnell, San Francisco......... KO 8
Apr. 11–Jimmy Duffy, Oakland .... LF 9
June 8–Billy Light, Chicago .... W 8
July 11–Russie LeRoy, Chicago .... KO 5
Aug. 10–Eddie Dempsey, Chicago............... KO 4
Aug. 22–Gene Cardi, Cleveland .... KO 6
Aug. 30–Joe Dundee, Chicago .... KO 2
Oct. 1–Jackie Fields, San Francisco .... L 10
Oct. 31–Danny Gordon, Chicago .... KO 2
Dec. 7–Red Bragan, Buffalo .... KO 4
       –Sam Bruce, Buffalo .... KO 10

1929

Jan. 25–Red Herring, Buffalo .... KO 7
Jan. 30–Harry Dudley, Kansas City............. KO 5
Feb. 18–Ham Jenkins, Kansas City............. W 10
Mar. 8–Heavy Andrews, Buffalo .... W 10
Mar. 25–Jackie Fields, Chicago .... L 10
       (For NBA Welterweight Title)
June 24–Jimmy Evans, San Francisco .... KO 9
Aug. 7–Jimmy Duffy, Oakland................. W 10
Oct. 2–Jimmy Duffy, Oakland .... KO 10
Oct. 9–Freddie Fitzgerald, Oakland............. L 10
Nov. 18–Billy White, Pittsburgh .... KO 8
Dec. 10–Billy Wells, Minneapolis .... W 10

1930

Jan. 10–Tommy Freeman, Detroit................ L 10
Feb. 3–Bucky Lawless, Rochester .... L 10
Mar. 2–Freddie Fltzgerald, Chicago .... W 10
Mar. 28–Jimmy McLarnin, New York .... L 10
May 9–Jackie Fields, Detroit................. W 15
       (Won World Welterweight Title)
June 6–Billy Wells, Omaha .... KO 2
June 9–Jerry Dolan, Portland, Ore.............. KO 3

June 17–Joe Cordoza, Los Angeles .... KO 3
July 4–Young Corbett III, San Francisco .... L 10
Sept. 5–Tommy Freeman, Cleveland.............. L 15
       (Lost World Welterweight Title)

1931

Mar. 4–Babe Anderson, Oakland .... KO 9
Mar. 19–Larry (Kid) Kaufman, Moline, Ill. .... KO 3
Apr. 14–Tommy Freeman, Cleveland............. KO 12
       (Regained World Welterweight Title)
May 8–Bucky Lawless, Chicago................. L 10
May 27–Pete August, Newark .... W 10
June 19–Speedball Turner, Little Rock .... KO 3
July 23–Lou Brouillard, Boston .... L 10
Sept. 6–Tommy Jones, Flint, Mich. .... KO 3
Oct. 23–Lou Brouillard, Boston .... L 15
       (Lost World Welterweight Title)

1932

Jan. 27–Jimmy Evans, Oakland................. L 10
Mar. 4–Billy Wells, Stockton.................. KO 6
Mar. 11–Al Trulmans, San Diego .... W 10
Mar. 25–Charlie Cobb, San Diego .... L 10
May 25–Leonard Bennet, Seattle .... W 6

TB	KO	WD	WF	D	LD	LF	KOBO	ND	NC
97	43	18	0	11	23	1	1	0	0

Died April 9 1946 Los Angeles Calif.

JACKIE WILSON
(Jack Benjamin Wilson)
Born, 1911, Arkansas. Weight, 115-131 lbs. Height, 5 ft. 5 in.
Managed by Billy Daly, Jack Laken, Pete Reilly, Harry Burnkrant.

1929

Dec. 6–Jimmy Thomas, Pittsburgh .... W 6
Dec. 20–Young Ketchell, Pittsburgh .... W 6

1930

Mar. 18–Lefty Foster, Johnstown, Pa. .... W 4
Apr. 17–Ross Fields, McKeesport, Pa. .... D 4
Apr. 24–Jack Benton, McKeesport .... W 6
May 5–Mose Butch, Pittsburgh .... D 6
July 14–Jackie Ward, North Braddock, Pa. .... L 6
Aug. 14–Mose Butch, Millvale, Pa. .... W 6
Sept. 11–Mose Butch, Millvale, Pa. .... L 6
Nov. 28–Bid Maloney, Pittsburgh .... KO 4

1931

	–Tony Marino, Pittsburgh	W 6
	–Babe Peleco, Pittsburgh	W 6
	–Tony Marino, Pittsburgh	D 6
	–Marty Gold, Pittsburgh	W 6
Sept.	24–Johnny Datto, Pittsburgh	KO by 3
Dec.	–Steve Senich, Pittsburgh	W 6

1932

Jan.	1–Ross Fields, Pittsburgh	W 6
Feb.	26–Willie Davies, Pittsburgh	W 10
Mar.	–Mose Butch, Pittsburgh	W 10
Mar.	21–Baby Face Mathison, Pittsburgh	W 8
May	16–Steve Senich, Pittsburgh	W 8
June	–Johnny Cataline, Pittsburgh	W 8
June	23–Chico Cisneros, Pittsburgh	L 10
Sept.	–Joey Bozak, Pittsburgh	W 8
Dec.	–Ross Fields, Pittsburgh	KO by 10

1933

Jan.	–Billy Landers	D 8
Feb.	3–Midget Wolgast, Pittsburgh	D 10
Mar.	3–Ross Fields, Pittsburgh	W 10
Mar.	17–Johnny Mitchell, Pittsburgh	W 10
Apr.	3–Tommy Paul, Pittsburgh	W 10
Apr.	13–Johnny Pena, Chicago	W 10
May	8–Eddie Shea, Pittsburgh	W 10
June	5–Tommy Paul, Pittsburgh	KO 8
July	20–Benny Britt, Fort Hamilton	W 10
Aig.	18–Ernie Ratner, Long Branch	W 10
Nov.	22–Johnny Fitzpatrick, Chicago	W 8
Dec.	4–Dario Moreno, Chicago	KO 6
Dec.	20–Everett Rightmire, Sioux City	D 8

1934

Jan.	8–Johnny Mitchell, Chicago	KO 6
	–Jimmy Gilligan, Toronto	W 6
	–Bud Dempsey	KO 1
July	19–Mose Butch, Pittsburgh	W 10
Oct.	–Joe Conde, Mexico City	L 10
Dec.	23–Mose Butch, Pittsburgh	W 10

1935

May	27–Al Farrone, Pittsburgh	W 6
June	10–Frankie Wolfram, Pittsburgh	W 8
July	4–Sammy Crocetti, Dubois	W
July	22–Sammy Angott, Pittsburgh	W 6
Oct.	10–Billy Gannon, Liverpool	W 10
Oct.	24–Spike Robinson, Belfast	W 12

Nov.	7–Cuthbert Taylor, Liverpool	W 10
Dec.	12–Gilbert Johnston, Liverpool	KO 5

1936

Jan.	12–Ronnie James, London	L 10
Jan.	27–Jane Linehan, Cork	W 10
Feb.	21–Stan, Jehu, Manchester	W 10
Mar.	6–Douglas Kestress, Manchester	W 10
Mar.	31–Johnny McGrory, Glasgow	KO 10
May	8–Jack Middleton, Plymouth	KO 2
May	22–George Gee, Plymouth	KO 7
June	16–Tommy Rogers, Wolverhampton	KO 4
Oct.	12–Bobby Dean, Pittsburgh	KO 2
Dec.	3–Lee Sheppard, Pittsburgh	W 10

1937

Feb.	9–Freddie Miller, Pittsburgh	W 10
Feb.	22–Mike Belloise, Pittsburgh	W 10
Mar.	22–Charley Burns, Lancaster	W 8
Apr.	12–Armando Sicilia, Springfield	D 8
Apr.	26–Freddie Miller, Cincinnati	W 10
May	10–Joey Brown, Lancaster	KO 4
June	15–Pete DeGrasse, Los Angeles	W 10
July	6–Speedy Dado, Stockton	W 10
July	26–Ritchie Fontaine, Los Angeles	L 10
Aug.	6–Al Manriquez, Sioux City	W 10
Aug.	19–Leo Rodak, St. Louis	D 10
Sept.	17–Leo Rodak, St. Louis	D 15
Oct.	12–Everett Rightmire, St. Louis	L 10

1938

Jan.	10–Leo Rodak, Chicago	D 10
Jan.	21–Varias Millig, Chicago	W 10
Mar.	22–Sammy Angott, Milwaukee	L 10
May	9–Norment Quarles, Baltimore	W 10
June	17–Leo Rodak, Baltimore	L 15
	(For Vacant Maryland World Featherweight Title)	
Nov.	4–Jiggs McKnight, Clarksburg	KO 8

1939

Feb.	4–Mickey Miller, Melbourne	KO 4
Feb.	13–Joe Hall, Sydney	W 12
Feb.	25–Joe Hall, Melbourne	W 12
Mar.	3–Sammy Garcia, Brisbane	W 12
Mar.	11–Claude Varner, Melbourne	W 12
Mar.	31–Henry Moreno, Brisbane	W 12
Apr.	11–Koe Velasco, Sydney	WF 8
Apr.	26–Joe Hall, Melbourne	WF 10
May	31–Mickey Miller, Melbourne	W 12

June 28–Henry Moreno, Melbourne . . . . W 12
July 6–Kui Kong, Sydney . . . . WF 8
Aug. 3–Kui Kong Young, Sydney . . . . W 12
Nov. 8–Armando Sicilia, Pittsburgh . . . . W 10
Nov. 20–Emil Joseph, Pittsburgh . . . . W 10

1940

Feb. 12–Frank Covelli, Chicago . . . . W 10
Mar. 31–Harris Blake, New Orleans . . . . L 10
Apr. 25–Bobby Green, Lancaster . . . . W 10
June 3–Leo Rodak, Chicago . . . . L 10
Aug. 20–Harry Jeffra, Youngstown . . . . L 10
Dec. 12–Frank Terranova, Baltimore . . . . W 8

1941

Jan. 23–Maxie Shapiro, Baltimore . . . . W 10
Feb. 11–Joe Marinelli, Youngstown . . . . W 10
Mar. 31–Matt Perfecti, Baltimore . . . . W 10
Apr. 21–Leo Rodak, Cincinnati . . . . L 10
May 19–Baby Arizmendi, Los Angeles . . . . KO 8
July 17–Chalky Wright, Baltimore . . . . L 10
Oct. 27–Leo Rodak, Toledo, Ohio . . . . L 10
Nov. 18–Richie Lemos, Los Angeles . . . . W 12
　　　　　(Won NBA Featherweight Title)
Dec. 16–Richie Lemos, Los Angeles . . . . W 12
　　　　　(Retained NBA Featherweight Title)

1942

Feb. 20–Abe Denner, Boston . . . . L 10
Mar. 2–Terry Young, New York . . . . L 8

1943

Jan. 18–Jackie Callura, Providence . . . . L 15
　　　　　(Lost NBA Featherweight Title)
Mar. 18–Jackie Callura, Boston . . . . L 15
　　　　　(For NBA Featherweight Title)
Apr. 26–Willie Pep. Pittsburgh . . . . L 12
May 17–Danny Petro, Washington, D.C. . . . . KO 10
June 7–Jimmy Phillips, Washington, D.C. . . . . W 10
June 28–Lew Hanbury, Washington, D.C. . . . . KO 7
July 26–Tony Costa, Providence . . . . W 10

Aug. 30–Lulu Costantino, Washington . . . . W 10
Oct. 4–Larry Bolvin, Providence . . . . L 10
Oct. 22–Freddie Pope, Cleveland . . . . L 10
Dec. 6–Tony Costa, Providence . . . . LF 6

1944

Sept. 19–Cleo Shans, Washington, D.C. . . . . W 10
Oct. 17–Pedro Hernandez, Washington . . . . L 10

1945

Jan. 8–Harry Jeffs, Baltimore . . . . W 10
Jan. 22–Pedro Hernandez, Washington . . . . W 10
Mar. 12–Cleo Shans, Baltimore . . . . W 10
Apr. 9–Chalky Wright, Baltimore . . . . NC 7
June 25–Freddie Russo, Baltimore . . . . L 10

1946

Mar. 11–Willie Joyce, Washington . . . . KO by 5
Mar. 26–Willie Pep, Kansas City . . . . L 10
May 3–Jackie Graves, Minneapolis . . . . L 8
June 18–Enrique Bolanos, Los Angeles . . . . KO by 7
Sept. 11–Star Misamis, Oakland . . . . L 10
Sept. 25–Star Misamis, Oakland . . . . L 10
Oct. 22–Luis Castillo, San Jose . . . . W 10
Nov. 18–Luis Castillo, San Jose . . . . L 10
Dec. 17–Mario Trigo, San Jose . . . . L 10

1947

Jan. 8–Speedy Cabanella, Sacramento . . . . L 10
Jan. 20–Buddy Jacklich, San Francisco . . . . L 10
Apr. 7–Freddie Steele, Vancouver . . . . KO 7
Apr. 25–Manny Ortega, El Paso . . . . KO by 10
May 12–Jackie Turner, Vancouver . . . . L 10
May 30–Jackie Turner, Vancouver . . . . L 10
Sept. 1–Joey Dolan, Spokane, Wash . . . . L 10
Sept. 22–Simon Vegara, Ocean Park . . . . KO by 9

TB	KO	WD	WF	D	LD	LF	KOBO	ND	NC
147	18	72	3	10	36	1	6	0	1

Died, December 2, 1966, Torrance, Pa.

BEAU JACK

(Sidney Walker)
Born, April 1, 1921, Augusta, Georgia. Weight, 132-145 lbs.
Height, 5 ft. 6 in. Managed by Joe Caron (1940-1941). Bowman
Milligan (1941-1942). Chick Wergeles (1942-1951).

1940

May	20–Frankie Allen, Holyoke	D	4
May	27–Billy Bannick, Holyoke	KO	3
June	17–Jackie Parker, Holyoke	L	4
July	14–Joe Polowitzer, New Haven	L	6
July	21–Joe Polowitzer, New Haven	W	6
Aug.	19–Jackie Parker, Holyoke	L	4
Aug.	26–Carlo Daponde, Holyoke	W	4
Sept.	2–Jackie Small, Holyoke	KO	4
Sept.	16–Ollie Barbour, Holyoke	KO	3
Sept.	30–Tony Dupre, Holyoke	KO	2
Oct.	14–Abe Cohen, Holyoke	KO	3
Oct.	21–Ritchie Jones, Holyoke	KO	3
Nov.	14–Joey Stack, Holyoke	W	6
Dec.	2–Jimmy Fox, Holyoke	W	6
Dec.	16–Young Johnny Buff, Holyoke	KO	1
Dec.	30–Mel Neary, Holyoke	KO	5

1941

Jan.	27–Joey Silva, Holyoke	L	6
Feb.	10–Mexican Joe Rivers, Holyoke	KO	4
Feb.	24–Lenny Isrow, Holyoke	KO	3
Mar.	10–Nickey Jerome, Holyoke	KO	3
Mar.	24–Joey Silva, Holyoke	W	6
Apr.	7–Tony Iacovacci, Holyoke	KO	6
Apr.	21–Bob Reilly, Holyoke	KO	7

Apr.	28–Harry Gentile, Holyoke	KO	1
May	5–Chester Rico, Holyoke	D	8
May	19–George Salamone, Holyoke	KO	8
June	2–Tommy Spiegel, Holyoke	W	8
June	16–George Zengaras, Holyoke	W	8
Aug.	5–Minnie DeMore, Brooklyn	KO	3
Aug.	14–Al Roth, Brooklyn	KO	6
Aug.	26–Guillermo Puente, New York	W	6
Sept.	19–Al Reid, New York	KO	7
Oct.	14–Tommy Spiegel, Brooklyn	W	8
Oct.	31–Guillermo Puente, New York	W	8
Dec.	1–Mexican Joe Rivers, Brooklyn	KO	3
Dec.	8–Freddie Archer, New York	L	8
Dec.	29–Freddie Archer, New York	L	8

1942

Jan.	5–Carmelo Fenoy, Holyoke	W	10
May	22–Bobby (Poison) Ivy, New York	W	8
June	23–Guillermo Puente, New York	KO	1
July	3–Bobby McIntire, Fort Hamilton	KO	6
July	7–Cosby Linson, Long Island City	KO	8
Aug.	1–Ruby Garcia, Elizabeth, N.J.	KO	6
Aug.	18–Carmine Fatta, New York	KO	1
Aug.	28–Billy Murray, New York	W	10
Sept.	22–Joe Torres, Washington, D.C.	KO	4
Oct.	2–Chester Rico, New York	W	8

Oct.   12–Terry Young, New York . . . . W 10
Nov. 13–Allie Stolz, New York . . . . KO 7
Dec. 18–Tippy Larkin, New York. . . . . KO 3
      (Won Vacant New York World Lightweight Title)

1943

Feb.   5–Fritzie Zivic . . . . W 10
Mar.   5–Fritzie Zivic, New York . . . . W 12
Apr.   2–Henry Armstrong, New York . . . . W 10
May 21–Bob Montgomery, New York. . . . . L 15
      (Lost New York World Lightweight Title)
June 21–Maxie Starr, Washington, D.C. . . . . KO 6
July 19–Johnny Hutchinson, Philadelphia . . . . KO 6
Oct.   4–Bobby Ruffin, New York. . . . . L 10
Nov. 19–Bob Montgomery, New York . . . . W 15
      (Regained New York World Lightweight Title)

1944

Jan.   7–Lulu Costantino, New York . . . . W 10
Jan. 28–Sammy Angott, New York . . . . D 10
Feb. 15–Maxie Berger, Cleveland. . . . . W 10
Mar.   3–Bob Montgomery, New York . . . . L 15
      (Lost New York World Lightweight)
Mar. 17–Al Davis, New York. W 10
Mar. 31–Juan Zurita, New York . . . . W 10
Aug.   4–Bob Montgomery, New York . . . . W 10

1945

Dec. 14–Willie Joyce, New York. . . . . W 10

1946

Jan.   4–Morris Reif, New York . . . . KO 4
Feb.   8–Johnny Greco, New York. . . . . D 10
May 31–Johnny Greco, New York. . . . . W 10
July   8–Sammy Angott, Washington . . . . KO 7
Aug. 19–Danny Kapilow, Washington. . . . . W 10
Oct. 22–Bustler Tyler, Elizabeth . . . . L 10

1947

Feb. 21–Tony Janiro, New York . . . . KO by 4
Nov.   3–Humberto Zavala, St. Louis. . . . . KO 4
Dec. 16–Frankie, Vigeant, Hartford . . . . W 10
Dec. 29–Billy Kearns, Providence. . . . . W 10

1948

Jan.   5–Jimmy Collins, New Haven . . . . KO 2
Jan. 28–Johnny Bratton, Chicago . . . . KO 8
Feb. 20–Terry Young, New York . . . . L 10
Apr.   9–Johnny Greco, Montreal. . . . . W 10

May 24–Tony Janiro, Washington . . . . W 10
July 12–Ike Williams, Philadelphia. . . . . KO by 6
      (For World Lightweight Title)
Oct. 28–Eric Boon, Washington, D.C.. . . . . KO 3
Nov. 23–Chuck Taylor, Philadelphia. . . . . KO 3
Dec. 17–Leroy Willis, Detroit. . . . . W 10

1949

Jan. 17–Jackie Weber, Boston. . . . . W 10
Mar. 28–Johnny Greco, Montreal . . . . L 10
July 19–Eddie Giosa, Washington . . . . W 10
Aug. 31–Johnny Gonsalves, Oakland . . . . W 10
Sept. 6–Tote Martinez, Los Angeles . . . . W 10
Sept. 30–Livie Minelli, Chicago. . . . . W 10
Oct. 14–Kid Gavilan, Chicago . . . . L 10
Dec. 16–Tuzo Portugez, New York . . . . L 10

1950

Apr.   3–Joey Carkido, Hartford . . . . L 10
Apr. 14–Lew Jenkins, Washington . . . . KO 5
May   8–Jackie Weber, Providence . . . . KO 7
May 22–Johnny Potenti, Boston. . . . . W 10
JUne 28–Ronnie Harper, Indianapolis . . . . KO 5
July 17–Bobby Timpson, Atlanta . . . . KO 6
Oct.   4–Philip Kim, Honolulu . . . . W 10
Nov. 14–Frankie Fernandez, Honolulu. . . . . L 10

1951

Jan.   1–Fitzie Pruden, Milwaukee . . . . L 10
Jan. 18–Del Flanagan, Minneapolis. . . . . L 10
Jan. 31–Emil Barao, Oakland, Calif. . . . . W 10
Mar.   5–Ike Williams, Providence. . . . . L 10
Mar. 30–Leroy Williams, New Orleans . . . . W 10
Apr. 16–Gil Turner, Philadelphia. . . . . L 10
May 21–Gil Turner, Philadelphia . . . . KO by 8

1952-1954

(Inactive)

1955

Jan. 20–Eddie Green, Columbia, S.C. . . . . W 10
Apr.   9–Ike Williams, Augusta, Ga. . . . . D 10
July   4–Willie Johnson, Dayton Beach. . . . . W 10
Aug. 12–Ike Williams, Augusta, Ga. . . . . KO by 9

TB	KO	WD	WF	D	LD	LF	KOBO	ND	NC
112	40	43	0	5	20	0	4	0	0

Elected to Boxing Hall of Fame, 1972

BOB MONTGOMERY

Born, February 10, 1919, Sumter, South Carolina. Weight,
133-134 lbs. Height, 5 ft. 8 in. Managed by Frankie Thomas
(1938-1944), Joe Gramby (1944-1947).

1938

Oct.	23–Young Johnny Buff, Atlantic City	KO 2
Oct.	27–Pat Patucci, Atlantic City	KO 2
Nov.	4–Eddie Stewart, Philadelphia	KO 2
Nov.	10–Joe Beltrante, Atlantic City	KO 3
Nov.	17–Red Rossi, Atlantic City	KO 2
Dec.8	–Jackie Sheppard, Atlantic City	W 8

1939

Jan.	19–Harvey Jacobs, Atlantic City	KO 1
Feb.	2–Charley Burns, Atlantic City	W 8
Feb.	23–Jay Macedon, Atlantic City	W 8
Mar.	9–Billy Miller, Atlantic City	KO 2
Mar.	16–Frankie Saia, Philadelphia	KO 4
Mar.	30–Benny Berman, Atlantic City	W 8
Apr.	13–Young Raspi, Atlantic City	KO 6
Apr.	20–Eddie Guerra, Atlantic City	W 8
May	1–George Zengaras, Philadelphia	D 10
May	23–Norment Quarles, Philadelphia	KO 4
June	15–Charley Burns, Atlantic City	KO 2
June	21–Tommy Rawson, Philadelphia	KO 1
July	3–Frankie Wallace, Philadelphia	W 10
Aug.	14–Jimmy Murray, Philadelphia	KO 3
Aug.	24–Ray Ingram, Atlantic City	W 10
Oct.	5–Charles Gilley, Atlantic City	KO 6
Oct.	23–Mike Evans, Philadelphia	W 10
Nov.	10–Tommy Spiegel, Philadelphia	L 10
Nov.	17–Mike Evans, Philadelphia	KO 1

1940

Jan.	29–Al Nettlow, Philadelphia	D 10
Mar.	11–Al Nettlow, Philadelphia	W 10
June	3–Al Nettlow, Philadelphia	W 12
July	5–Jimmy Vaughn, Atlantic City	KO 2
Sept.	16–Lew Jenkins, Philadelphia	L 10
Nov.	7–Norment Quarles, Atlantic City	D 10
Nov.	25–Sammy Angott, Philadelphia	L 10

1941

Jan.	29–Julie Kogon, Brooklyn	W 8
Feb.	7–Al Nettlow, New York	W 8
Mar.	3–George Zengaras, Philadelphia	KO 3
Apr.	28–Nick Peters, Philadelphia	KO 3

May	16–Lew Jenkins, New York	W 10
June	16–Manuel Villa, Baltimore	KO 1
June	30–Wishy Jones, Washington, D.C.	KO 6
July	3–Frankie Wallace, Atlantic City	KO 3
July	14–Luther (Slugger) White, Baltimore	W 10
Sept.	8–Mike Kaplan, Philadelphia	W 10
Oct.	10–Davey Day, Chicago, Ill.	KO 1
Oct.	24–Julie Kogon, Chicago, Ill.	W 10
Oct.	30–Frankie Wallace, Williamsport	KO 5
Dec.	8–Jimmy Garrison, Philadelphia	KO 4

1942

Jan.	5–Mayon Padlo, Philadelphia	KO 8
Mar.	6–Sammy Angott, New York	L 12
Apr.	20–Joey Peralta, Philadelphia	W 10
May	8–Carmen Notch, Toledo, Ohio	W 10
July	7–Sammy Angott, Philadelphia	L 12
Aug.	13–Bobby Ruffin, New York	W 10
Oct.	6–Maxie Shapiro, Philadelphia	L 10
Dec.	1–Maxie Shapiro, Philadelphia	W 10

1943

Jan.	8–Chester Rico, New York	KO 8
Feb.	22–Lulu Costantino, Philadelphia	W 10
Apr.	5–Roman Alvarez, Philadelphia	KO 4
Apr.	30–Gene Johnson, Scranton, Pa.	W 10
May	3–Henry Vasquez, Holyoke, Mass.	W 8
May	21–Beau Jack, New York	W 15
	(Won New York World Lightweight Title)	
July	4–Al Reasoner, New Orleans	KO 6
July	30–Frankie Wills, Washington	W 10
Aug.	23–Fritzie Zivic, Philadelphia	W 10
Oct.	25–Petey Scalzo, Philadelphia	KO 6
Nov.	19–Beau Jack, New York	L 15
	(Lost New York World Lightweight Title)	

1944

Jan.	7–Joey Peralta, Detroit	W 10
Jan.	25–Ike Williams, Philadelphia	KO 12
Feb.	18–Al Davis, New York	KO by 1
Mar.	3–Beau Jack, New York	W 15
	(Regained New York World Lightweight Title)	
Apr.	28–Joey Peralta, Chicago	W 10
Aug.	4–Beau Jack, New York	L 10

1945

Feb. 13–Cecil Hudson, Los Angeles . . . . W 10
Mar. 20–Genaro Rojo, Los Angeles . . . . KO 8
May 8–Nick Moran, Los Angeles . . . . L 10
July 9–Nick Moran, Philadelphia . . . . W 10

1946

Feb. 3–Bill Parsons, New Orleans . . . . W 10
Feb. 15–Leo Rodak, Chicago, Ill. . . . . W 10
Mar 8–Tony Pellone, New York . . . . W 10
Mar. 21–Ernie Petrone, New Haven . . . . KO 4
June 28–Allie Stolz, New York . . . . KO 13
(Retained New York World Lightweight Title)
July 29–George LaRover, Springfield, Mass. . . . . W 10
Aug. 19–Wesley Mouzon, Philadelphia . . . . KO by 2
Nov. 26–Wesley Mouzon, Philadelphia . . . . KO 8
(Retained New York World Lightweight Title)

1947

Jan. 20–Eddie Giosa, Philadelphia . . . . KO 5
Feb. 7–Tony Pellone, Detroit . . . . L 10

Feb. 25–Joey Barnum, Los Angeles . . . . KO 7
Mar. 31–Jesse Flores, San Francisco . . . . KO 3
May 12–George LaRover, Philadelphia . . . . W 10
June 2–Julie Kogon, New Haven, Conn. . . . . W 10
June 9–Frankie Cordino, Springfield . . . . W 10
Aug. 4–Ike Williams, Philadelphia . . . . KO by 6
(For Vacant World Lightweight Title)
Nov. 24–Livio Minelli, Philadelphia . . . . L 10
Dec. 22–Joey Angelo, Boston, Mass. . . . . L 10

1948-1949
(Inactive)

1950

Feb. 3–Aldo Minelli, Washington . . . . L 10
Feb. 27–Johnny Greco, Montreal . . . . L 10
Mar. 9–Don Williams, Worcester . . . . L 10
Mar. 27–Eddie Giosa, Philadelphia . . . . L 10

TB	KO	WD	WF	D	LD	LF	KOBO	ND	NC
97	37	38	0	3	16	0	3	0	0

ISIAH (IKE) WILLIAMS
Born, August 2, 1923, Brunswick, Georgia. Weight, 125-150
lbs. Height, 5 ft. 9 ½ in. Managed by Connie McCarthy
(1940-1946), Frank (Blinky) Palermo (1946-1955).

1940

Mar. 15–Carmine Fiotti, New Brunswick . . . . W 4
Mar. 29–Billy George New Brunswick . . . . W 4
Apr. 1–Patsy Gall, Hazleton, Pa . . . . D 6
may 10–Billy Hildebrand, Morristown . . . . L 6
June 17–Billy Hildebrand, Mt. Freedom . . . . KO 6
July 19–Joe Romero, Mt. Freedom, N.J. . . . . KO 2
Sept. 9–Pete Kelly, Trenton, N.J. . . . . KO 2
Nov. 11–Tony Maglione, Trenton . . . . L 8

1941

Jan. 6–Tommy Fontana, Trenton . . . . W 8
Feb. 19–Carl Zullo, Perth Amboy . . . . KO 2
Mar. 5–Joey Zodda, Perth Amboy . . . . L 6
Mar. 19–Joe Genovese, Perth Amboy . . . . W 5
Apr. 9–Johnny Rudolph, Perth Amboy . . . . W 6
Apr. 14–Hugh Civatte, Trenton . . . . KO 3
Oct. 1–Freddie Archer, Perth Amboy . . . . L 8
Oct. 27–Benny Williams, Newark . . . . D 6

Nov. 3–Vince DiLeo, Newark, N.J. . . . . W 6
Dec. 16–Eddie Dowl, Perth Amboy . . . . W 6

1942

–Ruby Garcia, Atlantic City . . . . W 6
Mar. 26–Pedro Firpo, Atlantic City . . . . W 8
Apr. 10–Angelo Panatellas, Atlantic City . . . . KO 5
Apr. 24–Willie Roache, Perth Amboy . . . . W 8
May 7–Abie Kaufman, Atlantic City . . . . W 8
June 29–Ivan Christie, Newark . . . . KO 5
July 29–Angelo Maglione, Trenton . . . . KO 3
Sept. 10–Charley Davis, Elizabeth . . . . W 8
Oct. 20–Gene Burton, White Plains . . . . KO 4
Dec. 7–Bob Gunther, Trenton . . . . W 8
Dec. 21–Sammy Daniels, Baltimore . . . . W 6

1943

Jan. 29–Jerry Moore, New York . . . . W 6
Feb. 22–Sammy Daniels, Philadelphia . . . . KO 2

Feb. 23–Bobby McQuillar, Cleveland. . . . . KO   3
Mar.   8–Bill Speary, Philadelphia . . . . KO   2
Apr.   2–Rudy Giscombe, New York . . . . KO   3
Apr.   5–Ruby Garcia, Philadelphia . . . . W   8
Apr. 21–Joe Genovese, Cleveland . . . . KO   4
May   7–Maurice LaChance, Boston . . . . W   8
May   17–Ray Brown, Philadelphia . . . . W 10
July 19–Jimmy Hatcher, Philadelphia . . . . KO   6
Aug. 24–Tommy Jessup, Hartford . . . . KO   5
Aug. 31–Johnny Bellus, Hartford . . . . W 10
Sept. 13–Jerry Moore, W. Springfield . . . . W 10
Oct.   1–Maurice LaChance, Boston . . . . KO   4
Oct. 22–Ed Perry, New Orleans . . . . KO   2
Oct. 29–Gene Johnson, New Orleans . . . . W 10
Nov.   8–Johnny Hutchinson, Philadelphia . . . . KO   3
Dec. 13–Mayon Padlo, Philadelphia . . . . W 10

1944

Jan. 25–Bob Montgomery, Philadelphia . . . . KO by 12
Feb. 28–Ellis Phillips, Trenton, N.J. . . . . KO   1
Mar. 13–Leo Francis, Trenton, N.J. . . . . W   8
Mar. 27–Joey Peralta, Philadelphia . . . . KO   9
Apr. 10–Leroy Saunders, Holyoke . . . . KO   5
Apr. 17–Mike Delis, Philadelphia . . . . KO   1
May   16–Slugger White, Philadelphia . . . . W 10
June   7–Sammy Angott, Philadelphia . . . . W 10
June 23–Cleo Shans, New York . . . . KO 10
July 10–Joey Pirrone, Philadelphia. . . . . KO   1
July 20–Julie Kogon, New York . . . . W 10
Aug. 29–Jimmy Hatcher, Washington . . . . W 10
Sept. 6–Sammy Angott, Philadelphia . . . . W 10
Sept. 19–Freddie Dawson, Philadelphia . . . . KO   4
Oct. 18–Johnny Green, Buffalo, N.Y. . . . . KO   2
Nov.   2–Ruby Garcia, Baltimore, Md. . . . . KO   7
Nov. 13–Willie Joyce, Philadelphia . . . . L 10
Dec.   5–Lulu Costantino, Cleveland . . . . W 10
Dec. 12–Dave Castilloux, Buffalo . . . . KO   5

1945

Jan.   8–Willie Joyce, Philadelphia . . . . W 12
Jan. 22–Mike Berger, Philadelphia . . . . KO   4
Mar.   2–Willie Joyce, New York . . . . L 12
Mar. 26–Dorsey Lay, Philadelphia . . . . KO   3
Apr. 18–Juan Zurita, Mexico City . . . . KO   2
        (Won NBA Lightweight Title)
June   8–Willie Joyce, New York . . . . L 10
Aug. 14–Charley Smith, Union City . . . . W 10

Aug. 28–Gene Burton, Philadelphia . . . . W 10
Sept. 7–Nick Moran, New York . . . . W 10
Sept. 19–Sammy Angott, Pittsburgh . . . . KO by 6
Nov. 26–Wesley Mouzon, Philadelphia. . . . . D 10

1946

Jan.   8–Charley Smith, Trenton. . . . . W 10
Jan. 20–Johnny Bratton, New Orleans . . . . W 10
Jan. 28–Freddie Dawson, Philadelphia . . . . D 10
Feb. 14–Cleo Shans, Orange, N.J. . . . . W 10
Feb. 22–Ace Miller, Detroit, Mich. . . . . W 10
Mar. 11–Eddie Giosa, Philadelphia . . . . KO   1
Apr.   8–Eddie Giosa, Philadelphia . . . . KO   4
Apr. 30–Enrique Bolanos, Los Angeles. . . . . KO   8
        (Retained NBA Lightweight Title)
June 12–Bobby Ruffin, Brooklyn, N.Y. . . . . KO   5
Aug.   6–Ivan Christie, Norwalk, Conn. . . . . KO   2
Sept. 4–Ronnie James, Cardiff, Wales . . . . KO   9
        (Retained NBA Lightweight Title)

1947

Jan. 27–Gene Burton, Chicago, III . . . . L 10
Apr. 14–Frankie Conti, Allentown, Pa. . . . . KO   7
Apr. 25–Willie Russell, Columbus, Ohio. . . . . W 10
May   9–Ralph Zannelli, Boston, Mass. . . . . W 10
May   26–Juste Fontaine, Philadelphia . . . . KO   4
June 20–Tippy Larkin, New York. . . . . KO   4
Aug.   4–Bob Montgomery, Philadelphia . . . . KO   6
        (Won Vacant World Lightweight Title)
Sept. 29–Doll Rafferty, Philadelphia . . . . KO   4
Oct. 10–Talmadge Bussey, Detroit . . . . KO   9
Dec. 12–Tony Pellone, New York . . . . W 10

1948

Jan. 13–Doug Carter, Camden, N.J. . . . . W 10
Jan. 26–Freddie Dawson, Philadelphia. . . . . W 10
Feb.   9–Livio Minelli, Philadelphia. . . . . W 10
Feb. 27–Kid Gavilan, New York . . . . W 10
May   5–Rudy Cruz, Oakland, Calif. . . . . W 10
May   25–Enrique Bolanos, Los Angeles . . . . W 15
        (Retained World Lightweight Title)
July 12–Beau Jack, Philadelphia . . . . KO   6
        (Retained World Lightweight Title)
Sept. 23–Jesse Flores, New York . . . . KO 10
        (Retained World Lightweight Title)
Nov.   8–Buddy Garcia, Philadelphia . . . . KO   1
Nov. 18–Billy Nixon, Philadelphia . . . . KO   4

1949

Jan.   17–Johnny Bratton, Philadelphia . . . . W 10
Jan.   28–Kid Gavilan, New York . . . . L 10
Apr.   1–Kid Gavilan, New York . . . . L 10
Apr.   23–Vince Turpin, Cleveland . . . . KO 6
June   21–Irvin Steen, Los Angeles . . . . W 10
July   21–Enrique Bolanos, Los Angeles . . . . KO 4
       (Retained World Lightweight Title)
Aug.   3–Benny Walker, Oakland . . . . W 10
Sept. 30–Doug Ratford, Philadelphia . . . . W 10
Oct.   24–Al Mobley, Trenton, N.J. . . . . W 10
Nov.   14–Jean Walzack, Philadelphia . . . . W 10
Dec.   5–Freddie Dawson, Philadelphia . . . . W 15
       (Retained World Lightweight Title)

1950

Jan.   20–Johnny Bratton, Chicago . . . . KO 8
Feb.   17–Sonny Boy West, New York . . . . KO 8
Feb.   27–John L. Davis, Seattle . . . . W 10
June   2–Lester Felton, Detroit . . . . W 10
July   12–George Costner, Philadelphia . . . . L 10
Aug.   7–Charley Salas, Washington . . . . L 10
Sept. 26–Charley Salas, Washington . . . . W 10
Oct.   2–Joe Miceli, Milwaukee . . . . L 10
Nov.   23–Joe Miceli, Milwaukee . . . . W 10
Dec.   12–Dave Marsh, Akron, Ohio . . . . KO 9
Dec.   18–Rudy Cruz, Philadelphia . . . . W 10

1951

Jan.   5–Jose Marcia Gatica, New York . . . . KO 1
Jan.   22–Ralph Zannelli, Providence . . . . KO 5
Jan.   31–Vic Cardell, Detroit, Mich. . . . . KO 9

Feb.   19–Joe Miceli, Philadelphia . . . . L 10
Mar.   5–Beau Jack, Providence . . . . W 10
Apr.   11–Fitzie Pruden, Chicago . . . . W 10
May   25–James Carter, New York . . . . KO by 14
       (Lost World Lightweight Title)
Aug.   2–Don Williams, Worcester . . . . L 10
Sept. 10–Gil Turner, Philadelphia . . . . KO by 10

1952

Mar.   17–Johnny Cunningham, Baltimore . . . . KO 5
Mar.   26–Chuck Davey, Chicago . . . . KO by 5
Nov.   24–Pat Manzi, Syracuse . . . . KO 7

1953

Jan.   12–Carmen Basilio, Syracuse . . . . L 10
Mar.   9–Claude Hammond, Trenton . . . . W 10
Mar.   28–Vic Cardell, Philadelphia . . . . W 10
Apr.   20–Billy Andy, Trenton . . . . W 10
May   18–Billy Andy, Erie, Pa . . . . W 10
June   8–George Johnson, Trenton . . . . KO by 8
Sept. 17–Dom Zimbardo, Newark . . . . KO 2
Nov.   9–Jed Black, Fort Wayne . . . . L 10

1954

July   2–Rafael Lastre, Havana . . . . L 10

1955

Apr.   9–Beau Jack, Augusta . . . . D 10
Aug.   12–Beau Jack, Augusta . . . . KO 9

TB	KO	WD	WF	D	LD	LF	KOBO	ND	NC
153	60	64	0	5	18	0	6	0	0

Elected to Boxing Hall of Fame, 1978.

HAROLD DADE

Born Oct. 9, 1924, Chicago, Ill. Height 5 ft. 5 in. Bantam
weight. Managed by Gus Wilson. Fought as amateur, 1940-1941

1940 National Golden Gloves Bantamweight Champion

1942

Dec.   18–Caferino Robleto, Hollywood . . . . W 4

1943

Jan.   4–Joe Robleto, Ocean Pk., Cal. . . . . D 6
Jan.   8–Orville Young, Hollywood . . . . KO 4
Jan.   18–Ceferino Robleto, Ocean Pk., Cal. . . . . D 8

Feb.   19–Chester Ellis, San Diego . . . . W 10
Mar.   22–Victor Flores, Ocean Pk., Cal. . . . . W 8
Apr.   22–Victor Flores, San Diego . . . . W 10
May   11–Dave Hernandez, Los Angeles . . . . W 10
May   14–Joey Dolan, Portland, Ore. . . . . W 10
       –Ceferino Robleto, Los Angeles . . . . W 4
       –Pedro Ramirez, Hollywood . . . . L 6
       –Joe Robleto, Hollywood . . . . W 10

1944
U.S. Marines
-Al Gregorio, Overseas .... KO 2
-Mc. Don, Overseas .... KO 1

1946
Apr. 9-Ruperto Garcia, San Jose .... KO 3
Apr. 16-Billy Clark, Fresno .... KO 2
Apr. 26-Jess Salazar, Hollywood .... KO 3
Apr. 30-Joe Borjon, Fresno .... W 8
May 7-Billy Gibson, Fresno................... W 8
Sept. 9-Juan Leanos, Ocean Park .... W 10
Dec. 13-Joey Dolan, Portland .... W 10
     -Chivo Carvajal, San Diego .... KO 7

1947
Jan. 6-Manuel Ortiz, San Francisco............ W 15
          (Won Bantamweight Title)
Feb. 12-Speedy Cabanella, Oakland.............. W 10
Mar. 11-Manuel Ortiz, Los Angeles .... L 15
          (Lost Bantamweight Title)
Apr. 2-Tony Olivera, Oakland .... W 10
May 6-Carlos, Chavez, Los Angeles .... D 12
May 27-Jackie McCoy, San Jose .... W 10
July 22-Carlos Chavez, Los Angeles............ L 12
Aug. 26-Simon, Los Angeles .... L 10
Oct. 18-Spedy Cabanella, Manila .... W 10
Nov. 19-Star Navan, Manila.................... W 10
Dec. 23-Manny Ortega, Los Angeles .... W 10

1948
Jan. 6-Bobby Jackson, Los Angeles .... KO 7
Mar. 3-Lauro Salas, Sacramento .... W 10
Mar. 16-Jackie McCoy, San Jose .... W 10
Apr. 3-Luis Galvani, Havana .... L Dis. 8
Apr. 14-Carlos Chavez, Los Angeles............. L 10
June 3-Jackie Graves, Minneapolis .... L 10
June 21-Charley Riley, Chicago .... W 10
Juky 12-Charley Riley, St. Louis............... D 10
Aug. 28-Luis Galvani, Havana .... L 10
Sept. 28-Henry Davis, Honolulu .... L 10
Oct. 29-Charley Riley, Chicago .... W 8
Dec. -Lauro Salas, Los Angeles .... W 12

1949
Jan. 18-Joey Clemo, Seattle................... W 10

Feb. 16-Joe Valdez, Spokane 3 10
Mar. 1-Aaron Joshua, Portland .... KO 5
Apr. 14-Joey Ortega, Tacoma .... W 10
May 31-Jesus Fonseca, Los Angeles .... W 10
July 21-Corky Gonzales, Denver .... L 10
Sept. 2-Sandy Saddler, Chicago .... L 10
Sept. 30-Frank Flannery, Melbourne............. W 12
Oct. 17-Elley Bennett, Sydney .... W 12
Nov. 22-Cork Gonzalez, St. Paul............... L 10
Dec. 12-Willie Pep, St. Louis................. L 10

1950
Jan. 2-Keith Nuttall, Salt Lake City .... L 10
Jan. 18-Baby Leroy, Sacramento .... D 10
Jan. 31-Keith Nuttall, Salt Lake City .... L 10
Feb. 14-Chico Rosa, San Jose .... D 10
Mar. 7-Manuel Ortiz, Los Angeles .... L 10
Apr. 4-Eddie Chavez, San Jose .... KO by 5
Apr. 24-Eddie Chavez, San Francisco........... L 10
July 14-Rudy Garcia, Hollywood .... KO by 11
Sept. -Kid Chocolate, Panama................. W 10
Oct. 4-Rocky McKay, Panama .... L 10
Dec. 3-Rocky McKay, Balboa.................. L 10

1951
Jan. 30-Percy Bassett, Phila................. KO by 8
Mar. 6-Felix Ramirez, San Jose .... L 10
Apr. 22-Memo Valero, Mex. City............. L Dis. 5
June 1-Fabala Chavez, Hollywood .... L 10
June 28-Diego Sosa, Havana .... L 10

1952
Feb. 28-Bobby Woods, Spokane .... W 10
June 22-Lauro Salas, Monterey .... KO by 3
Nov. 27-Bobby Woods, Vancouver................ L 10

1953
Apr. 9-Ernie Kemick, Calgary................. L 10

1955
Mar. 29-Paul Jorgensen, Houston .... KO by 4

TB	KO	WD	WF	D	LD	LF	KOBO	ND	NC
77	9	32	0	6	23	2	5	0	0

Died, July 17, 1962, Los Angeles, Calif.

SUGAR RAY ROBINSON

(Walker Smith, Jr.)

Born, May 3, 1921, Detroit, Mich. Weight, 145-157 lbs.
Height, 5 ft. 11½ in. Managed by George Gainford.

1939 New York Golden Gloves Featherweight
  Champion.
1940 New York Golden Gloves Lightweight Champion
1939, 1940 New York vs. Chicago Inter-City Golden
  Gloves Lightweight Champion

1940

Oct.	4–Joe Escheverria, New York	KO	2
Oct.	8–Silent Stefford, Savannah	KO	2
Oct.	22–Mistos Grispos, New York	W	6
Nov.	11–Bobby Woods, Philadelphia	KO	1
Dec.	9–Norment Quarles, Philadelphia	KO	4
Dec.	12–Oliver White, New York	KO	3

1941

Jan.	4–Henry LaBarba, Brooklyn	KO	1
Jan.	13–Frankie Wallace, Philadelphia	KO	1
Jan.	31–George Zengaras, New York	W	6
Feb.	8–Benny Cartegena, Brooklyn	KO	1
Feb.	21–Bobby McIntire, New York	W	6
Feb.	27–Gene Spencer, Detroit	KO	5
Mar.	3–Jimmy Tygh, Philadelphia	KO	8
Apr.	14–Jimmy Tygh, Philadelphia	KO	1
Apr.	24–Charley Burns, Atlantic City	KO	1
Apr.	30–Joe Ghnouly, Washington, D.C.	KO	3
May	10–Vic Troise, Brooklyn	KO	1
May	19–Nick Castiglione, Philadelphia	KO	1
June	16–Mike Evans, Philadelphia	KO	2
July	2–Pete Lello, New York	KO	4
July	21–Sammy Angott, Philadelphia	W	10
Aug.	27–Carl (Red) Guggino, Long Island City	KO	3
Aug.	29–Maurice Arnault, Atlantic City	KO	1
Sept.	19–Maxie Shapiro, New York	KO	3
Sept.	25–Marty Servo, Philadelphia	W	10
Oct.	31–Fritzie Zivic, New York	W	10

1942

Jan.	16–Fritzie Zivic, New York	KO	10
Feb.	20–Maxie Berger, New York	KO	2
Mar.	20–Norman Rubio, New York	KO	7
Apr.	17–Harvey Dubs, Detroit	KO	6
Apr.	30–Dick Banner, Minneapolis	KO	2
May	28–Marty Servo, New York	W	10
July	31–Sammy Angott, New York	W	10

Aug.	21–Ruben Shank, New York	KO	2
Aug.	27–Tony Motisi, Chicago	KO	1
Oct.	2–Jake LaMotta, New York	W	10
Oct.	19–Izzy Jannazzo, Philadelphia	W	10
Nov.	6–Vic Dellicurti, New York	W	10
Dec.	1–Izzy Jannazzo, Cleveland	KO	8
Dec.	14–Al Nettlow, Philadelphia	KO	3

1943

Feb.	5–Jake LaMotta, Detroit	L	10
Feb.	19–Jackie Wilson, New York	W	10
Feb.	26–Jake LaMotta, Detroit	W	10
Apr.	30–Freddie Cabral, Boston	KO	1
July	1–Ralph Zannelli, Boston	W	10
Aug.	27–Henry Armstrong, New York	W	10

1944

Oct.	13–Izzy Jannazzo, Boston	KO	2
Oct.	27–Sgt. Lou Woods, Chicago	KO	9
Nov.	17–Vic Dellicurti, Detroit	W	10
Dec.	12–Sheik Rangel, Philadelphia	KO	2
Dec.	22–Georgia Martin, Boston	KO	7

1945

Jan.	10–Billy Furrone, Washington, D.C.	KO	2
Jan.	16–Tommy Bell, Cleveland	W	10
Feb.	14–George Costner, Chicago	KO	1
Feb.	24–Jake LaMotta, New York	W	10
May	14–Jose Basora, Philadelphia	D	10
June	15–Jimmy McDaniels, New York	KO	2
Sept.	18–Jimmy Mandell, Buffalo	KO	5
Sept.	26–Jake LaMotta, Chicago	W	12
Dec.	4–Vic Dellicurti, Boston	W	10

1946

Jan.	14–Dave Clark, Pittsburgh	KO	2
Feb.	5–Tony Riccio, Elizabeth	KO	4
Feb.	15–O'Neill Bell, Detroit	KO	2
Feb.	26–Cliff Beckett, St. Louis	KO	4
Mar.	4–Sammy Angott, Pittsburgh	W	10
Mar.	14–Izzy Jannazzo, Baltimore	W	10
Mar.	21–Freddy Flores, New York	KO	5
June	12–Freddy Wilson, Worcester	KO	2
June	25–Norman Rubio, Union City	W	10

July   12–Joe Curcio, New York . . . . KO 2
Aug.   15–Vinnie Vines, Albany . . . . KO 6
Sept.   25–Sidney Miller, Elizabeth . . . . KO 3
Oct.   7–Ossie Harris, Pittsburgh . . . . W 10
Nov.   1–Cecil Hudson,Detroit . . . . KO 6
Nov.   6–Artie Levine, Cleveland . . . . KO 10
Dec.   20–Tommy Bell,New York . . . . W 15
        (Won Vacant World Welterweight Title)

1947

Mar.   27–Bernie Miller, Miami . . . . KO 3
Apr.   3–Fred Wilson, Akron . . . . KO 3
Apr.   8–Eddie Finazzo, Kansas City . . . . KO 4
May   16–Georgia Abrams, New York . . . . W 10
June   24–Jimmy Doyle, Cleveland . . . . KO 8
        (Retained World Welterweight Title)
Aug.   21–Sammy Secreet, Akron . . . . KO 1
Aug.   29–Flashy Sebastian, New York . . . . KO 1
Oct.   28–Jackie Wilson, Los Angeles . . . . KO 7
Dec.   10–Billy Nixon, Elizabeth . . . . KO 6
Dec.   19–Chuck Taylor, Detroit . . . . KO 6
        (Retained World Welterweight Title)

1948

Mar.   4–Ossie Harris, Toledo . . . . W 10
Mar.   16–Henry Brimm, Buffalo . . . . W 10
June   28–Bernard Docusen, Chicago . . . . W 15
        (Retained World Welterweight Title)
Sept.   23–Kid Gavilan, New York . . . . W 10
Nov.   15–Bobby Lee, Philadelphia . . . . W 10

1949

Feb.   10–Gene Buffalo, Wilkes-Barre . . . . KO 1
Feb.   15–Henry Brimm, Buffalo . . . . D 10
Mar.   25–Bobby Lee, Chicago . . . . W 10
Apr.   11–Don Lee, Omaha . . . . W 10
Apr.   20–Earl Turner, Oakland . . . . KO 8
May   16–Al Tribuani, Wilmington . . . . Exh. 4
June   7–Freddie Flores, New Bedford . . . . KO 3
June   20–Cecil Hudson, Providence . . . . KO 5
July   11–Kid Gavilan, Philadelphia . . . . W 15
        (Retained World Welterweight Title)
Aug.   24–Steve Belloise, New York . . . . KO 7
Sept.   2–Al Mobley, Chicago . . . . Exh. 4
Sept.   9–Benny Evans, Omaha . . . . KO 5
Sept.   12–Charley Dotson, Houston . . . . KO 3
Nov.   9–Don Lee, Denver . . . . W 10
Nov.   13–Vern Lester, New Orleans . . . . KO 5

Nov.   15–Gene Burton, Shreveport . . . . Exh. 6
Nov.   16–Gee Burton, Dallas . . . . Exh. 6

1950

Jan.   30–George LaRover, New Haven . . . . KO 4
Feb.   13–Al Mobley, Miami . . . . KO 6
Feb.   22–Aaron Wade, Savannah . . . . KO 3
Feb.   27–Jean Walzack, St Louis . . . . W 10
Mar.   22–George Costner, Philadelphia . . . . KO 1
Apr.   21–Cliff Beckett, Columbus . . . . KO 3
Apr.   28–Ray Barnes, Detroit . . . . W 10
June   5–Robert Villemain, Philadelphia . . . . W 15
        (Won Vacant Pennsylvania World Middleweight Title)
Aug.   9–Charley Fusari, Jersey City . . . . W 15
        (Retained World Welterweight Title)
Aug.   25–Jose Basora, Scranton . . . . KO 1
        (Retained Pennsylvania World Middleweight Title)
Sept.   4–Billy Brown, New York . . . . W 10
Oct.   16–Joe Rindone, Boston . . . . KO 6
Oct.   28–Carl (Bobo) Olson, Philadelphia . . . . KO 12
        (Retained Pennsylvania World Middleweight Title)
Nov.   8–Bobby Dykes, Chicago . . . . W 10
Nov.   27–Jean Stock, Paris . . . . KO 2
Dec.   9–Luc Van Dam, Brussels . . . . KO 4
Dec.   16–Jean Walzack, Geneva . . . . W 10
Dec.   22–Robert Villemain, Paris . . . . KO 9
Dec.   25–Hans Stretz, Frankfort . . . . KO 5

1951

Feb.   14–Jake LaMotta, Chicago . . . . KO 13
        (Won World Middleweight Title)
Apr.   5–Holley Mims, Miami . . . . W 10
Apr.   9–Don Ellis, Oklahoma City . . . . KO 1
May   21–Kid Marcel, Paris . . . . KO 5
May   26–Jean Wanes, Zurich . . . . W 10
June   10–Jan de Bruin, Antwerp . . . . KO 8
June   16–Jean Walzack, Liege . . . . KO 6
June   24–Gerhard Hecht, Berlin . . . . NC 2
July   1–Cyrille Delannoit, Turin . . . . KO 3
July   10–Randy Turpin, London . . . . L 15
        Lost World Middleweight Title)
Sept.   12–Randy Turpin, New York . . . . KO 10
        (Regained World Middleweight Title)

1952

Mar.   13–Carl (Bobo) Olson, San Francisco . . . . W 15
        (Retained World Middleweight Title)

Apr.   16–Rocky Graziano, Chicago . . . . KO   3
       (Retained World Middleweight Title)
June   25–Joey Maxim, New York . . . . KO by 14
       (For World Light Heavyweight Title)
Dec.   18–Announced retirement

1953

(Inactive)

1954

Oct.   20–Announced return to ring
Nov.   29–Gene Burton, Hamilton . . . . Exh.   6

1955

Jan.   5–Joe Rindone, Detroit . . . . KO   6
Jan.   19–Ralph (Tiger) Jones, Chicago . . . . L 10
Mar.   29–Johnny Lombardo, Cincinnati . . . . W 10
April 14–Ted Olla, Milwaukee . . . . TKO   3
May   4–Garth Panter, Detroit . . . . W 10
July   22–Rocky Castellani, San Francisco . . . . W 10
Dec.   9–Carl (BoBo) Olson, Los Angeles . . . . KO   4
       (Regained World Middleweight Title)

1956

May   18–Carl (Bobo) Olson, Los Angeles . . . . KO   4
       (Retained World Middleweight Title)
Nov.   10–Bob Provizzi, New Haven . . . . W 10

1957

Jan.   2–Gene Fullmer, New York . . . . L 15
       (Lost World Middleweight Title)
May   1–Gene Fullmer, Chicago . . . . KO   5
       (Regained World Middleweight Title)
Sept. 10–Otis Woodard, Philadelphia . . . . Exh.   2
Sept. 10–Lee Williams, Philadelphia . . . . Exh.   2
Sept. 23–Carmen Basilio, New York . . . . L 15
       (Lost World Middleweight Title)

1958

Mar.   25–Carmen Basilio, Chicago . . . . W 15
       (Regained World Middleweight Title)

1959

Dec.   14–Bob Young, Boston . . . . TKO   2

1960

Jan.   22–Paul Pender, Boston . . . . L 15
       (Lost World Middleweight Title)
Apr.   2–Tony Baldoni, Baltimore . . . . KO   1

June   10–Paul Pender, Boston . . . . L 15
       (For World Middleweight Title)
Dec.   3–Gene Fullmer, Los Angeles . . . . D 15
       (For the National Boxing Association Middleweight Title)

1961

Mar.   4–Gene Fullmer, Las Vegas . . . . L 15
       (For the National Boxing Association Middleweight Title)
Sept. 25–Wilf Greaves, Detroit . . . . W 10
Oct.   21–Denny Moyer, New York . . . . W 10
Nov.   20–Al Hauser, Providence . . . . TKO   6
Dec.   8–Wilf Greaves, Pittsburgh . . . . KO   8

1962

Feb.   17–Denny Moyer, New York . . . . L 10
Apr.   27–Bobby Lee, Port of Spain . . . . KO   2
July   9–Phil Moyer, Los Angeles . . . . L 10
Sept. 25–Terry Downes, London . . . . L 10
Oct.   17–Diego Infantes, Vienna . . . . KO   2
Nov.   10–George Estatoff, Lyons . . . . TKO   6

1963

Jan.   30–Ralph Dupas, Miami Beach . . . . W 10
Feb.   25–Bernie Reynolds, Santo Domingo . . . . KO   4
Mar.   11–Billy Thornton, Lewiston . . . . KO   3
May   5–Maurice Robinet, Sherbrooke . . . . KO   3
June   24–Joey Giadello, Philadelphia . . . . L 10
Oct.   14–Armand Vanucci, Paris . . . . W 10
Nov.   9–Fabio Bettini, Lyons . . . . D 10
Nov.   16–Emile Saerens, Brussels . . . . KO   8
Nov.   29–Armand Davier, Grenoble . . . . W 10
Dec.   9–Armand Vanucci, Paris . . . . W 10

1964

May   19–Gaylord Barnes, Portland . . . . W 10
July   8–Clarence Riley, Pittsfield . . . . KO   6
July   27–Art Hernandez, Omaha . . . . D 10
Sept.   3–Mick Leahy, Paisley, Scot. . . . . L 10
Sept. 28–Yolande Leveque, Paris . . . . W 10
Oct.   12–Johnny Angel, London . . . . TKO   6
Oct.   24–Jackie Cailleau, Nice . . . . W 10
Nov.   7–Jean Baptiste Roland, Caen . . . . W 10
Nov.   14–Jean Beltritti, Marseilles . . . . W 10
Nov.   27–Fabio Bettini, Rome . . . . D 10

1965

Mar.   6–Jimmy Beecham, Kingston . . . . KO   2
Apr.   4–East Basting, Savannah . . . . KO   1

Apr. 28–Rocky Randall, Norfolk . . . . KO 3
May   5–Rocky Randall, Jacksonville . . . . W 8
May   24–Memo Ayon, Tijuana . . . . L 10
June 1–Stan Harrington, Honolulu . . . . L 10
June 24–Harvey McCullough, Richmond . . . . W 10
July 12–Ferd Hernandez, Las Vegas . . . . L 10
Aug. 10–Stan Harrington, Honolulu . . . . L 10
Sept. 15–Bill Henderson, Norfolk . . . . NC 2
Sept. 23–Harvey McCullough, Philadelphia . . . . W 10

Oct. 1–Peter Schmidt, Johnstown . . . . W 10
Oct. 5–Neil Morrison, Richmond . . . . TKO 2
Oct. 20–Rudolph Bent, Steubenville . . . . KO 3
Nov. 10–Joey Archer, Pittsburgh . . . . L 10
Dec. 10–Announced retirement

TB	KO	WD	WF	D	LD	LF	KOBO	ND	NC
202	110	65	0	6	18	0	1	0	2

Elected to Boxing Hall of Fame, 1967

ARCHIE MOORE

(Archibald Lee Wright)
(The Old Mongoose)

Born, December 13, 1913, Benoit, Mississippi. Weight,
157-192 lbs, Height, 5 ft. 11 in. Managed by Kid Bandy, George
Wilsman, Cal Thompson, Felix Thurman, Jack Richardson
Jimmy Johnson, Charley Johnston, Jack Kearns.

1935

–Piano Man Jones, Hot Springs . . . . KO 2

1936

Jan. 31–Pocohontas Kid, Hot Springs . . . . KO 2
Feb. 7–Dale Richards, Poplar Bluffs . . . . KO 1
Feb. 18–Ray Halford, St. Louis . . . . KO 3
Feb. 20–Willie Harper, St. Louis . . . . KO 3
Feb. 21–Courtland Sheppard, St. Louis . . . . L 6
      –Kneibert Davidson . . . . KO 2
      –Ray Brewster . . . . KO 3
      –Billy Simms . . . . KO 2
      –Johnny Leggs . . . . KO 1
Apr. 15–Peter Urban, Cleveland . . . . KO 6
Apr. 16–Frankie Nelson, Cleveland . . . . L 6
May   4–Tiger Brown, St. Louis . . . . L 6
May   18–Thurman Martin, St. Louis . . . . W 5
      –Ferman Burton . . . . KO 1
      –Billy Simms . . . . KO 1
July 14–Murray Allen, Quincy, Ill. . . . . KO 6
      –Julius Kemp . . . . KO 3
      –Four H. Posey . . . . KO 6
Oct. 9–Sammy Jackson, St. Louis . . . . W 6
      –Dick Putnam . . . . KO 3
Dec. 8–Sammy Jackson, St. Louis . . . . D 6
Dec. –Sammy Christian, St. Louis . . . . KO 6

1937

Jan. 5–Dynamite Payne, St. Louis . . . . KO 1
Jan. 18–Johnny Davis, Quincy, Ill . . . . KO 3
Feb. 2–Joe Huff, St. Louis . . . . KO 2
      –Murray Allen, Keokuk, Iowa . . . . KO 2
Apr. 9–Charley Dawson, Indianapolis . . . . KO 5
Apr. 23–Karl Martin, Indianapolis . . . . KO 1
      –Frank Hatfield . . . . KO 1
      –Al Dublinsky . . . . KO 1
Aug. 19–Deacon Logan, St. Louis . . . . KO 3
Sept. 9–Sammy Slaughter, Indianapolis . . . . W 10
      –Sammy Slaughter, Jenkins . . . . W 10
      –Billy Adams, Cincinnati . . . . L 10
Nov. 16–Sammy Christian, St. Louis . . . . W 5
      –Sammy Jackson . . . . KO 8

1938

Jan. 7–Carl Lautenschlager, St. Louis . . . . KO 2
May   20–Jimmy Brent, San Diego . . . . KO 1
May   27–Ray Vargas, San Diego . . . . KO 3
June 24–Johnny Romero, San Diego . . . . L 10
July 22–Johnny Sykes, San Diego . . . . KO 1
Aug. 5–Lorenzo Pedro, San Diego . . . . W 10
Sept. 2–Johnny Romero, San Diego . . . . KO 8
Sept. 16–Frank Rowsey, San Diego . . . . KO 3
Sept. 27–Tom Henry, Los Angeles . . . . KO 4
      –Bobby Yannes . . . . KO 2

Nov. 22–Ray Lyle, St. Louis . . . . KO 2
Dec. 8–"Irish" Bob Turner, St. Louis . . . . KO 2

1939

Jan. 20–Jack Moran, St. Louis . . . . KO 1
Mar. 2–Domenic Ceccarelli, St. Louis . . . . KO 1
Mar. 16–Marty Simmons, St. Louis . . . . W 10
Apr. 20–Teddy Yarosz, St. Louis . . . . L 10
July 21–Jack Coggins, San Diego . . . . NC 8
Sept. 1–Jack Coggins, San Diego . . . . W 10
Sept. 22–Bobby Seaman, San Diego . . . . KO 7
Dec. 7–Honeyboy Jones, St. Louis . . . . W 10
Dec. 29–Shorty Hogue, San Diego . . . . L 6

1940

Mar. 30–Jack McNamee, Melbourne . . . . KO 4
Apr. 18–Ron Richards, Sydney . . . . Ko 10
May 9–Atiloio, Sabatino, Sydney . . . . KO 5
May 12–Joe Delaney, Adelaide . . . . KO 7
June 2–FrankLindsay, Tasmania . . . . KO 4
June 27–Fred Henneberry, Sydney . . . . KO 7
July 11–Ron Richards, Sydney . . . . W 12
Oct. 18–Pancho Ramirez, San Diego . . . . KO 5

1941

Jan. 17–Clay Rowan, San Diego . . . . KO 1
Jan. 31–Shorty Hogue, San Diego . . . . L 10
Feb. 21–Eddie Booker, San Diego . . . . D 10
       –Freddie Dixon, Phoenix . . . . KO 5

1942

Jan. 28–Bobby Britton, Phoenix . . . . KO 3
Feb. 27–Guero Martinez, San Diego . . . . KO 2
Mar. 17–Jimmy Casino, Oakland . . . . KO 5
Oct. 30–Shorty Hogue, San Diego . . . . KO 2
Nov. 6–Tabby Romero, San Diego . . . . KO 2
Nov. 27–Jack Chase, San Diego . . . . W 10
Dec. 11–Eddie Booker, San Diego . . . . D 12

1943

May 8–Jack Chase, San Diego . . . . W 15
       (Won California Middleweight Title)
July 22–Big Boy Hogue, San Diego . . . . KO 5
July 28–Eddie Cerda, San Diego . . . . KO 3
Aug. 2–Jack Chase, San Francisco . . . . L 15
       (Lost California Middleweight Title)
Aug. 16–Aaron (Tiger) Wade, San Francisco . . . . L 10
Nov. 5–Kid Hermosillo, San Diego . . . . KO 5
Nov. 26–Jack Chase, Hollywood . . . . W 10

1944

Jan. 7–Amado Rodriguez, San Diego . . . . KO 1
Jan. 21–Eddie Booker, Hollywood . . . . KO by 8
Mar. 24–Roman Starr, Hollywood . . . . KO 2
Apr. 21–Charley, Burley, Hollywood . . . . L 10
May 19–Kenny LaSalle, San Diego . . . . W 10
Aug. 11–Louie Mays, San Diego . . . . KO 3
Aug. 18–Jimmy Hayden, San Diego . . . . KO 5
Sept. 1–Battling Monroe, San Diego . . . . KO 6
Dec. 18–Nate Bolden, New York . . . . W 10

1945

Jan. 11–Joey Jones, Boston . . . . KO 1
Jan. 29–Bob Jacobs, New York . . . . KO 9
Feb. 12–Nap Mitchell, Boston . . . . KO 6
Apr. 2–Nate, Bolden, Baltimore . . . . W 10
Apr. 23–Teddy Randolph, Baltimore . . . . KO 9
May 21–Lloyd Marshall, Baltimore . . . . W 10
June 18–George Kochan, Baltimore . . . . KO 6
June 26–Lloyd Marshall, Cleveland . . . . KO 10
Aug. 22–Jimmy Bivins, Cleveland . . . . KO by 6
Sept. 17–Cocoa Kid, Baltimore . . . . KO 8
Oct. 22–Holman Williams, Baltimore . . . . L 10
Nov. 12–Odell Riley, Detroit . . . . KO 6
Nov. 26–Holman Williams, Baltimore . . . . KO 11
Dec. 13–Colion Chaney, St. Louis . . . . KO 5

1946

Jan. 28–Curtis Sheppard, Baltimore . . . . W 12
Feb. 5–Georgie Parks, Washington, D.C. . . . . KO 1
May 2–Verne Escoe, Orange, N.J. . . . . KO 7
May 20–Ezzard Charles, Pittsburgh . . . . L 10
Aug. 19–Buddy Walker, Baltimore . . . . KO 4
Sept. 9–Shamus O'Brien, Baltimore . . . . KO 2
Oct. 23–Billy Smith, Oakland . . . . D 12
Nov. 6–Jack Chase, Oakland . . . . D 10

Mar. 18–Jack Chase, Los Angeles . . . . KO 9
Apr. 11–Rusty Payne, San Diego . . . . W 10
May 5–Ezzard Charles, Cincinnati . . . . L 10
June 16–Curtis Sheppard, Washington, D.C. . . . . W 10
July 14–Bert Lytell, Baltimore . . . . W 10
July 30–Bobby Zander, Oakland . . . . W 12
Sept. 8–Jimmy Bivins, Baltimore . . . . KO 9
Nov. 10–George Fitch, Baltimore . . . . KO 6

1947

Jan. 13–Ezzard Charles, Cleveland . . . . KO by 8
Apr. 12–Dusty Wilkerson, Baltimore . . . . KO 7

Apr.	19–Doc Williams, Newark	KO 7
May	5–Billy Smith, Cincinnati	W 10
June	2–Leonard Morrow, Oakland	KO by 1
June	28–Jimmy Bivins, Baltimore	W 10
Aug.	2–Ted Lowry, Baltimore	W 10
Sept.	20–Billy Smith, Baltimore	KO 4
Oct.	15–Henry Hall, New Orleans	L 10
Nov.	1–Lloyd Gibson, Washington, D.C.	LF 4
Nov.	15–Henry Hall, Baltimore	W 10
Dec.	6–Bob Amos, Washington, D.C.	W 10
Dec.	27–Charley Williams, Baltimore	KO 7

1949

Jan.	10–Alabama Kid, Toledo	KO 4
Jan.	31–Bob Satterfield, Toledo	KO 3
Mar.	4–Alabama Kid, Columbus	KO 3
Mar.	23–Dusty Wilkerson, Philadelphia	KO 6
Apr.	11–Jimmy Bivins, Toledo	KO 8
Apr.	26–Harold Johnson, Philadelphia	W 10
June	13–Clinton Bacon, Indianapolis	LF 6
June	27–Bob Sikes, Indianapolis	KO 3
July	29–Esco Greenwood, North Adams	KO 2
Oct.	4–Bob Amos, Toledo	W 10
Oct.	24–Phil Muscato, Toledo	KO 6
Dec.	6–Doc Williams, Hartford	KO 8
Dec.	13–Leonard Morrow, Toledo	KO 10

1950

Jan.	31–Bert Lytell, Toledo	W 10
July	31–Vernon Williams, Chicago	KO 2

1951

Jan.	2–Billy Smith, Portland, Ore.	TKO 8
Jan.	28–John Thomas, Panama City	KO 1
Feb.	21–Jimmy Bivins, New York	TKO 9
Mar.	13–Abel Cestac, Toledo	W 10
Apr.	26–Herman Harris, Flint	TKO 4
May	14–Art Henri, Baltimore	TKO 4
June	9–Abel Cestac, Buenos Aires	TKO 10
June	23–Karel Sys, Buenos Aires	D 10
July	8–Alberto Lovell, Buenos Aires	KO 1
July	15–Vincente Quiroz, Montevideo	KO 6
July	26–Victor Carabajal, Cordoba	TKO 3
July	28–Americo Capitanelli, Tucuman	TKO 3
Aug.	5–Rafael Miranda, Argentina	TKO 4
Aug.	17–Alfredo Lagay, Bahia Blanca	KO 3
Sept.	3–Embrell Davison, Detroit	KO 1
Sept.	24–Harold Johnson, Philadelphia	W 10
Oct.	29–Chubby Wright, St. Louis	TKO 7

Dec.	10–Harold Johnson, Milwaukee	L 10

1952

Jan.	29–Harold Johnson, Toledo	W 10
Feb.	27–Jimmy Slade, St. Louis	W 10
May	19–Bob Dunlap, San Francisco	KO 6
June	26–Clarence Henry, Baltimore	W 10
July	25–Clint Bacon, Denver	TKO 4
Dec.	17–Joey Maxim, St. Louis	W 15
	(Won World Light Heavyweight Title)	

1953

Jan.	27–Toxie Hall, Toledo	KO 4
Feb.	16–Leonard Dugan, San Francisco	TKO 8
Mar.	3–Sonny Andrews, Sacramento	TKO 5
Mar.	11–Nino Valdes, St. Louis	W 10
Mar.	17–Al Spaulding, Spokane	KO 3
Mar.	30–Frank Buford, San Diego	TKO 9
June	24–Joey Maxim, Ogden, Utah	W 15
	(Retained World Light Heavyweight Title)	
Aug.	22–Reinaldo Ansaloni, Buenos Aires	TKO 4
Sept.	12–Dogomar Martinez, Buenos Aires	W 10

1954

Jan.	27–Joey Maxim, Miami	W 15
	(Retained World Light Heavyweight Title)	
Mar.	9–Bob Baker, Miami Beach	TKO 9
June	7–Bert Whitehurst, New York	KO 6
Aug.	11–Harold Johnson, New York	TKO 14
	(Retained World Light Heavyweight Title)	

1955

May	2–Nino Valdes, Las Vegas	W 15
June	22–Carl (Bobo) Olson, New York	KO 3
	(Retained World Light Heavyweight Title)	
Sept.	21–Rocky Marciano, New York	KO by 9
	(For World Heavyweight Title)	
Oct.	22–Dale Hall, Philadelphia	Exh. 4

1956

Feb.	2–Dale Hall, Fresno	Exh. 4
Feb.	20–Howard King, San Francisco	W 10
Feb.	27–Bob Dunlap, San Diego	KO 1
Mar.	17–Frankie Daniels, Hollywood	W 10
Mar.	27–Howard King, Sacramento	W 10
Apr.	10–Willie Bean, Richmond, Cal.	TKO 5
Apr.	16–George Parmenter, Seattle	TKO 3
Apr.	26–Sonny Andrews, Edmonton	KO 4
Apr.	30–Gene Thompson, Tucson	TKO 3

June 5-Yolande Pompey, London . . . . TKO 10
      (Retained World Light Heavyweight Title)
July 25-James J. Parker, Toronto . . . . TKO 9
Sept. 8-Roy Shire, Ogden, Utah . . . . TKO 3
Nov. 30-Floyd Patterson, Chicago . . . . KO by 5
      (For Vacant World Heavyweight Title)

1957

May   1-Hans Kalbfell, Essen . . . . W 10
June 2-Alain Cherville, Stuttgart . . . . TKO 6
Sept. 20-Tony Anthony, Los Angeles . . . . TKO 7
      (Retained World Light Heavyweight Title)
Oct. 31-Bob Mitchell, Vancouver . . . . TKO 5
Nov. 5-Eddie Cotton, Seattle . . . . W 10
Nov. 29-Roger Rischer, Portland . . . . KO 4

1958

Jan. 18-Luis Ignacio, Sao Paulo . . . . W 10
Feb. 1-Julio Neves, Rio de Janeiro . . . . KO 3
Mar. 4-Bert Whitehurst, San Bernardino . . . . TKO 10
Mar. 10-Bob Albright, Vancouver . . . . TKO 7
May   2-Willi Besmanoff, Louisville . . . . W 10
May   17-Howard King, San Diego . . . . W 10
May   26-Charlie Norkus, San Francisco . . . . W 10
June 9-Howard King, Sacramento . . . . W 10
Aug. 4-Howard King, Reno . . . . D 10
Dec. 10-Yvon Durelle, Montreal . . . . KO 11
      (Retained World Light Heavyweight Title)

1959

Feb. 5-Eddie Cotton, Victoria . . . . Exh. 5
Mar. 9-Sterling Davis, Odessa, Texas . . . . TKO 3
Aug. 12-Yvon Durelle, Montreal . . . . KO 3
      (Retained World Light Heavyweight Title)

1960

May   25-Willi Besmanoff, Indianapolis . . . . TKO 10
Sept. 13-George Abinet, Dallas . . . . TKO 3
Oct. 25-National Boxing Association vacated Light Heavy-
          weight Title . . . .
Oct. 29-Giulio Rinaldo, Rome . . . . L 10
Nov. 28-Buddy Turman, Dallas . . . . W 10

1961

Mar. 25-Buddy Turman, Manila . . . . W 10
May   8-Dave Furch, Tucson . . . . Exh. 4
May   12-Clifford Gray, Nogales . . . . KO 4
June 10-Giulio Rinaldi, New York . . . . W 15
      (Retained World Light Heavyweight Title)
Oct. 23-Pete Rademacher, Baltimore . . . . TKO 6

1962

Feb. 10-New York State Athletic Commission vacates
          Light Heavyweight Title . . . .
Mar. 30-Alejandro Lavorante, Los Angeles . . . . TKO 10
May   7-Howard King, Tijuana . . . . KO 1
May   28-Willie Pastrano, Los Angeles . . . . D 10
Nov. 15-Cassius Clay, Los Angeles . . . . KO by 4

1963

Mar. 15-Mike DiBiase, Phoenix . . . . KO 3

1964

(Inactive)

1965

Aug. 27-Nap Mitchell, Michigan City . . . . Exh. KO 3

TB	KO	WD	WF	D	LD	LF	KOBO	ND	NC
215	129	54	0	9	13	2	7	0	1

Elected to Boxing Hall of Fame, 1966

FLOYD PATTERSON

Born, January 4, 1935, Waco, North Carolina. Weight, 164-196
lbs. Height, 5 ft. 11 in. Managed by Cus D'Amato

1952 United States National Amateur Athletic Union
Middleweight Champion
1952 United States Olympic Middleweight
Gold Medalist

1952

Sept.	12–Eddie Godbold, New York	KO	4
Oct.	6–Sammy Walker, Brooklyn	KO	2
Oct.	21–Lester, Jackson, New York	KO	3
Dec.	29–Lalu Sabotin, Brooklyn	KO	5

1953

Jan.	28–Chester Mieszala, Chicago	KO	5
Apr.	3–Dick Wagner, Brooklyn	W	8
June	1–Gordon Wallace, Brooklyn	KO	3
Oct.	19–Wes Bascom, Brooklyn	W	8
Dec.	14–Dick Wagner, Brooklyn	KO	5

1954

Feb.	15–Yvon Durelle, Brooklyn	W	8
Mar.	30–Sam Brown, Washington, D.C.	KO	2
Apr.	19–Alvin Williams, Brooklyn	W	8
May	10–Jesse Turner, Brooklyn	W	8
June	7–Joey Maxim, Brooklyn	L	8
July	12–Jacques Royer-Crecy, New York	KO	7
Aug.	2–Tommy Harrison, Brooklyn	KO	1
Oct.	11–Esau Ferdinand, New York	W	8
Oct.	22–Joe Gannon, New York	W	8
Nov.	19–Jimmy Slade, New York	W	8

1955

Jan.	7–Willie Troy, New York	KO	5
Jan.	17–Don Grant, Brooklyn	KO	5
Mar.	17–Esau Ferdinand, Oakland	KO	10
June	23–Yvon Durelle, Newcastle	KO	5
July	6–Archie McBride, New York	KO	7
Sept.	8–Alvin Williams, Moncton	KO	8
Sept.	29–Dave Whitlock, San Francisco	KO	3
Oct.	13–Calvin Brad, Las Angeles	KO	1
Dec.	8–Jimmy Slade, Los Angeles	KO	7

1956

Mar.	12–Jimmy Walls, New Britain	KO	2
Apr.	10–Alvin Williams, Kansas City	KO	3
June	8–Tommy Jackson, New York	W	12

Nov.	30–Archie Moore, Chicago	KO	5
	(Won Vacant World Heavyweight Title)		

1957

July	29–Tommy Jackson, New York	KO	10
	(Retained World Heavyweight Title)		
Aug.	22–Pete Rademacher, Seattle	KO	6
	(Retained World Heavyweight Title)		

1958

Aug.	18–Roy Harris, Los Angeles	KO	12
	(Retained World Heavyweight Title)		

1959

May	1–Brian London, Indianapolis	KO	11
	(Retained World Heavyweight Title)		
June	26–Ingemar Johansson, New York	KO by	3
	(Lost World Heavyweight Title)		

1960

June	20–Ingemar Johansson, New York	KO	4
	(Regained World Heavyweight Title)		

1961

Mar.	13–Ingemar Johansson, Miami Beach	KO	6
	(Retained World Heavyweight Title)		
Dec.	4–Tom McNeeley, Toronto	KO	4
	(Retained World Heavyweight Title)		

1962

Sept.	25–Sonny Liston, Chicago	KO by	1
	(Lost World Heavyweight Title)		

1963

July	22–Sonny Liston, Las Vegas	KO by	1
	(For World Heavyweight Title)		

1964

Jan.	6–Sante Amonti, Stockholm	KO	8
July	5–Eddie Machen, Stockholm	W	12
Dec.	12–Charley Powell, San Juan	KO	6

1965

Feb.	1–George Chuvalo, New York	W	12
May	14–Tod Herring, Stockholm	KO	3

Nov. 22–Muhammad Ali, Las Vegas .... KO by 12
       (For World Heavyweight Title)

1966

Sept. 20–Henry Cooper, London .... KO   4

1967

Feb. 13–Willie Johnson, Miami Beach .... KO   3
Mar. 30–Bill McMurray, Pittsburgh .... KO   1
June   9–Jerry Quarry, Los Angeles .... D 10
Oct. 28–Jerry Quarry, Los Angeles............... L 12
       (WBA Heavyweight Elimination Tournament)

1968

Sept. 14–Jimmy Ellis, Stockholm .... L 15
       (For WBA Heavyweight Title)

1969

       (Inactive)

1970

Sept. 15–Charlie Green, New York .... KO 10

1971

Jan. 16–Levi Forte, Miami Beach .... KO   2
Mar. 29–Roger Russell, Philadelphia............. KO   9
May   26–Terry Daniels, Cleveland................ W 10
July 17–Charlie Polito, Erie .... W 10
Aug. 21–Vic Brown, Buffalo..................... W 10
Nov. 23–Charlie Harris, Portland .... KO   6

1972

Feb. 11–Oscar Bonavena, New York............... W 10
May   16–Charlie Harris, Washington, D.C. .... Exh. 5
July 14–Pedro Agosto, New York .... KO   6
Sept. 20–Muhammad Ali, New York .... KO by 7
       (For NABF Heavyweight Title)

TB	KO	WD	WF	D	LD	LF	KOBO	ND	NC
64	40	15	0	1	3	0	5	0	0

Elected to Boxing Hall of Fame, 1976.

BOB FOSTER

Born, December 15, 1938, Albuquerque, New Mexico.
Weight, 170-188 lbs. Height, 6 ft. 3 in.

1959 Pan American Games Middleweight
Silver Medalist

1961

Mar. 27–Duke Williams, Washington, D.C. .... KO   2
Apr.   3–Clarence Ryan, New York .... W   4
May   8–Billy Johnson, New York................ W   4
June 22–Ray Bryan, Montreal................... KO   2
Aug.   8–Floyd McCoy, Montreal.................. W   6
Nov. 22–Ernie Knox, Norfolk .... KO   4
Dec.   4–Clarence Floyd, Toronto .... KO   4

1962

May   19–Billy Tisdale, New York................. KO   2
June 27–Bertt Whitehurst, New York .... W   8
Oct. 20–Doug Jones, New York .... KO by 8

1963

Feb. 18–Richard Benjamin, Washington .... KO   1
Apr. 29–Curtis Bruce, Washington, D.C........... KO   4

Nov.   6–Mauro Mina, Lima, Peru .... L 10
Dec. 11–Willi Besmanoff, Norfolk............... KO   3

1964

Feb. 25–Dave Bailey, Miami Beach .... KO   1
May   8–Allen Thomas, Chicago .... KO   1
July 10–Ernest Terrell, New York .... KO by 7
Nov. 12–Don Quinn, Norfolk .... KO   1
Nov. 23–Norm Letcher, San Francisco .... KO   1
Dec. 11–Henry Hank, Norfolk................... KO 10

1965

Feb. 15–Roberto Rascon, Albuquerque........... KO   2
Mar. 21–Dave Russell, Norfolk .... KO   6
May   24–Chuck Leslie, New Orleans............. KO   3
July 26–Henry Hank, New Orleans .... W 12
Dec.   6–Zora Folley, New Orleans .... L 10

1966

Dec.   6–Leroy Green, Norfolk .... KO   2

1967

Jan.	16–Jim Robinson, Washington, D.C.	KO	1
Feb.	27–Andres Selpa, Washington, D.C.	KO	2
May	8–Eddie Cotton, Washington, D.C.	KO	3
June	9–Henry Mathews, Roanoke, Va.	KO	2
Oct.	25–Levan Roundtree, Washington	KO	8
Nov.	20–Eddie Vick, Providence	W	10
Dec.	5–Sonny Moore, Washington, D.C.	KO	2

1968

May	24–Dick Tiger, New York	KO	4
	(Won World Light Heavyweight Title)		
July	29–Charley Polite, West Springfield	KO	3
Aug.	26–Eddie Vick, Albuquerque	KO	9
Sept.	9–Roger Rouse, Washington, D.C.	KO	5

1969

Jan.	22–Frank DePaula, New York	KO	1
	(Retained World Light Heavyweight Title)		
May	24–Andy Kendall, West Springfield	KO	4
	(Retained World Light Heavyweight Title)		
June	19–Levan Roundtree, Atlanta	KO	4
Nov.	2–Chuck Leslie, New Orleans	KO	5

1970

Feb	24–Bill Hardney, Orlando	KO	4
Mar.	9–Cookie Wallace, Tampa	KO	6
Apr.	4–Roger Rouse, Missoula	KO	4
	(Retained World Light Heavyweight Title)		
June	27–Mark Tessman, Baltimore	KO	10
	(Retained World Light Heavyweight Title)		
Nov.	18–Joe Frazier, Detroit	KO by	2
	(For World Heavyweight Title)		

1971

Mar.	2–Hal Carroll, Scranton	KO	4
	(Retained World Light Heavyweight Title)		
Apr.	24–Ray Anderson, Tampa	W	15
	(Retained World Light Heavyweight Title)		
Aug.	17–Vernon McIntosh, Miami Beach	KO	3
Oct.	29–Tommy Hicks, Scranton	KO	8
	(Retained World Light Heavyweight Title)		

Dec.	16–Brian Kelly, Oklahoma City	KO	3
	(Retained World Light Heavyweight Title)		

1972

Apr.	7–Vicente Rondon, Miami Beach	KO	2
	(Retained World Light Heavyweight Title)		
June	27–Mike Quarry, Las Vegas	KO	4
	(Retained World Light Heavyweight Title)		
Sept.	26–Chris Finnegan, London	KO	14
	(Retained World Light Heavyweight Title)		
Nov.	21–Muhammad Ali, Stateline	KO by	8
	(For NABF Heavyweight Title)		

1973

Aug.	21–Pierre Fourie, Albuquerque	W	15
	(Retained World Light Heavyweight Title)		
Dec.	1–Pierre Fourier, Johannesburg	W	15
	(Retained World Light Heavyweight Title)		

1974

June	17–Jorge Ahumada, Albuquerque	D	15
	(Retained World Light Heavyweight Title)		
Sept.	16–Announced retirement		

1975

June	28–Bill Hardney, Santa Fe	KO	3

1976

May	8–Al Bolden, Missoula	KO	3
Aug.	28–Harold Carter, Missoula	W	10
Sept.	25–Al Bolden, Spokane	KO	6

1977

Sept.	2–Bob Hazelton, Curacao	KO	10

1978

Feb.	9–Mustapha Wassaja, Copenhagen	KO by	5
June	3–Bob Hazelton, Wichita	KO by	2

TB	KO	WD	WF	D	LD	LF	KOBO	ND	NC
65	46	10	0	1	2	0	6	0	0

Elected to Boxing Hall of Fame, 1983.

MUHAMMAD ALI
(Cassius Marcellus Clay, Jr.)
(The Louisville Lip)
Born, January 17, 1942, Louisville, Ky. Weight, 186-230 lbs.
Height, 6 ft. 3 in.

1959 National Golden Gloves Light Heavyweight
   Champion
1959, 1960 United States National Amateur Athletic
   Union Light Heavyweight Champion
1960 United States Olympic Light Heavyweight
   Gold Medalist

1960
Oct. 29–Tunney Hunsaker, Louisville . . . . W 6
Dec. 27–Herb Siler, Miami Beach. . . . . KO 4

1961
Jan. 17–Tony Esperti, Miami Beach . . . . KO 3
Feb. 7–Jim Robinson, Miami Beach . . . . KO 1
Feb. 21–Donnie Fleeman, Miami Beach . . . . KO 7
Apr. 19–Lamar Clark, Louisville. . . . . KO 2
June 26–Duke Sabedong, Las Vegas . . . . W 10
July 22–Alonzo Johnson, Louisville . . . . W 10
Oct. 7–Alex Miteff, Louisville. . . . . KO 6
Nov. 29–Willi Besmanoff, Louisville . . . . KO 7

1962
Feb. 10–Sonny Banks, New York . . . . KO 4
Feb. 28–Don Warner, Miami Beach. . . . . KO 4
Apr. 23–George Logan, Los Angeles . . . . KO 4
May 19–Billy Daniels, New York. . . . . KO 7
July 20–Alejandro Lavorante, Los Angeles . . . . KO 5
Nov. 15–Archie Moore, Los Angeles. . . . . KO 4

1963
Jan. 24–Charlie Powell, Pittsburgh . . . . KO 3
Mar. 13–Doug Jones, New York . . . . W 10
June 18–Henry Cooper, London . . . . KO 5

1964
Feb. 25–Sonny Liston, Miami Beach. . . . . KO 7
(Won World Heavyweight Title)

1965
May 25–Sonny Liston, Lewiston, Me . . . . KO 1
(World Heavyweight Title)
July 31–Jimmy Ellis, San Juan P.R. . . . . Exh. 3
July 31–Cody Jones, San Juan, P.R. . . . . Exh. 3

Aug. 16–Cody Jones, Gothenburg . . . . Exh. 2
Aug. 16–Jimmy Ellis, Gothenburg. . . . . Exh. 2
Aug. 20–Jimmy Ellis, London, England . . . . Exh. 4
Aug. 20–Cody Jones, Paisley, Scotland . . . . Exh. 4
Nov. 22–Floyd Patterson, Las Vegas . . . . KO 12
(Retained World Heavyweight Title)

1966
Mar. 29–George Chuvalo, Toronto . . . . W 15
(Retained World Heavyweight Title)
May 21–Henry Cooper, London, England . . . . KO 6
(Retained World Heavyweight Title)
Aug. 6–Brian London, London, England . . . . KO 3
(Retained World Heavyweight Title)
Sept. 10–Karl Mildenberger, Frankfurt. . . . . KO 12
(Retained World Heavyweight Title)
Nov. 14–Cleveland Williams, Houston. . . . . KO 3
(Retained World Heavyweight Title)

1967
Feb. 6–Ernest Terrell, Houston . . . . W 15
(Retained World Heavyweight Title)
Mar. 22–Zora Folley, New York. . . . . KO 7
(Retained World Heavyweight Title)
June 15–Alvin (Blue) Lewis, Detroit. . . . . Exh. 3
June 15–Orvill Qualls, Detroit . . . . Exh. 3

1968-1969
(Inactive)

1970
Feb. 3–Announced retirement. . . . .
Oct. 26–Jerry Quarry, Atlanta . . . . KO 3
Dec. 7–Oscar Bonavena, New York . . . . KO 15

1971
Mar. 8–Joe Frazier, New York . . . . L 15
(For World Heavyweight Title)
June 25–J.D.McCauley, Dayton. . . . . Exh. 2
June 25–Eddie Brooks, Dayton . . . . Exh. 3
June 25–Rufus Brassell, Dayton. . . . . Exh. 3
June 30–Alex Mack, Charleston . . . . Exh. 3
June 30–Eddie Brooks, Charleston. . . . . Exh. 4

July 26–Jimmy Ellis, Houston .... KO 12
(Won Vacant NABF Heavyweight Title)
Aug. 21–Lancer Johnson, Caracas .... Exh. 4
Aug. 21–Eddie Brooks, Caracas .... Exh. 4
Aug. 23–Lancer Johnson, Port of Spain .... Exh. 4
Aug. 23–Eddie Brooks, Port of Spain .... Exh. 2
Nov. 6–James Summerville, Buenos Aires....... Exh. 5
Nov. 6–Miguel Angel Paez, Buenos Aires .... Exh. 5
Nov. 17–Buster Mathis, Houston .... W 12
(Retained NABF Heavyweight Title)
Dec. 26–Jurgen Blin, Zurich, Switzerland .... KO 7

1972

Apr. 1–Mac Foster, Tokyo, Japan .... W 15
May 1–George Chuvalo,Vancouver, B.C.......... W 12
(Retained NABF Heavyweight Title)
June 27–Jerry Quarry, Las Vegas .... KO 7
(Retained NABF Heavyweight Title)
July 1–Lonnie Bennett, Los Angeles.......... Exh. 2
July 1–Eddie Jones, Los Angeles .... Exh. 2
July 1–Billy Ryan, Los Angles .... Exh. 2
July 1–Charley James, Los Angeles .... Exh. 2
July 1–Rahaman Ali, Los Angeles .... Exh. 2
July 19–Alvin (Blue) Lweis, Dublin .... KO 11
Aug. 24–Obie English, Baltimore.............. Exh. 4
Aug. 24–Ray Anderson, Baltimore .... Exh. 2
Aug. 24–Alonzo Johnson, Baltimore .... Exh. 2
Aug. 24–George Hill, Baltimore................ Exh. 2
Aug. 28–Alonzo Johnson, Cleveland .... Exh. 2
Aug. 28–Amos Johnson, Cleveland............. Exh. 2
Sept. 20–Floyd Patterson, New York .... KO 7
(Retained NABF Heavyweight Title)
Oct. 11–John (Dino) Denis, Boston............ Exh. 2
Oct. 11–Cliff McDonald, Boston .... Exh. 2
Oct. 11–Doug Kirk, Boston .... Exh. 2
Oct. 11–Ray Anderson, Boston .... Exh. 2
Oct. 11–Paul Raymond, Boston .... Exh. 2
Nov. 21–Bob Foster, Stateline, Nev. .... KO 8
(Retained NABF Heavyweight Title)

1973

Feb. 14–Joe Bugner, Las Vegas .... W 12
Mar. 31–Ken Norton, San Diego .... L 12
(Lost NABF Heavyweight Title)
Sept. 10–Ken Norton, Los Angeles .... W 12
(Regained NABF Heavyweight Title)
Oct. 20–Rudi Lubbers, Jakarta .... W 12

1974

Jan. 28–Joe Frazier, New York .... W 12
(Retained NABF Heavyweight Title)
Oct. 30–George Foreman, Kinshasa, Zaire .... KO 8
(Regained World Heavyweight Title)

1975

Mar. 24–Chuck Wepner, Cleveland .... KO 15
(Retained World Heavyweight Title)
May 16–Ron Lyle, Las Vegas .... KO 11
(Retained World Heavyweight Title)
July 1–Joe Bugner, Kuala Lumpur .... W 15
(Retained World Heavyweight Title)
Oct. 1–Joe Frazier, Manila .... KO 14
(Retained World Heavyweight Title)

1976

Feb. 20–Jean Pierre Coopman, San Juan .... KO 5
(Retained World Heavyweight Title)
Apr. 30–Jimmy Young, Landover .... W 15
(Retained World Heavyweight Title)
May 24–Richard Dunn, Munich .... KO 5
(Retained World Heavyweight Title)
June 25–Antonio Inoki, Tokyo .... Exh. D 15
(Above match was a boxer against a wrestler.)
Sept. 28–Ken Norton, New York .... W 15
(Retained World Heavyweight Title)

1977

Jan. 29–Peter Fuller, Boston.................. Exh. 4
Jan. 29–Walter Haines, Boston................. Exh. 1
Jan. 29–Jeyy Houston, Boston................. Exh. 2
Jan. 29–Ron Drinkwater, Boston .... Exh. 2
Jan. 29–Matt Ross, Boston .... Exh. 2
Jan. 29–Frank Smith, Boston .... Exh. 1
May 16–Alfredo Evangelista, Landover........... W 15
(Retained World Heavyweight Title)
Sept. 29–Earnie Shavers, New York .... W 15
(Retained World Heavyweight Title)
Dec. 2–Scott LeDoux, Chicago............... Exh. 5

1978

Feb. 15–Leon Spinks, Las Vegas................ L 15
(Lost World Heavyweight Title)
Sept. 15–Leon Spinks, New Orleans .... W 15
(Regained World Heavyweight Title)

1979
–Announced retirement..................

1980
Oct.   2–Larry Holmes, Las Vegas .... KO by 11
(For World Heavyweight Title)

1981
Dec. 11–Trevor Berbick, Nassau .... L 10

TB	KO	WD	WF	D	LD	LF	KOBO	ND	NC
61	37	19	0	0	4	0	1	0	0

Elected to the Boxing Hall of Fame, 1987

JOSEPH FRAZIER
(Smokin' Joe)

Born, January 12, 1944, Beaufort, S.C. Weight, 205 lbs.
Height, 5 ft. 11½ in.

1964 United States Olympic Heavyweight Gold Medalist

1965
Aug.   16–Woody Goss, Philadelphia .... KO   1
Sept. 20–Mike Bruce, Philadelphia .... KO   3
Sept. 28–Ray Staples,Philadelphia .... KO   2
Nov.   11–Abe Davis, Philadelphia................ KO   1

1966
Jan.   17–Mel Turnbow, Philadelphia .... KO   1
Mar.   4–Dick Wipperman, New York.............. KO   5
Apr.   4–Charley Polite, Philadelphia............. KO   2
Apr.   28–Don (Toro) Smith, Pittsburgh .... KO   3
May   19–Chuck Leslie, Los Angeles .... KO   3
May   26–Memphis Al Jones, Los Angeles .... KO   1
July   25–Billy Daniels, Philadelphia.............. KO   6
Sept. 21–Oscar Bonavena, New York.............. W 10
Nov.   21–Eddie Machen, Los Angeles .... KO 10

1967
Feb.   21–Doug Jones, Philadelphia .... KO   6
Apr.   11–Jeff Davis, Miami Beach .... KO   5
May   4–George Johnson, Los Angeles............ W 10
July   19–George Chuvalo, New York .... KO   4
Oct.   17–Tony Doyle, Philadelphia............... KO   2
Dec.   18–Marion Connors, Boston................ KO   3

1968
Mar.   4–Buster Mathis, New York .... KO 11
(Won Vacant New York World Heavyweight Title)
June   24–Manuel Ramos, New York .... KO   2
(Retained New York World Heavyweight Title)
Dec.   10–Oscar Bonavena, Philadelphia............ W 15
(Retained New York World Heavyweight Title)

1969
Apr.   22–Dave Zyglewicz, Houston............... KO   1
(Retained New York World Heavyweight Title)
June   23–Jerry Quarry, New York .... KO   7
(Retained New York World Heavyweight Title)

1970
Feb.   16–Jimmy Ellis, New York .... KO   5
(Won Vacant World Heavyweight Title)
Nov.   18–Bob Foster, Detroit .... KO   2
(Retained World Heavyweight Title)

1971
Mar.   8–Muhammad Ali, New York.............. W 15
(Retained World Heavyweight Title)
July   15–Cleveland Williams, Houston.......... Exh.   3
July   15–James Helwig, Houston .... Exh.   3

1972
Jan.   15–Tery Daniels, New Orleans .... KO   4
(Retained World Heavyweight Title)
May   25–Ron Stander, Omaha.................. KO   5
(Retained World Heavyweight Title)

1973
Jan.   22–George Foreman, Kingston .... KO by   2
(Lost World Heavyweight Title)
July   2–Joe Bugner, London................... W 12

1974
Jan.   28–Muhammad Ali, New York .... L 12
(For NABF Heavyweight Title)
June   17–Jerry Quarry, New York .... KO   5

1975

Mar. 1–Jimmy Ellis, Melbourne .... KO 9
Oct. 1–Muhammad Ali, Manila .... KO by 14
      (For World Heavyweight Title)

1976

June 15–George Foreman, Uniondale .... KO by 5

1977-1980

(Inactive)

1981

Dec. 3–Jumbo Cummings, Chicago .... D 10

TB	KO	WD	WF	D	LD	LF	KOBO	ND	NC
37	27	5	0	1	1	0	3	0	0

Elected to Boxing Hall of Fame, 1980.

LARRY HOLMES

(The Easton Assassin)

Born, November 3, 1949, Cuthbert, Georgia. Weight, 196-224 lbs. Height, 6 ft. 3 in.

1973

Mar. 21–Rodell Dupree, Scranton .... W 4
May   2–Art Savage, Scranton .... KO 3
June 20–Curtis Whitner, Scranton .... KO 1
Aug. 22–Don Branch, Scranton .... W 6
Sept. 10–Bob Bozic, New York .... W 6
Nov. 14–Jerry Judge, Scranton .... W 6
Nov. 28–Kevin Isaac, Cleveland .... KO 3

1974

Apr. 24–Howard Darlington, Scranton .... KO 4
May   29–Bob Mashburn, Scranton .... KO 7
Dec. 11–Joe Hathaway, Scranton .... KO 1

1975

Mar. 24–Charley Green, Cleveland .... KO 2
Apr. 10–Oliver Wright, Honolulu .... KO 3
Apr. 26–Robert Yarborough, Toronto .... KO 3
May   16–Ernie Smith, Las Vegas................. KO 3
Aug. 16–Obie English, Scranton................. KO 7
Aug. 26–Charlie James, Honolulu................ W 10
Oct. 1–Rodney Bobick, Manila .... KO 6
Dec. 9–Leon Shaw, Washington D.C............. KO 1
Dec. 20–Billy Joiner, San Juan .... KO 3

1976

Jan. 29–Joe Gholston, Easton .... KO 8
Apr. 5–Fred Ashew, Landover .... KO 2
Apr. 30–Roy Williams, Landover .... W 10

1977

Jan. 16–Tom Prater, Pensacola .... W 8
      (U.S. Championship Tournament)
Mar. 17–Horacio Robinson, San Juan .... KO 5
Sept. 14–Young Sanford Houpe, Las Vegas......... KO 7
Nov. 5–Ibar Arrington, Las Vegas .... KO 10

1978

Mar. 25–Earnie Shavers, Las Vegas .... W 12
June 9–Ken Norton, Las Vegas................. W 15
      (Won WBC Heavyweight Title)
Nov. 10–Alfredo Evangelista, Las Vegas .... KO 7
      (Retained WBC Heavyweight Title)

1979

Mar. 23–Osvaldo Ocasio, Las Vegas .... KO 7
      (Retained WBC Heavyweight Title)
June 22–Mike Weaver, New York .... KO 12
      (Retained WBC Heavyweight Title)
Sept. 28–Earnie Shavers, Las Vegas .... KO 11
      (Retained WBC Heavyweight Title)

1980

Feb. 3–Lorenzo Zanon, Las Vegas.............. KO 6
      (Retained WBC Heavyweight Title)
Mar. 31–Leroy Jones, Las Vegas................ KO 8
      (Retained WBC Heavyweight Title)
July 7–Scott LeDoux, Bloomington .... KO 7
      (Retained WBC Heavyweight Title)

Oct.   2–Muhammad Ali, Las Vegas . . . . KO 11
       (Won Vacant World Heavyweight Title)

1981

Apr.   11–Trevor Berbick, Las Vegas . . . . W 15
       (Retained World Heavyweight Title)
June   12–Leon Spinks, Detroit . . . . TKO   3
       (Retained World Heavyweight Title)
Nov.   6–Renaldo Snipes, Pittsburgh . . . . TKO 11
       (Retained World Heavyweight Title)

1982

June   11–Gerry Cooney, Las Vegas . . . . TKO 13
       (Retained World Heavyweight Title)
Nov.   26–Randall (Tex) Cobb, Houston . . . . W 15
       (Retained World Heavyweight Title)

1983

Mar.   27–Lucien Rodriguez, Scranton . . . . W 12
       (Retained World Heavyweight Title)
May   20–Tim Witherspoon, Las Vegas . . . . W 12
       (Retained World Heavyweight Title)
Sept. 10–Scott Frank, Atlantic City . . . . TKO   5
       (Retained World Heavyweight Title)
Nov.   25–Marvis Frazier, Las Vegas . . . . TKO   1
       (Retained World Heavyweight Title)

1984

Nov.   9–James Smith, Las Vegas . . . . TKO 12
       (Retained World Heavyweight Title)

1985

Mar.   15–David Bey, Las Vegas . . . . TKO 10
       (Retained World Heavyweight Title)

May   20–Carl Williams, Reno 15
       (Retained World Heavyweight Title)
Sept. 22–Michael Spinks, Las Vegas . . . . L 15
       (Lost World Heavyweight Title)

1986

Apr.   19–Michael Spinks, Las Vegas . . . . L 15
       (For World Heavyweight Title)

1988

Jan.   22–Mike Tyson, Atlantic City . . . . KO by   4
       (World Heavyweight Title)

1991

Apr.   7–Tim Anderson, Florida . . . . TKO   1
Aug.   13–Eddie Gonzales, Florida . . . . WD 10
Aug.   24–Michael Greer, Hawaii . . . . KO   4
Sept. 17–Art Card, Florida . . . . WD 10
Nov.   12–Jamie Howe, Florida . . . . TKO   1

1992

Feb.   7–Ray Mercer, Atlantic City . . . . WD 12
June   19–Evander Holyfield, Las Vegas . . . . LD 12
       (World Heavyweight Title)

1993

Jan.   5–Everett Martin, Mississippi . . . . WD 10
Mar.   9–Rocky Pepeli, Mississippi . . . . TKO   5
Apr.   13–Ken Lakusta, Mississippi . . . . TKO   7
May   18–Paul Poirier, Mississippi . . . . TKO   6

TB	KO	WD	WF	D	LD	LF	KOBO	ND	NC
62	40	18	0	0	3	0	1	0	0

THOMAS HEARNS

(The Motor City Cobra)
(Hit Man)
Born, October 18, 1958, Memphis, Tenn. Weight, 145–175 lbs.
Height, 6 ft. 1 in.

*1977 U.S. National Amateur Athletic Union Light
   Welterweight Champion*
1977 National Golden Gloves Welterweight Champion

1977

Nov.   25–Jerone Hill, Detroit . . . . KO   2
Dec.   7–Jerry Strickland, Mt. Clemens . . . . KO   3
Dec.   16–Willie Wren, Detroit . . . . KO   3

1978

Jan.   29–Anthony House, Detroit . . . . KO   2
Feb.   10–Robert Adams, Detroit . . . . KO   3
Feb.   17–Billy Goodman, Detroit . . . . KO   2
Mar.   17–Ray Fields, Detroit . . . . KO   2
Mar.   31–Tyrone Phelps, Saginaw . . . . KO   3
June   8–Jimmy Rothwell, Detroit . . . . KO   1
July   20–Raul Aguirre, Detroit . . . . KO   3

Aug.	3-Eddie Marcelle, Detroit	KO 2
Sept.	7-Bruce Finch, Detroit	KO 3
Oct.	26-Pedro Rojas, Detroit	KO 1
Dec.	9-Rudy Barro, Detroit	KO 4

1979

Jan.	13-Clyde Gray, Detroit	KO 10
Jan.	31-Sammy Ruckard, Detroit	KO 8
Mar.	3-Segundo Murillo, Detroit	KO 8
Apr.	3-Alfonso Hayman, Philadelphia	W 10
May	20-Harold Weston Jr., Las Vegas	KO 6
June	28-Bruce Curry, Detroit	KO 3
Aug.	23-Mao DeLa Rosa, Detroit	KO 2
Sept.	22-Jose Figueroa, Los Angeles	KO 3
Oct.	18-Saensak Muangsurin, Detroit	KO 3
Nov.	30-Mike Colbert, New Orleans	W 10

1980

Feb.	3-Fighting Jim Richards, Las Vegas	KO 3
Mar.	2-Angel Espada, Detroit	KO 4
	(Won Vacant USBA Welterweight Title)	
Mar.	31-Santiago Valdez, Las Vegas	KO 1
May	3-Eddie Gazo, Detroit	KO 1
Aug.	2-Pipino, Cuevas, Detroit	KO 2
	(Won WBA Welterweight Title)	
Nov.	29-William (Cavemen) Lee, L.A.	Exh.
Dec.	6-Luis Primera, Detroit	KO 6
	(Retained WBA Welterweight Title)	

1981

Apr.	25-Randy Shields, Phoenix	KO 13
	(Retained WBA Welterweight Title)	
June	25-Pablo Baez, Houston	KO 4
	(Retained WBA Welterweight Title)	
Sept.	16-Ray Leonard, Las Vegas	KO by 14
	(For World Welterweight Title)	
Dec.	11-Ernie Singletary, Nassau	W 10

1982

Feb.	27-Marcos Geraldo, Las Vegas	KO 1
July	25-Jeff McCracken, Detroit	KO 8
Dec.	3-Wilfred Benitez, New Orleans	W 15
	(Won WBC Junior Middleweight Title)	

1983

July	10-Murray Sutherland, Atlantic City	W 10

1984

Feb.	11-Luigi Minchillo, Detroit	W 12
	(Retained WBC Junior Middleweight Title)	
June	15-Roberto Duran, Las Vegas	KO 2
	(Won Vacant World Junior Middleweight Title)	

Sept.	15-Fred Hutchings, Saginaw	KO 3
	(Retained World Junior Middleweight Title)	

1985

Apr.	15-Marvin Hagler, Las Vegas	TKO by 3
	(For World Middleweight Title)	

1986

Mar.	10-James Shuler, Las Vegas	KO 1
	(Won NABF Middleweight Title)	
June	23-Mark Medal, Las Vegas	TKO 8
	(Retained World Junior Middleweight Title)	
Sept.	-Relinquished World Junior Middleweight Title	
Oct.	17-Doug DeWitt, Detroit	W 12
	(Retained NABF Middleweight Title)	

1987

Feb.	-Dennis Andries, Detroit	TKO 10
	(Won WBC Light Heavyweight Title)	
Oct.	29-Juan Roldan, Las Vegas	KO 4
	(World Boxing Council Middleweight Title)	

1988

June	6-Iran Barkley, Las Vegas	TKO by 3
	(World Boxing Council Middleweight Title)	
Nov.	4-James Kinchen, Las Vegas	WD 12
	(World Boxing Organization Super Middleweight Title)	
June	12-Ray Leonard, Las Vegas	D 12
	(World Boxing Council Super Middleweight Title)	

1990

Apr.	28-Michael Olajide, Atlantic City	WD 12
	(World Boxing Organization Super Middleweight Title)	

1991

Feb.	11-Kemper Morton, Los Angeles	KO 2
Apr.	6-Ken Atkin, Hawaii	TKO 3
June	3-Virgil Hill, Las Vegas	WD 12
	(World Boxing Association Light-Heavyweight Title)	

1992

Mar.	20-Iran Barkley, Las Vegas	LD 12
	(World Boxing Association Light-Heavyweight Title)	

TB	KO	WD	WF	D	LD	LF	KOBO	ND	NC
55	40	10	0	1	0	0	3	0	0

SUGAR RAY LEONARD

(Ray Charles Leonard)
Born, May 17, 1956, Wilmington, N.C. Weight 141–153 lbs.
Height, 5 ft. 10 in.

1973 National Golden Gloves Lightweight Champion
1974 National Golden Gloves Light Welterweight
  Champion
1974, 1975 United States National Amateur Athletic
  Union Light Welterweight Champion
1975 Pan American Games Light Welterweight
  Gold Medalist
1976 United States Olympic Light Welterweight
  Gold Medalist

1977

Feb.	5–Luis Vega, Baltimore	W 6
May	14–Willie Rodriguez, Baltimore	W 6
June	10–Vinnie DeBarros, Hartford	KO 3
Sept.	24–Frank Santore, Baltimore	KO 5
Nov.	5–Augustin Estrada, Las Vegas	KO 5
Dec.	17–Hector Diaz, Washington D.C.	KO 2

1978

Feb.	4–Rocky Ramon, Baltimore	W 8
Mar.	1–Art McKnight, Dayton	KO 7
Mar.	19–Javier Muniz, New Haven	KO 1
Apr.	13–Bobby Haymon, Landover	KO 3
May	13–Randy Milton, Utica	KO 8
June	3–Rafael Rodriguez, Baltimore	W 10
July	18–Dick Eckland, Boston	W 10
Sept.	9–Floyd Mayweather, Providence	KO 9
Oct.	6–Randy Shields, Baltimore	W 10
Nov.	3–Bernardo Prada, Portland, Me	W 10
Dec.	9–Armando Muniz, Springfield	KO 6

1979

Jan.	11–Johnny Gant, Landover	KO 8
Feb.	11–Fernand Marcotte, Miami Beach	KO 8
Mar.	24–Daniel Gonzales, Tuscan	KO 1
Apr.	21–Adolfo Viruet, Las Vegas	W 10
May	20–Marcos Geraldo, New Orleans	W 10
June	24–Tony Chiaverini, Las Vegas	KO 4
Aug.	12–Pete Ranzany, Las Vegas	KO 4
	(Won NABF Welterweight Title)	
Sept.	28–Andy Price, Las Vegas	KO 1
	(Retained NABF Welterweight Title)	
Nov.	30–Wilfred Benitez, Las Vegas	KO 15
	(Won World Welterweight Title)	

1980

Mar.	31–Dave (Boy) Green, Landover	KO 4
	(Retained World Welterweight Title)	
June	20–Roberto Duran, Montreal	L 15
	(Lost World Welterweight Title)	
Nov.	25–Roberto Duran, New Orleans	KO 8
	(Regained World Welterweight Title)	

1981

Mar.	28–Larry Bonds, Syracuse	KO 10
	(Retained World Welterweight Title)	
June	25–Ayub Kalule, Houston	KO 9
	(Won World Junior Middleweight Title)	
Sept.	16–Thomas Hearns, Las Vegas	KO 14
	(Retained World Welterweight Title)	

1982

Feb.	15–Bruce Finch, Reno, Nev.	KO 3
	(Retained World Welterweight Title)	
Nov.	9–Announced retirement.	

1983

(Inactive)

1984

May	11–Kevin Howard, Worcester	KO 9

1987

Apr.	6–Marvin Hagler, Las Vegas	W 12
	(Won WBC Middleweight Title)	

1988

Nov.	7–Donnie LaLonde, Las Vegas	TKO 9
	(World Boxing Council Light-Heavyweight Title)	

1989

June	12–Thomas Hearns, Las Vegas	D 12
	(World Boxing Council Super Middleweight Title)	
Dec.	7–Roberto Duran, Las Vegas	WD 12
	(World Boxing Council Super Middleweight Title)	

		TB	KO	WD	WF	D	LD	LF	KOBO	ND	NC
	1991	39	25	11	0	1	1	0	2	0	0
Feb.	2–Terry Norris, New York .... LD 12										
	(World Boxing Council Junior Middleweight Title)										

MARVIN HAGLER
(Marvelous Marvin)
Born, May 23, 1954, Newark, N.J. Weight, 155-162 lbs.
Height, 5 ft. 9½ in. Southpaw. Managed by Goody and Pat
Petronelli.

1973 U.S. National AAU Middleweight Champion

1973

May 18–Terry Ryan, Brockton .... KO 2
July 25–Sonny Williams, Boston .... W 6
Aug. 8–Muhammad Smith, Boston .... KO 2
Oct. 6–Don Wigfall, Brockton .... W 8
Oct. 26–Cove Green, Brockton .... KO 4
Nov. 18–Cocoa Kid, Brockton.................. KO 2
Dec. 7–Manny Freitas, Portland, Me .... KO 1
Dec. 18–James Redford, Boston................ KO 4

1974

Feb. 5–Bob Harrington, Boston .... KO 5
Apr. 5–Tracy Morrison, Boston .... KO 8
May 4–Jim Redford, Brockton .... KO 2
May 30–Curtis Phillips, Portland .... KO 5
July 16–Robert Williams, Boston.............. KO 3
Aug. 13–Peachy Davis, New Bedford............ KO 1
Aug. 30–Ray Seales, Boston .... W 10
Oct. 29–Morris Jordan, New Bedford........... KO 4
Nov. 16–George Green, Brockton.............. KO 1
Nov. 26–Ray Seales, Seattle.................... D 10
Dec. 20–D.C. Walker, Boston.................. KO 2

1975

Feb. 15–Don Wigfall, Brockton................. KO 5
Mar. 31–Joey Blair, Boston .... KO 2
Apr. 14–Jimmy Owens, Boston .... W 10
May 24–Jimmy Owens, Boston............. W disq 6
Aug. 7–Jesse Bender, Portland................ KO 1
Sept. 30–Lamont Lovelady, Boston .... KO 7
Dec. 20–Johnny Baldwin, Boston .... W 10

1976

Jan. 13–Bobby Watts, Philadelphia .... L 10

Feb. 7–Matt Donovan, Boston .... KO 2
Mar. 9–Willie Monroe, Philadelphia.............. L 10
June 2–Bob Smith, Taunton .... KO 5
Aug. 3–D.C. Walker, Providence............... KO 6
Sept. 14–Eugene Hart, Philadelphia.............. KO 8
Dec. 21–George Davis, Boston.................. KO 6

1977

Feb. 15–Willie Monroe, Boston .... KO 12
Mar. 16–Reginald Ford, Boston .... KO 3
June 10–Roy Jones, Hartford .... KO 3
Aug. 23–Willie Monroe, Philadelphia .... KO 2
Sept. 24–Ray Phillips, Boston .... KO 7
Oct. 15–Jim Henry, Providence .... W 10
Nov. 26–Mike Colbert, Boston .... KO 12

1978

Mar. 4–Kevin Finnegan, Boston .... KO 9
Apr. 7–Doug Demmings, Los Angeles.......... KO 8
May 13–Kevin Finnegan, Boston .... KO 7
Aug. 24–Bennie Briscoe, Philadelphia .... W 10
Nov. 11–Willie Warren, Boston................. KO 7

1979

Feb. 3–Ray Seales, Boston.................... KO 1
Mar. 12–Bob Patterson, Providence .... KO 3
May 26–Jaime Thomas, Portland, Me .... KO 3
June 30–Norberto Cabrera, Monte Carlo.......... KO 8
Nov. 30–Vito Antuofermo, Las Vegas .... D 15
(For World Middleweight Title)

1980

Feb. 16–Loucif Hammani, Portland.............. KO 2
Apr. 19–Bobby Watts, Portland .... KO 2
May 17–Marcos Geraldo, Las Vegas............. W 10
Sept. 27–Alan Minter, London.................. KO 3
(Won World Middleweight Title)

1981

Jan.　17–Fulgencio Obelmejias, Boston . . . . KO　8
　　　　(Retained World Middleweight Title)
June　13–Vito Antuoferno, Boston . . . . KO　5
　　　　(Retained World Middleweight Title)
Oct.　3–Mustafa Hamsho, Rosemont . . . . KO　11
　　　　(Retained World Middleweight Title)

1982

Mar.　7–Wm. (Caveman) Lee, Atlantic City . . . . KO　1
　　　　(Retained World Middleweight Title)
Oct.　30–Fulgencio Obelmejias, San Remo . . . . KO　5
　　　　(Retained World Middleweight Title)

1983

Feb.　11–Tony Sibson, Worcester, Mass . . . . KO　6
　　　　(Retained World Middleweight Title)
May　27–Wilford Scypion, Providence . . . . KO　4
　　　　(Retained World Middleweight Title)
Nov.　10–Roberto Duran, Las Vegas . . . . W　15
　　　　(Retained World Middleweight Title)

1984

Mar.　30–Juan Domingo Roldan, Las Vegas . . . . KO　10
　　　　(Retained World Middleweight Title)
Oct.　19–Mustafa Hamsho, New York . . . . KO　3
　　　　(Retained World Middleweight Title)

1985

Apr.　15–Thomas Hearns, Las Vegas . . . . TKO　3
　　　　(Retained World Middleweight Title)

1986

Mar.　10–John Mugabi, Las Vegas . . . . KO　11
　　　　(Retained World Middleweight Title)

1987

Apr.　6–Sugar Ray Leonard, Las Vegas . . . . LD　12
　　　　(Lost WBC Middleweight Title)

TB	KO	WD	WF	D	LD	LF	KOBO	ND	NC
67	52	9	1	2	3	0	0	0	0

Elected to the Boxing Hall of Fame, 1993

MICHAEL SPINKS

Born, July 13, 1956, St. Louis, Mo. Weight, 165-200 lbs.
Height, 6 ft. 2½ in. Managed by Butch Lewis.

1976 National Golden Gloves Middleweight Champion
1976 United States Olympic Middleweight Gold
Medalist

1977

Apr.　17–Eddie Benson, Las Vegas . . . . KO　1
May　9–Luis Rodriguez, St. Louis . . . . W　6
June　1–Joe Borden, Montreal, Qbc. . . . . KO　2
Aug.　23–Jasper Brisbane, Philadelphia . . . . KO　1
Sept.　13–Ray J. Elson, Los Angeles . . . . KO　1
Oct.　21–Gary Summerhays, Las Vegas . . . . W　8

1978

Feb.　15–Tom Bethea, Las Vegas, Nev. . . . . W　8
Dec.　15–Eddie Phillips, White Plains . . . . KO　4

1979

Nov.　24–Marc Hans, Bloomington. . . . . KO　1

1980

Feb.　1–Johnny Wilburn, Louisville, Ky . . . . W　8
Feb.　24–Ramon Ronquillo, Atlantic City . . . . TKO　6
May　4–Murray Sutherland, Kiamesha Lake . . . . W　10
Aug.　2–David Conteh, Baton Rouge, La. . . . . KO　9

Oct.　18–Yaqui Lopez, Atlantic City . . . . KO　7

1981

Jan.　24–Willie Taylor, Philadelphia . . . . KO　8
Mar.　28–Marvin Johnson, Atlantic City . . . . KO　4
July　18–Mustafa Muhammad, Las Vegas. . . . . W　15
　　　　(Won WBA Light Heavyweight Title)
Nov.　7–Vonzell Johnson, Atlantic City . . . . TKO　7
　　　　(Retained WB Light Heavyweight Title)

1982

Feb.　13–Mustapha Wasajja, Atlantic City . . . . TKO　6
　　　　(Retained WBA Light Heavyweight Title)
Apr.　11–Murray Sutherland, Atlantic City . . . . TKO　8
　　　　(Retained WBA Light Heavyweight Title)
June　12–Jerry Celestine, Atlantic City. . . . . TKO　8
　　　　(Retained WBA Light Heavyweight Title)
Sept.　18–Johnny Davis, Atlantic City . . . . TKO　9
　　　　(Retained WBA Light Heavyweight Title)

1983

Mar.　18–Dwight Braxton, Atlantic City . . . . W　15
　　　　(Won Vacant World Light Heavyweight Title)

Nov. 25-Oscar Rivadeneyra, Vancouver.......... TKO 10
(Retained World Light Heavyweight Title)

1984

Feb. 25-Eddie Davis, Atlantic City............... W 12
(Retained World Light Heavyweight Title)

1985

Feb. 23-David Sears, Atlantic City .... TKO 3
(Retained World Light Heavyweight Title)

June   6-Jim MacDonald, Las Vegas .... TKO 8
(Retained World Light Heavyweight Title)

Sept. 22-Larry Holmes, Las Vegas .... W 15
(Won World Heavyweight Title)

1986

Apr. 19-Larry Holmes, Las Vegas .... W 15
(Retained World Heavyweight Title)

Sept. 6-Steffen Tangstad, Las Vegas .... TKO 4
(Retained World Heavyweight Title)

1987

June 15-Gerry Cooney, Atlantic City............ TKO 5
(Retained World Heavyweight Title)

June 27-Michael Tyson, 1988 Atlantic City .... KO by 1

TB	KO	WD	WF	D	LD	LF	KOBO	ND	NC
31	21	10	0	0	0	0	1	0	0

MICHAEL GERALD TYSON

Born, June 30, 1966, Brooklyn, N.Y. Weight, 212-221 lbs.
Height, 5 ft. 11 in. Managed by Don King.

1984 National Golden Gloves Heavyweight Champion

1985

Mar.   6-Hector Mercedes, Albany .... TKO 1
Apr. 10-Trent Singleton, Albany .... TKO 1
May   23-Don Halpin, Albany .... KO 4
June 20-Rick Spain, Atlantic City .... KO 1
July 11-John Alderson, Altantic City........... TKO 2
July 19-Larry Sims, Poughkeepsie, N.Y........... KO 3
Aug. 15-Lorenzo Canady, Atlantic City.......... TKO 1
Sept. 5-Mike Johnson, Atlantic City............. KO 1
Oct.   9-Donnie Long, Atlantic City.............. KO 1
Oct. 25-Robert Colay, Atlantic City............. KO 1
Nov.   1-Sterling Benjamin, Latham, N.Y. .... TKO 1
Nov. 13-Eddie Richardson, Houston............. KO 1
Nov. 22-Conroy Nelson, Latham, N.Y............ TKO 2
Dec.   6-Sammy Scaff, New York................ TKO 1
Dec. 27-Mark Young, Latham, N.Y. .... TKO 1

1986

Jan. 11-David Jaco, Albany .... TKO 1
Jan. 24-Mike Jameson, Atlantic City........... TKO 5
Feb. 16-Jesse Ferguson, Troy, N.Y.............. TKO 6
Mar. 10-Steve Zouski, E. Rutherford .... KO 3
May   3-James Tillis, Glens Falls .... W 10
May   20-Mitchell Green, New York............... W 10
June 13-Reggie Gross, New York .... TKO 1
June 28-William Hosea, Troy, N.Y. .... KO 1
July 11-Lorenzo Boyd, Swan Lake .... KO 2
July 26-Marvis Frazier, Glens Falls .... KO 1

Aug. 17-Jose Ribalta, Atlantic City .... TKO 10
Sept. 6-Alfonzo Ratliff, Las Vegas .... TKO 2
Nov. 22-Trevor Berbick, Las Vegas .... TKO 2
(Won WBC Heavyweight Title)

1987

Mar.   3-James Smith, Las Vegas .... W 12
(Unified WBC & WBA Heavyweight Titles)

May   30-Pinklon Thomas, Las Vegas .... KO 6
(Retained the WBC & WBA Heavyweight Titles)

Aug.   1-Tony Tucker, Las Vegas................. W 12
(Won the IBF Heavyweight Title)

Oct. 16-Tyrell Biggs, Atlantic City .... TKO 7
(World Heavyweight Title)

1988

Jan. 22-Larry Holmes, Atlantic City .... TKO 4
(World Heavyweight Title)

Mar. 21-Tony Tubbs, Tokyo, Japan .... KO 2
(World Heavyweight Title)

June 27-Michael Spinks, Atlantic City .... KO 1
(World Heavyweight Title)

1989

Feb. 25-Frank Bruno, Las Vegas .... TKO 5
(World Heavyweight Title)

July 21-Carl Williams, Atlantic City .... TKO 1
(World Heavyweight Title)

1990

Feb.	11–James Douglas, Tokyo, Japan	KO	10
	(Lost World Heavyweight Title)		
June	16–Henry Tillman, Las Vegas	KO	1
Dec.	8–Alex Stewart, Atlantic City	TKO	1

1991

Mar.	18–Donovan Ruddock, Las Vegas	TKO	7
June	28–Donovan Ruddock, Las Vegas	WD	12

TB	KO	WD	WF	D	LD	LF	KOBO	ND	NC
41	35	5	0	0	0	0	1	0	0

SANDY SADDLER

Born, June 23, 1926. Boston, Mass. Weight, 124–130 lbs. Height,
5 ft. 8½ in. Managed by Charley Johnston.

1944

Mar.	7–Earl Roys, Hartford	W	8
Mar.	21–Jock Leslie, Hartford	KO by	3
Mar.	27–Al King, Holyoke, Mass.	KO	2
Apr.	17–Joe Landry, Holyoke, Mass.	KO	1
May	8–Jose Aponte Torres, Trenton	W	6
May	15–Jose Aponte Torres, Holyoke	W	6
May	23–Domingo Diaz, Jersey City	W	6
June	13–Jose Aponte Torres, Union City	W	8
June	15–Lou Alter, Fort Hamilton	L	6
June	23–Lou Alter, New York	D	4
July	11–Clyde English, Dexter	W	6
July	18–Benny Saladino, Brookyln	KO	3
July	25–Al Pennino, Brooklyn	W	6
Aug.	8–Georgie Knox, Brooklyn	KO	3
Aug.	18–Clifford Smith, New York	W	6
Nov.	11–Manuel Torres, Brooklyn	W	6
Nov.	13–Ken Tompkins, Newark	KO	1
Nov.	24–Manuel Torres, New York	KO	5
Nov.	28–Percy Lewis, Jersey City	KO	1
Dec.	12–Tony Oshiro, Jersey City	KO	2
Dec.	16–Earl Mintz, Brooklyn	KO	2
Dec.	26–Midget Mayo, Newark	KO	3

1945

Jan.	13–Tony Oshiro, Brooklyn	W	6
Jan.	15–Mickey Johnson, Newark	KO	1
Jan.	22–Joey Puig, New York	KO	1
Jan.	26–Benny May, New Brunswick	W	6
Feb.	19–Joey Gatto, New York	KO	1
Mar.	10–Harold Gibson, Brooklyn	W	6
Mar.	19–Joe Montiero, New York	KO	4
Mar.	22–Georgie Knox, Camden	KO	4
Apr.	2–Jimmy Allen, Newark	KO	1
Apr.	19–Willie Anderson, Detroit	KO	5
Apr.	30–Chilindrina Valencia, Detroit	KO	9

June	18–Caswell Harris, Baltimore	KO	3
June	25–Bobby Washington, Allentown	KO	2
June	29–Leo Methot, New York	KO	1
July	23–Herbert Jones, Baltimore	KO	3
July	24–Joe Montiero, Brooklyn	KO	5
July	30–Luis Rivera, New York	KO	4
Aug.	16–Louis Langley, Brooklyn	KO	1
Aug.	20–Bobby English, Providence	KO	3
Aug.	27–Earl Mintz, Providence	KO	1
Sept.	21–Richie Myashiro, New York	W	6
Dec.	3–Benny Daniels, Holyoke	W	6
Dec.	14–Joe Montiero, Boston	W	8
Dec.	21–Filberto Osario, New York	W	6

1946

Jan.	17–Sam Zelman, Orange, N.J.	KO	1
Feb.	18–Bobby McQuillar, Detroit	L	10
Apr.	8–Ralph LaSalle, New York	KO	1
Apr.	11–Johnny Wolgast, Atlantic City	W	8
Apr.	25–Pedro Firpo, Atlantic City	W	8
June	13–Cedric Flournoy, Detroit	KO	4
July	10–George Cooper, Brooklyn	KO	7
July	23–Phil Terranova, Detroit	L	10
Aug.	5–Dom Ameroso, Providence	KO	2
Aug.	22–Pedro Firpo, Brooklyn	W	10
Oct.	10–Jose Rodriguez, Atlantic City	KO	3
Nov.	12–Art Price, Detroit, Mich.	W	10
Dec.	9–Clyde English, Holyoke	KO	3
Dec.	26–Luis Marquez, Jamaica	KO	2
Dec.	30–Leonard Caesar, Newark	KO	2

1947

Jan.	20–George Brown, Holyoke	KO	4
Jan.	27–Humberto Zavala, New York	KO	7
Feb.	7–Larry Thomas, Asbury Park	KO	2
Mar.	8–Leonardo Lopez, Mexico City	KO	2

Mar.	29–Carlos Malacara, Mexico City	W	10
Apr.	14–Charley (Cabey) Lewis, New York	W	10
May	2–Joe Brown, New Orleans, La.	KO	3
May	9–Melvin Bartholomew, New Orleans	W	10
June	3–Jimmy Carter, Washington, D.C.	D	10
July	26–Oscar Calles, Caracas, Vez.	KO	5
Aug.	14–Lesile Harris, Atlantic City	KO	5
Aug.	29–Miguel Acevedo, New York	KO	8
Sept.	17–Angelo Ambrosano, Jamaica	KO	2
Oct.	3–Humberto Sierra, Minneapolis	L	10
Oct.	13–Al Pennino, New York	KO	4
Oct.	26–Lino Garcia, Caracas	KO	5
Nov.	9–Emilio Sanchez, Caracas	KO	5
Dec.	5–Lino Garcia, Havana	KO	3
Dec.	13–Orlando Zulueta, Havana	W	10

1948

Feb.	2–Charley Noel, Holyoke	W	10
Feb.	9–Joey Angelo, New York	W	10
Mar.	5–Archie Wilmer, New York	W	8
Mar.	8–Thompson Harmon, Holyoke	TKO	8
Mar.	23–Bobby Thompson, Hartford	W	10
Apr. 10–	Luis Monagas, Caracas	KO	3
Apr.	17–Jose Diaz, Caracas	KO	8
Apr.	26–Young Tanner, Aruba	KO	5
May	24–Harry LaSane, Holyoke	W	10
June	29–Chico Rosa, Honolulu	L	10
Aug.	16–Kid Zefine, Panama City	KO	2
Aug.	23–Aguilino Allen, Panama City	KO	2
Oct.	11–Willie Roache, New Haven	TKO	3
Oct.	29–Willie Pep, New York	KO	4
	(Won World Featherweight Title)		
Nov.	19–Tomas Beato, Bridgeport	KO	2
Nov.	29–Dennis Pat Brady, Boston	W	10
Dec.	7–Eddie Giosa, Cleveland	KO	2
Dec.	17–Terry Young, New York	KO	10

1949

Jan.	17–Young Finnegan, Panama City	KO	5
Feb.	11–Willie Pep, New York	L	15
	(Lost World Featherweight Title)		
Mar.	21–Felix Ramirez, Newark	W	10
Apr.	18–Ermano Bonetti, Philadelphia	KO	2
June	2–Jim Keery, London, Eng.	KO	4
June	23–Luis Ramos, New York	KO	5
July	15–Gordon House, New York	TKO	5
Aug.	2–Chuck Burton, Pittsfield	KO	5
Aug.	8–Johnny Rowe, Brooklyn, N.Y.	KO	8
Aug.	24–Alfredo Escobar, Los Angeles	KO	9

Sept.	2–Harold Dade, Chicago, Ill.	W	10
Sept.	20–Proctor Heinold, Schenectady	KO	2
Oct.	28–Paddy DeMarco, New York	TKO	9
Nov.	7–Leroy Willis, Toledo, Ohio	W	10
Dec.	6–Orlando Zulueta, Cleveland	W	10
	(Won Vacant World Junior Lightweight Title)		

1950

Jan.	16–Paulie Jackson, Caracas	KO	1
Jan.	22–Pedro Firpo, Caracas	KO	1
Feb.	6–Chuck Burton, Holyoke	KO	1
Feb.	20–Luis Ramos, Toronto	TKO	3
Apr.	10–Reuben Davis, Newark	TKO	7
Apr.	18–Lauro Salas, Cleveland	TKO	9
	(Retained World Junior Lightweight Title)		
Apr.	29–Jesse Underwood, Waterbury	W	10
May	25–Miguel Acevedo, Minneapolis	TKO	6
June	19–Johnny Forte, Toronto	KO	3
June	30–Leroy Willis, Long Beach	TKO	2
Sept.	8–Willie Pep, New York	TKO	8
	(Regained World Featherweight Title)		
Oct.	12–Harry LaSane, St. Loius	W	10
Nov.	1–Charley Riley, St. Louis	W	10
Dec.	6–Del Flanagan, Detroit	L	10

1951

Jan.	23–Jesse Underwood Buffalo	W	10
Feb.	28–Diego Sosa, Havana, Cuba	KO	2
	(Retained World Junior Lightweight Title)		
Mar.	27–Lauro Salas, Los Angeles	TKO	6
Apr.	3–Freddie Herman, Los Angeles	TKO	5
May	5–Harry LaSane, Hershey, Pa.	W	10
June	2–Alfredo Prada, Buenos Aires	KO	4
June	16–Oscar Flores, Buenos Aires	KO	1
June	22–Mario Salinas, Santiago	KO	5
June	30–Angel Olivieri, Buenos Aires	KO	5
Aug.	20–Hermie Freeman, Philadelphia	TKO	5
Aug.	27–Paddy DeMarco, Milwaukee	L	10
Sept.	26–Willie Pep, New York	TKO	9
	(Retained World Featherweight Title)		
Dec.	7–Paddy DeMarco, New York	L	10

1952

Jan.	14–George Araujo, Boston	L	10
Mar.	3–Armand Savoie, Montrel	L disq.	4
Mar.	17–Tommy Collins, Boston	TKO	5

1953
(Inactive)

1954

Jan.	15–Bill Bossio, New York	TKO	9
Mar.	4–Charlie Slaughter, Akron	TKO	4
Apr.	1–Augie Salazar, Boston	TKO	7
May	17–Hoacine Khalfi, New York	L	10
July	5–Libby Manzo, New York	KO	10
Aug.	30–Jackie Blair, Caracas	TKO	1
Sept.	27–Baby Ortiz, Caracas	TKO	3
Oct.	25–Ray Famechon, Paris	TKO	6
Dec.	10–Bobby Woods, Spokane	W	10

1955

Jan.	17–Lulu Perez, Boston	KO	4
Feb.	25–Teddy Davis, New York	W	15
	(Retained World Featherweight Title)		
Apr.	5–Kenny Davis, Butte	TKO	5
May	24–Joe Lopes, Sacramento	L	10

July	8–Shigeji Kaneko, Tokyo	TKO	6
July	20–Flash Elorde, Manila	L	10
Dec.	12–Dave Gallardo, San Fran	TKO	7

1956

Jan.	18–Flash Elorde, San Francisco	TKO	13
	(Retained World Featherweight Title)		
Feb.	13–Curley Monroe, Providence	TKO	3
Apr.	14–Larry Boardman, Boston	L	10

1957

Jan.   21–Announced retirement.

TB	KO	WD	WF	D	LD	LF	KO BY	ND	NC
162	103	41	0	2	14	1	1	0	0

Elected to Boxing Hall of Fame, 1971.

JEFF CHANDLER

Born, September 3, 1956, Philadelphia, Pa. Weight, 114–121 lbs.
Height, 5 ft. 7 in. Managed by K. O. Becky O'Neill.

1976

Feb.	25–Mike Dowling, Scranton	D	4
Apr.	13–Chico Vivas, Philadelphia	W	4
June	8–Mike Frazier, Philadelphia	W	4
Aug.	6–John Glover, Atlantic City	W	4
Oct.	14–Larry Huffin, Wilmington	KO	3
Nov.	30–Pee Wee Stokes, Philadelphia	W	4

1977

Feb.	21–Fernando Sanchez, Philadelphia	W	6
June	15–John Glover, Philadelphia	W	6
Oct.	25–Tony Reed, Philadelphia	W	8

1978

Mar.	14–Tony Hernandez, Philadelphia	KO	2
May	24–Jose Luis Garcia, Philadelphia	KO	5
June	19–Roque Moreno, Philadelphia	TKO	5
Aug.	24–Sergio Reyes, Philadelphia	W	8
Oct.	24–Andres Torres, Philadelphia	W	10
Dec.	5–Rafael Gandarillo, Philadelphia	TKO	9

1979

Apr.	3–Davey Vasquez, Philadelphia	W	10
May	14–Justo Garcia, Philadelphia	W	10
July	31–Alberto Cruz, Atlantic City	TKO	3

Sept.	26–Baby Kid Chocolate, Upper Darby	TKO	9
	(Won Vacant USBA Bantamweight Title)		
Dec.	4–Francisco Alvarado, Upper Darby	KO	7

1980

Feb.	1–Javier Flores, Philadelphia	TKO	10
	(Won Vacant NABF Bantamweight Title)		
Mar.	29–Andres Hernandez, Atlantic City	W	12
	(Retained USBA and NABF Bantamweight Titles)		
July	12–Gilberto Villacana, Atl. City	KO	4
July	31–Gustavo Martinez, Atl. City	KO	8
Nov.	14–Julian Solis, Miami, Fla.	TKO	14
	(Won World Bantamweight Title)		

1981

Jan.	31–Jorge Lujan, Philadelphia	W	15
	(Retained World Bantamweight Title)		
Apr.	5–Eijiro Murata, Tokyo	D	15
	(Retained World Bantamweight Title)		
July	25–Julian Solis, Atlantic City	KO	7
	(Retained World Bantamweight Title)		
Dec.	10–Eijiro Murata, Atlantic City	TKO	13
	(Retained World Bantamweight Title)		

1982

Mar. 27–Johnny Carter, Philadelphia .... TKO 6
(Retained World Bantamweight Title)
Oct. 27–Miguel Iriarte, Atlantic City .... TKO 9
(Retained World Bantamweight Title)

1983

Mar. 13–Gaby Canizales, Atlantic City .... W 15
(Retained World Bantamweight Title)
May 22–Hector Cortez, Atlantic City .... W 10
July 23–Oscar Muniz, Atlantic City .... L 10

Sept. 11–Eijiro Murata, Tokyo, Japan .... TKO 10
(Retained World Bantamweight Title)
Dec. 17–Oscar Muniz, Atlantic City .... TKO 7
(Retained World Bantamweight Title)

1984

Apr. 7–Richard Sandoval, Atlantic City .... TKO by 15
(Lost World Bantamweight Title)

TB	KO	WD	WF	D	LD	LF	KO BY	ND	NC
37	18	15	0	2	1	0	1	0	0

GEORGE FOREMAN

Born, January 22, 1948, Marshall, Texas. Weight, 215–225 lbs.
Height, 6 ft. 3 in. 1968 Olympic Heavyweight Gold Medalist

1969

June 23–Don Waldhelm, New York .... KO 3
July 1–Fred Askew, Houston, Texas .... KO 1
July 14–Sylvester Dullaire, Washington .... KO 1
Aug. 18–Chuck Wepner, New York .... KO 3
Sept. 18–John Carroll, Seattle .... KO 1
Sept. 23–Cookie Wallace, Houston .... KO 2
Oct. 7–Vernon Clay, Houston .... KO 2
Oct. 31–Roberto Davila, New York .... W 8
Nov. 5–Leo Peterson, Scranton .... KO 4
Nov. 18–Max Martinez, Houston .... KO 2
Dec. 6–Bob Hazelton, Las Vegas .... KO 1
Dec. 16–Levi Forte, Miami Beach .... W 10
Dec. 18–Gary Wiler, Seattle .... KO 1

1970

Jan. 6–Charlie Polite, Houston .... KO 4
Jan. 26–Jack O'Halloran, New York .... KO 5
Feb. 16–Gregorio Peralta, New York .... W 10
Mar. 31–Rufus Brassell, Houston .... KO 1
Apr. 17–James J. Woody, New York .... KO 3
Apr. 29–Aaron Easting, Cleveland .... KO 4
May 16–George Johnson, Los Angeles .... TKO 7
July 20–Roger Russell, Philadelphia .... KO 1
Aug. 4–George Chuvalo, New York .... KO 3
Nov. 3–Lou Bailey, Oklahoma City .... KO 3
Nov. 18–Boone Kirkman, New York .... KO 2
Dec. 19–Mel Turnbow, Seattle .... TKO 1

1971

Feb. 8–Charlie Boston, St. Paul .... KO 1

Apr. 3–Stamford Harris, Lake Geneva .... KO 2
May 10–Gregorio Peralta, Oakland .... TKO 10
Sept. 14–Vic Scott, El Paso, Texas .... KO 1
Sept. 21–Leroy Caldwell, Beaumont .... KO 3
Oct. 7–Ollie Wilson, San Antonio .... KO 2
Oct. 29–Luis Faustino Pires, New York .... TKO 4

1972

Feb. 29–Murphy Goodwin, Austin .... KO 2
Mar. 7–Clarence Boone, Beaumont .... KO 2
Apr. 10–Ted Gullick, Los Angeles .... KO 2
May 11–Miguel Angel Paez, Oakland .... KO 2
Oct. 10–Terry Sorrels, Salt Lake City .... KO 2

1973

Jan. 22–Joe Frazier, Kingston .... TKO 2
(Won World Heavyweight Title)
Sept. 1–Jose (King) Roman, Tokyo .... KO 1
(Retained World Heavyweight Title)

1974

Mar. 26–Ken Norton, Caracas .... TKO 2
(Retained World Heavyweight Title)
Oct. 30–Muhammad Ali, Kinshasa .... KO by 8
(Lost World Heavyweight Title)

1975

Apr. 26–Charley Polite, Toronto .... Exh. 3
Apr. 26–Boone Kirkman, Toronto .... Exh. 3
Apr. 26–Terry Daniels, Toronto .... Exh. 2
Apr. 26–Jerry Judge, Toronto .... Exh. 2

Apr.	26–Alonzo Johnson, Toronto	Exh.	2
Nov.	26–Jody Ballard, Kiamesha Lake	Exh.	2
Dec.	17–Eddie Brooks, San Francisco	Exh.	4

1976

Jan.	24–Ron Lyle, Las Vegas, Nev.	KO	4
June	15–Joe Frazier, Uniondale, N.Y.	KO	5
Aug.	14–Scott LeDoux, Utica, N.Y.	KO	3
Oct.	15–John Denis, Hollywood, Fla.	TKO	4

1977

Jan.	22–Pedro Agosta, Pensacola, Fla.	KO	4
Mar.	17–Jimmy Young, San Juan, P.R.	L	12

1987

Mar.	9–Steve Zouski, California	TKO	4
July	9–Charles Hostetter, California	KO	3
Sept.	15–Bobby Crabtree, Missouri	TKO	6
Nov.	21–Tim Anderson, Florida	TKO	4
Dec.	18–Rocky Sekorski, Nevada	TKO	3

1988

Jan.	23–Tom Trim, Florida	TKO	1
Feb.	5–Guido Trane, Las Vegas	TKO	5
Mar.	19–Dwight Qwai, Las Vegas	TKO	7
May	21–Frank Williams, Arkansas	KO	3
June	26–Carlos Hernanadez, Atlantic City	TKO	4
Aug.	25–Ladislao Mijangos, Florida	TKO	2
Sept.	10–Bobby Hitz, Michigan	KO	1
Oct.	27–Tony Fulilangi, Texas	TKO	2
Dec.	28–David Jaco, California	KO	1

1989

Jan.	26–Mark Young, New York	TKO	7
Feb.	16–Manuel De Almeida, Florida	TKO	3
Apr.	30–J. B. Williamson, Texas	TKO	5
June	1–Bert Cooper, Arizona	TKO	2
July	20–Everett Martin, Arizona	WD	10

1990

Jan.	15–Gerry Cooney, Atlantic City	KO	2
Apr.	17–Mike Jameson, Las Vegas	KO	4
June	16–Adilson Rodrigues, Las Vegas	KO	2
July	31–Ken Lakusta, Canada	KO	3
Sept.	25–Terry Anderson, England	KO	1

1991

Apr.	19–Evander Holyfield, Atlantic City	LD	12
	(World Heavyweight Title)		
Dec.	7–Jimmy Ellis, Las Vegas	TKO	3

1992

Apr.	11–Alex Stewart, Las Vegas	WD	10

1993

Jan.	16–Pierre Coetzer, Las Vegas	TKO	8
June	7–Tommie Morrison, Las Vegas	LD	12
	(World Boxing Organization Title)		

TB	KO	WD	WF	D	LD	LF	KO BY	ND	NC
76	67	5	0	0	3	0	1	0	0

EVANDER HOLYFIELD

Born, October 19, 1962, Atmore, Ala. Weight, 176–210 lbs. Height, 6 ft. 1 in.
1984 National Golden Gloves Light Heavyweight Champion
1984 Olympic Light Heavyweight Bronze Medalist

1984

Nov.	15–Lionel Byarm, New York	W	6

1985

Jan.	20–Eric Winbush, Atlantic City	W	6
Mar.	13–Fred Brown, Norfolk, Va.	TKO	1
Apr.	20–Mark Rivera, Corpus Christi	KO	2
July	20–Tyrone Booze, Norfolk, Va.	W	8
Aug.	29–Rick Myers, Atlanta, Ga.	TKO	1
Oct.	30–Jeff Meachum, Atlantic City	TKO	5
Dec.	21–Anthony Davis, Virginia Beach	TKO	4

1986

Mar.	1–Chisanda Mutti, Lancaster, Pa.	TKO	3
Apr.	6–Jesse Shelby, Corpus Christi	KO	3
July	12–Dwight Braxton, Atlanta, Ga.	W	15
	(Won WBA Junior Heavyweight Title)		
Dec.	8–Mike Brothers, Paris, France	KO	3
	(WBA & IBF Junior Heavyweight Title)		

1987

Feb.	14–Henry Tillman, Reno	TKO	7
	(WBA & IBF Junior Heavyweight Title)		

May	15–Rickey Parkey, Las Vegas	TKO	3
	(WBA & IBF Junior Heavyweight Title)		
Aug.	15–Ossie Ocasio, St. Tropez, France	TKO	11
	(WBA & IBF Junior Heavyweight Title)		
Dec.	5–Dwight Qwai, Atlantic City	TKO	4
	(WBA & IBF Junior Heavyweight Title)		

1988

Apr.	9–Carlos DeLeon, Las Vegas	KO	8
	(Won the World Boxing Council Junior Heavyweight Title)		
July	16–James Tillis, Lake Tahoe	KO	5
Dec.	9–Pinklon Thomas, Atlantic City	TKO	7

1989

Mar.	11–Michael Dokes, Las Vegas	TKO	10
July	15–Adilson Rodrigues, Lake Tahoe	KO	2
Nov.	4–Alex Stewart, Atlantic City	TKO	8

1990

| June | 1–Seamus McDonogh, Atlantic City | TKO | 4 |

| Oct. | 25–Buster Douglas, Las Vegas | KO | 3 |
| | (Won the World Heavyweight Title) | | |

1991

Apr.	19–George Foreman, Atlantic City	WD	12
	(World Heavyweight Title)		
Nov.	23–Bert Cooper, Atlanta, GA	TKO	57
	(World Heavyweight Title)		

1992

June	19–Larry Holmes, Las Vegas	WD	12
	(World Heavyweight Title)		
Nov.	13–Riddick Bowe, Las Vegas	LD	12
	(World Heavyweight Title)		

1993

| June | –Alex Stewart, Atlantic City | WD | 10 |

TB	KO	WD	WF	D	LD	LF	KO BY	ND	NC
29	22	7	0	0	1	0	0	0	0

RIDDICK BOWE

Born August 10, 1967, Brooklyn, New York. Weight, 226–245 lbs. Height, 6 ft. 5 in. Managed by Rock Newman. Trained by Eddie Futch.
1988 United States Olympic Super Heavyweight Silver Medalist

1989

Mar.	6–Lionel Butler, Las Vegas	TKO	2
Apr.	14–Thacy Thomas, Atlantic City	TKO	3
May	9–Garing Lane, Atlantic City	W	4
July	2–Antonio Whiteside, North Carolina	TKO	1
July	15–Lorenzo Canady, Atlantic City	TKO	2
Sept.	3–Lee Moore, Florida	KO	1
Sept.	15–Anthony Hayes, New York	KO	1
Sept.	19–Earl Lewis, Florida	KO	1
Oct.	19–Mike Acey, Atlantic City	TKO	1
Nov.	4–Garing Lane, Atlantic City	TKO	4
Nov.	18–Don Askew, Washington, D.C.	KO	1
Nov.	28–Art Card, New York	TKO	3
Dec.	14–Charles Woodard, Missouri	TKO	2

1990

Feb.	20–Mike Robinson, Atlantic City	TKO	3
Apr.	1–Robert Colay, Washington, D.C.	TKO	2
Apr.	14–Eddie Gonzales, Las Vegas	W	8
May	8–Manny Contreras, Atlantic City	KO	1

July	8–Art Tucker, Atlantic City	TKO	3
Sept.	7–Pinklon Thomas, Washington, D.C.	TKO	9
Oct.	25–Bert Cooper, Las Vegas	TKO	2
Dec.	14–Tony Morrison, Missouri	KO	1

1991

Mar.	2–Tyrell Biggs, Atlantic City	TKO	8
Apr.	20–Tony Tubbs, Atlantic City	W	10
June	28–Rodolfo Marin, Las Vegas	KO	2
July	23–Phillip Brown, Atlantic City	TKO	3
Aug.	9–Bruce Seldon, Atlantic City	KO	1
Oct.	29–Elijah Tillery, Washington, D.C.	WDSQ	1
Dec.	13–Elijah Tillery, Washington, D.C.	TKO	4

1992

Apr.	7–Conroy Nelson, Atlantic City	KO	1
May	8–Everett Martin, Las Vegas	TKO	5
July	18–Pierre Coetzer, Las Vegas	TKO	7
Nov.	13–Evander Holyfield, Las Vegas	WD	12
	(World Heavyweight Title)		

1993

			TB	KO	WD	D	LD	LF	KO BY	ND	NC
			34	29	5	0	0	0	0	0	0

Feb.　6–Michael Dokes, New York .... TKO 1
　　　(WBA & IBF Heavyweight Title)

May　22–Jesse Ferguson, Washington, D.C. .... KO 2
　　　(WBA Heavyweight Title)

AARON PRYOR

Born, October 20, 1955, Cincinnati, Ohio. Weight, 135–140 lbs.
Height, 5 ft. 6½ in.
1973 National AAU Lightweight Champion

1976

Nov.　12–Larry Smith, Cincinnati .... TKO 2

1977

Feb.　1–Larry Moore, Cincinnati .... TKO 4
Feb.　24–Harvey Wilson, Cincinnati .... KO 1
Mar.　12–Nicky Wills, Lincoln Hts. .... KO 1
Mar.　26–Isaac Vega, Cincinnati .... KO 2
May　7–Jose Resto, Cincinnati .... W 8
Sept.　3–Melvin Young, Covington .... KO 4
Oct.　7–Johnny Summerhays, Cinc. .... W 8
Nov.　4–Angel Cintron, Cincinnati .... KO 3

1978

Jan.　16–Robert Tijernia, Cincinnati .... KO 2
Mar.　1–Ron Pettigrew, Dayton, Ohio .... TKO 5
Mar.　10–Alfred Franklin, Cincinnati .... TKO 3
May　3–Scotty Foreman, Miami Beach .... TKO 6
July　18–Marion Thomas, Dayton, Ohio .... KO 8

1979

Mar.　16–Johnny Copeland, Cincinnati .... KO 7
Apr.　13–Norman Goins, Cincinnati .... KO 9
Apr.　27–Freddie Harris, Dayton .... KO 3
May　11–Al Ford, Cincinnati .... TKO 4
June　23–Jose Fernandez, Cinc. .... KO 1
Oct.　20–Alfonzo Frazer, Cinc. .... TKO 5

1980

Feb.　24–Juan Garcia, Las Vegas .... KO 1
Mar.　16–Julio Valdez, Miami, Fla. .... TKO 4
Apr.　13–Leonidas Asprilla, Kansas City .... TKO 10
June　20–Carl Crowley, Cincinnati .... KO 1
Aug.　2–Antonio Cervantes, Cincinnati .... KO 4
　　　(Won WBA Junior Welterweight Title)
Nov.　1–Danny Myers, Dayton, Ohio .... TKO 3

Nov.　22–Gaetan Hart, Cincinnati .... TKO 6
　　　(Retained WBA Junior Welterweight Title)

1981

June　27–Lennox Blackmoore, Las Vegas .... TKO 2
　　　(Retained WBA Junior Welterweight Title)
Nov.　14–Dujuan Johnson, Cleveland .... TKO 7
　　　(Retained WBA Junior Welterweight Title)

1982

Mar.　21–Miguel Montilla, Atlantic City .... TKO 12
　　　(Retained WBA Junior Welterweight Title)
July　4–Akio Kameda, Cincinnati .... TKO 6
　　　(Retained WBA Junior Welterweight Title)
Nov.　12–Alexis Arguello, Miami, Fla. .... TKO 14
　　　(Retained WBA Junior Welterweight Title)

1983

Apr.　2–Sang-Hyun Kim, Atlantic City .... TKO 3
　　　(Retained WBA Junior Welterweight Title)
Sept.　9–Alexis Arguello, Las Vegas .... KO 10
　　　(Retained WBA Junior Welterweight Title)
Dec.　–Relinquished WBA Jr. Welter Title.

1984

Jan.　–Proclaimed IBF jr. welter champion.
June　22–Nick Furlano, Toronto .... W 15
　　　(Retained IBF Junior Welterweight Title)

1985

Mar.　2–Gary Hinton, Atlantic City .... W 15
　　　(Retained IBF Junior Welterweight Title)
Dec.　–IBF vacated title.

1987

Aug.　8–Bobby Joe Young, Florida .... KO by 7

1988

Dec. 15–Herminio Morales, New York .... KO 3

1990

May 16–Darryl Jones, Wisconsin .... KO 3

Dec. 4–Roger Choate, Oklahoma .... TKO 7

TB	KO	WD	WF	D	LD	LF	KO BY	ND	NC
40	35	4	0	0	0	0	1	0	0

PERNELL WHITAKER
Norfolk, Va. Lightweight
Born: January 2, 1964, Norfolk, Va.
Height: 5 ft. 6 in. Southpaw
Managers: Lou Duva, Shelly Finkel
1984 Olympic Lightweight Gold Medalist

1984

Nov. 15–Farrain Comeaux, New York .... KO 2

1985

Jan. 20–Danny Avery, Atlantic City .... KO 4
Mar. 13–Mike Golden, Norfolk, Va. .... TKO 4
Apr. 20–Nick Parker, Corpus Christi .... W 6
July 20–John Senegal, Norfolk, Va. .... TKO 2
Aug. 29–Ted Hatfield, Atlanta, Ga. .... TKO 3
Nov. 12–Jesus de la Cruz, Houston .... KO 1

1986

Mar. 9–John Montes, Hampton, Va. .... W 10
Aug. 16–Rafael Williams, Atl. City .... W 10
Oct. 9–Rafael Candarilla, New York .... W 10
Dec. 20–Alfredo Layne, Norfolk .... W 10

1987

Mar. 28–Roger Mayweather, Norfolk .... WD 12
(North American Boxing Federation Lightweight
Title)
June 28–Jim Flores, Texas .... TKO 1
July 25–Miguel Santana, Norfolk .... TKO 6
(NABF & USBF Lightweight Title)
Dec. 19–Davey Montana, France .... TKO 4

1988

Mar. 12–Jose Ramirez, France .... LD 12
(WBC Lightweight Title)
Nov. 2–Antonio Carter, Norfolk .... TKO 1

1989

Feb. 18–Greg Haugen, Norfolk .... WD 12
(IBF Lightweight Title)

Apr. 30–Louie Lomeli, Norfolk .... TKO 3
(IBF Lightweight Title)
Aug. 20–Jose Ramirez, Norfolk .... WD 12
(WBC Lightweight Title)
Dec. 11–Martin Galvan, France .... TKO 3

1990

Feb. 3–Fred Pendleton, Atlantic City .... WD 12
(IBF Lightweight Title)
May 19–Azumah Nelson, Las Vegas .... WD 12
(WBC & IBF Lightweight Title)
Aug. 11–Juan Nazario, Las Vegas .... KO 1
(World Lightweight Title)
Nov. 22–Benji Marquez, Spain .... WD 10

1991

Feb. 23–Anthony Jones, Las Vegas .... WD 12
(World Lightweight Title)
July 27–Poli Diaz, Norfolk .... WD 12
(World Lightweight Title)
Oct. 5–Jorge Paez, Las Vegas .... WD 12
(World Lightweight Title)

1992

Jan. 18–Harold Brazier, Pennsylvania .... WD 10
May 22–Jerry Smith, Mexico .... KO 1
July 18–Rafael Pineda, Las Vegas .... WD 12
(World Junior Welterweight Title)
Dec. 1–Ben Baez, Norfolk .... KO 1

1993

Mar. 6–James McGirt, New York .... WD 12
(WBC Welterweight Title)

TB	KO	LD
33	15	1

AFRICAN-AMERICAN BOXING CHAMPIONS

Heavyweights	Title Held
Johnson, Jack	1908–1915
Louis, Joe	1937–1949
Charles, Ezzard	1949–1951
Walcott, Jersey Joe	1951–1952
Patterson, Floyd	1960–1962
Liston, Sonny	1962–1964
Clay, Cassius (Muhammad Ali)	1964–1970
Terrell, Ernest (W.B.A.)	1965–1967
Frazier, Joe (New York)	1968–1970
Ellis, Jimmy (W.B.A.)	1968–1970
Frazier, Joe	1970–1973
Foreman, George	1973–1974
Ali, Muhammad	1974–1978, 1978–1979
Spinks, Leon	1978
Norton, Ken (W.B.C.)	1978
Holmes, Larry (W.B.C.)	1978–1983
(I.B.F.)	1984–1985
Tate, John (W.B.A.)	1979–1980
Weaver, Michael (W.B.A.)	1980–1982
Dokes, Michael (W.B.A.)	1982–1983
Witherspoon, Tim (W.B.C.)	1984
Thomas, Pinklon (W.B.C.)	1984–1986
Page, Greg (W.B.A.)	1985
Tubbs, Tony (W.B.A.)	1985–1986
Spinks, Michael (I.B.F.)	1985–1987
Witherspoon, Tim (W.B.A.)	1986–1987
Tyson, Michael (W.B.C.)	1986–1987
Smith, James "Bonecrusher" (W.B.A.)	1986–1987
Tucker, Tony (I.B.F.)	1987
Tyson, Michael (W.B.C./W.B.A./I.B.F.)	1987–1990
Douglas, James "Buster" (W.B.C./W.B.A./I.B.F.)	1990
Holyfield, Evander (W.B.C./W.B.A./I.B.F.)	1990–1992

Heavyweights	Title Held
Bowe, Riddick (W.B.C.*/W.B.A./I.B.F.)	1992–

*Bowe gave up the W.B.C. title December 1992.

Cruiserweights	Title Held
Gordon, S.T. (W.B.C.)	1982–1983
Murphy, Leroy (I.B.F.)	1984–1986
Ratliff, Alonzo (W.B.C.)	1985
Qwai, Dwight Braxton (W.B.A.)	1985–1987
Parkey, Rick (I.B.F.)	1986–1987
Holyfield, Evander (W.B.A.)	1986–1987
(W.B.A./I.B.F.)	1987–1990
Daniels, Robert (W.B.A.)	1989–1991
Warring, James (I.B.F.)	1991–1992
Pritchard, James (I.B.F.)	1991
Cole, Alfred (I.B.F.)	1992–

Light Heavyweights	Title Held
Lewis, John Henry	1935–1938
Moore, Archie	1952–1962
Johnson, Harold	1961–1963
Foster, Bob	1968–1974
Johnson, Marvin (W.B.C.)	1978–1979
(W.B.A.)	1979–1981
(W.B.A.)	1986–1987
Franklin, Matthew (Matthew Saad Muhammad) (W.B.C.)	1979–1981
Gregory, Eddie (Eddie Mustafa Muhammad) (W.B.A.)	1980–1981
Spinks, Michael (W.B.A.)	1981
Qwai, Dwight Braxton (W.B.C.)	1981–1983
Spinks, Michael (W.B.A./W.B.C./I.B.F.)	1983–1985
Williamson, J.B. (W.B.C.)	1985–1986
Hill, Virgil (W.B.A.)	1987–1991
Williams, Prince Charles (I.B.F.)	1987–1993
Hearns, Thomas (W.B.C.)	1987–1993
Leonard, Sugar Ray (W.B.C.)	1988
Hearns, Thomas (W.B.A.)	1991–1992
Barkley, Iran (W.B.A.)	1992
Hill, Virgil (W.B.A.)	1992–

Middleweights	Title Held
Flowers, Tiger	1926
Jones, Gorilla	1931–1932
Robinson, Sugar Ray	1951, 1951–1952, 1955–1957, 1957, 1958–1960
Hagler, Marvin	1980–1987
Leonard, Sugar Ray	1987
Tate, Frank (I.B.F.)	1987–1988
Hearns, Thomas (W.B.C.)	1987–1988
Barkley, Iran (W.B.C.)	1988–1989
Nunn, Michael (I.B.F.)	1988–1991
Toney, James (I.B.F.)**	1991–1993
Johnson, Reginald (W.B.A.)	1992–
Jones, Roy (I.B.F.)	1993–
McClellan, Gerald (W.B.C.)	1993–

**Toney gave up the middleweight title to campaign as a Super Middleweight. As of July, 1993 he was the I.B.F. Super Middleweight Champion.

Junior Middleweights	Title Held
Leonard, Sugar Ray (W.B.A.)	1981–1982
Moore, Davey (W.B.A.)	1982–1983
Hearns, Thomas (W.B.C.)	1982–1984, 1984–1987
Thomas, Duane (W.B.C.)	1986–1987
Drayton, Buster (I.B.F.)	1986–1987
Hines, Robert (I.B.F.)	1988–1989
Norris, Terry (W.B.C.)	1990–

Welterweights	Title Held
Walcott, Joe (Barbados)	1901–1904
Brown, Aaron (The Dixie Kid)	1904–1905
Thompson, Cecil (Young Jack)	1930–1931
Robinson, Sugar Ray	1946–1951
Bratton, Johnny (N.B.A.)	1951
Saxton, John	1956
Akins, Virgil	1958
Jordon, Don	1958–1960
Cokes, Curtis	1966–1969
Lewis, Hedgman (New York)	1972–1973
Leonard, Sugar Ray (W.B.C.)	1979–1982
(W.B.C./W.B.A.)	1981–1982

Welterweights	Title Held
Hearns, Thomas (W.B.A.)	1980–1981
Curry, Donald (W.B.A.)	1983–1985
(W.B.A./W.B.C./I.B.F.)	1985–1986
McCrory, Milton (W.B.C.)	1983–1985
Breland, Mark (W.B.A.)	1987
Starling, Marlon (W.B.A.)	1987–1988
Breland, Mark (W.B.A.)	1989–1990
Starling, Marlon (W.B.C.)	1989–1990
Davis, Aaron (W.B.A.)	1990–1991
Blocker, Maurice (W.B.C.)	1990–1991
Taylor, Meldrick (W.B.A.)	1991–1992
Blocker, Maurice (I.B.F.)	1991–1993
McGirt, James "Buddy" (W.B.C.)	1991–1993
Whitaker, Pernell "Sweet Pea" (W.B.C.)	1993–

Junior Welterweights	Title Held
Pryor, Aaron (W.B.A.)	1980–1983
(W.B.A./I.B.F.)	1983–1985
Haley, Leroy (W.B.C.)	1982–1983
Curry, Bruce (W.B.C.)	1983–1984
Costello, Billy (W.B.C.)	1984
Bumphus, Johnny (W.B.A.)	1984
Smith, Lonnie (W.B.C.)	1985–1986
Hinton, Gary (I.B.F.)	1986
Manley, Joe Louis (I.B.F.)	1988–1990
Taylor, Meldrick (W.B.A.)	1988–1990
McGirt, James (I.B.F.)	1990
Whitaker, Pernell "Sweet Pea" (I.B.F.)	1992–1993
Murray, Charles (I.B.F.)	1993

Lightweights	Title Held
Gans, Joe	1902–1908
Armstrong, Henry	1938–1939
Walker, Sidney (Beau Jack) (New York)	1942–1943/1943–1944
Montgomery, Bob (New York)	1943–1944/1947
Williams, Ike (N.B.A.)	1945–1947
Carter, James	1951–1952
Smith, Wallace (Bud)	1955–1956
Brown, Joe	1956–1962

Lightweights	Title Held
Kenty, Hilmer (W.B.A.)	1980–1981
Paul, Jimmy (I.B.F.)	1985–1986
Whitaker, Pernell "Sweet Pea"	
(I.B.F./W.B.C.)	1989–1990
(W.B.A./W.B.C./I.B.F.)	1990–1992*
Pendleton, Fred (I.B.F.)	1993–

*Whitaker gave up the lightweight title to campaign as a junior welterweight.

Junior Lightweights	Title Held
Saddler, Sandy	1949–1950
Mayweather, Roger (W.B.A.)	1982–1984
Lockridge, Rocky (W.B.A.)	1984–1985

Featherweights	Title Held
Dixon, George (Canadian)	1898–1900
Armstrong, Henry	1937–1938

Featherweights	Title Held
Wright, Albert (Chalky)	1941–1942
Wilson, Jackie (N.B.A.)	1941–1943
Saddler, Sandy	1950–1957

Featherweights	Title Held
Bassey, Hogan (Kid)	1957–1959
Moore, Davey	1959–1963
Johnson, Tom (I.B.F.)	1993–

Junior Featherweights	Title Held
Patterson, Tracy Harris (W.B.C.)	1992–
McKinney, Kennedy (I.B.F.)	1993

Bantamweights	Title Held
Dade, Harold	1942
Chandler, Jeff	1980–1984
Cook, Eddie (W.B.A.)	1992–1993

RING MAGAZINE "FIGHTER OF THE YEAR" AWARD

Year	Name	Weight Class	Year	Name	Weight Class
1936	Joe Louis	Heavyweight	1967	Joe Frazier	Heavyweight
1937	Henry Armstrong	Featherweight	1970	Joe Frazier	Heavyweight
1938	Joe Louis	Heavyweight	1971	Joe Frazier	Heavyweight
1939	Joe Louis	Heavyweight	1972	Muhammad Ali	Heavyweight
1941	Joe Louis	Heavyweight	1973	George Foreman	Heavyweight
1941	Ray Robinson	Welterweight	1974	Muhammad Ali	Heavyweight
1944	Beau Jack	Lightweight	1975	Muhammad Ali	Heavyweight
1948	Ike Williams	Lightweight	1976	George Foreman	Heavyweight
1949	Ezzard Charles	Heavyweight	1978	Muhammad Ali	Heavyweight
1950	Ezzard Charles	Heavyweight	1979	Ray Leonard	Welterweight
1951	Ray Robinson	Middleweight	1980	Thomas Hearns	Welterweight
1956	Floyd Patterson	Heavyweight	1981	Ray Leonard (co-winner)	Welterweight
1960	Floyd Patterson	Heavyweight	1982	Larry Holmes	Heavyweight
1961	Joe Brown	Lightweight	1983	Marvin Hagler	Middleweight
1963	Cassius Clay (Muhammad Ali)	Heavyweight	1984	Thomas Hearns	Junior Middleweight

Year	Name	Weight Class	Year	Name	Weight Class
1985	Donald Curry (co-winner)	Welterweight	1988	Mike Tyson	Heavyweight
	Marvin Hagler (co-winner)	Middleweight	1989	Pernell Whitaker	Lightweight
1986	Mike Tyson	Heavyweight	1991	James Toney	Middleweight
1987	Evander Holyfield	Cruiserweight	1992	Riddick Bowe	Heavyweight

OLYMPIC AFRICAN-AMERICAN GOLD MEDALISTS
(Boxing)

Year	Fighter	Weight Class	Year	Fighter	Weight Class
1952	Nathan Brooks	Flyweight	1960	Edward Crook	Middleweight
1976	Leo Randolph	Flyweight	1976	Michael Spinks	Middleweight
1988	Kennedy McKinney	Bantamweight	1952	Norvel Lee	Light Heavyweight
1984	Meldrick Taylor	Featherweight	1956	James Boyd	Light Heavyweight
1968	Ronnie Harris	Lightweight	1960	Cassius Clay	Light Heavyweight
1976	Howard Davis	Lightweight	1976	Leon Spinks	Light Heavyweight
1984	Pernell Whitaker	Lightweight	1988	Andrew Maynard	Light Heavyweight
1952	Charles Adkins	Light Welterweight	1984	Henry Tillman	Heavyweight
1972	Ray Seales	Light Welterweight	1989	Ray Mercer	Heavyweight
1976	Ray Leonard	Light Welterweight	1952	Ed Sanders	Super Heavyweight
1984	Jerry Page	Light Welterweight	1964	Joe Frazier	Super Heavyweight
1984	Mark Breland	Welterweight	1968	George Foreman	Super Heavyweight
1984	Frank Tate	Light Middleweight	1984	Tyrell Biggs	Super Heavyweight
1952	Floyd Patterson	Middleweight			

AFRICAN-AMERICANS INDUCTED INTO THE INTERNATIONAL BOXING HALL OF FAME

Old Timers

Year Inducted	Name	Record	Weight Class
1990	George Dixon	50 wins, 28 losses, 45 draws	Featherweight
1990	Joe Gans	131 wins, 4 losses, 16 draws	Lightweight
1990	Peter Jackson	35 wins, 3 losses, 1 draw	Heavyweight
1990	Sam Langford	187 wins, 50 losses, 47 draws	Heavyweight
1991	Joe Walcott	74 wins, 30 losses, 22 draws	Welterweight
1992	Harry Wills	not available	Heavyweight
1990	Jack Johnson	86 wins, 4 losses, 11 draws	Heavyweight
1993	Theodore "Tiger" Flowers	133 wins, 15 losses, 7 draws	Middleweight

Modern Era

Year Inducted	Name	Record	Weight Class
1990	Muhammad Ali	56 wins, 5 losses	Heavyweight
1990	Henry Armstrong	152 wins, 21 losses	Featherweight, Lightweight, Welterweight
1992	Charley Burley	84 wins, 11 losses, 2 draws	Lightweight
1990	Ezzard Charles	96 wins, 25 losses, 1 draw	Heavyweight
1990	Bob Foster	56 wins, 12 losses, 1 draw	Light-Heavyweight
1990	Joe Frazier	32 wins, 4 losses, 1 draw	Heavyweight
1991	Beau Jack	83 wins, 24 losses, 5 draws	Lightweight
1991	Sonny Liston	50 wins, 4 losses	Heavyweight
1990	Joe Louis	63 wins, 3 losses	Heavyweight
1990	Archie Moore	183 wins, 22 losses, 9 draws	Light-Heavyweight
1992	Ken Norton	42 wins, 7 losses, 1 draw	Heavyweight
1991	Floyd Patterson	55 wins, 8 losses, 1 draw	Heavyweight
1990	Sugar Ray Robinson	175 wins, 19 losses, 6 draws	Welterweight/Middleweight
1990	Sandy Saddler	144 wins, 16 losses, 2 draws	Featherweight
1990	Jersey Joe Walcott	50 wins, 18 losses, 1 draw	Heavyweight
1990	Ike Williams	123 wins, 25 losses, 5 draws	Lightweight
1993	Harold Johnson	76 wins, 11 losses	Light-Heavyweight
1993	"Marvelous" Marvin Hagler	62 wins, 3 losses, 2 draws	Middleweight

Non-Participants

1992	Jack Blackburn, Trainer

AFRICAN AMERICAN OLYMPIC SILVER AND BRONZE MEDALISTS

1) Harlan Marbley, Light Flyweight, 1968 U.S. Olympic Silver Medalist
2) Jack Wilson, Bantamweight, 1936 U.S. Olympic Silver Medalist
3) Charles Mooney, Bantamweight, 1976 U.S. Olympic Silver Medalist
4) Albert Robinson, Featherweight, 1968 U.S. Olympic Silver Medalist
5) Ronald Allan Harris, Lightweight, 1964 U.S. Olympic Bronze Medalist
6) Romallis Ellis, Lightweight, 1988 U.S. Olympic Bronze Medalist
7) Quincey Daniels, Light-Welterweight, 1952 U.S. Olympic Bronze Medalist
8) Kenneth Gould, Welterweight, 1988 U.S. Olympic Bronze Medalist
9) Roy Jones, Light-Middleweight, 1988 U.S. Olympic Silver Medalist
10) Alfred Jones, Middleweight, 1968 U.S. Olympic Bronze Medalist
11) Marvin Johnson, Middleweight, 1972 U.S. Olympic Bronze Medalist
12) Evander Holyfield, Light-Heavyweight, 1984 U.S. Olympic Bronze Medalist
13) Riddick Bowe, Super Heavyweight, 1988 U.S. Olympic Silver Medalist

VAL BARKER CUP RECIPIENTS

(Awarded to the most outstanding boxer at the Olympic games,
who displays the best technique and style. The cup is named in
honor of the first General-Secretary of the International Amateur
Boxing Association.)

1) Norvel Lee, Light-Heavyweight, 1952
2) Howard Davis, Lightweight, 1976
3) Roy Jones, Light-Middleweight, 1988

EDWARD J. NEIL AWARD RECIPIENTS
Fighter of the Year

Year	Fighter	Weightclass	Year	Fighter	Weightclass
1940	Henry Armstrong	Featherweight	1977	Ken Norton	Heavyweight
1941	Joe Louis	Heavyweight	1978	Larry Holmes	Heavyweight
1948	Ike Williams	Lightweight	1979	Sugar Ray Leonard	Welterweight
1949	Ezzard Charles	Heavyweight	1980	Thomas Hearns	Welterweight
1950	Sugar Ray Robinson	Middleweight	1981	Sugar Ray Leonard	Welterweight
1951	Jersey Joe Walcott	Heavyweight	1982	Aaron Pryor	Junior Welterweight
1956	Floyd Patterson	Heavyweight	1983	Marvin Hagler	Middleweight
1958	Archie Moore	Light-Heavyweight	1984	Thomas Hearns	Junior Middleweight
1960	Floyd Patterson	Heavyweight	1985	Marvin Hagler	Middleweight
1965	Muhammad Ali	Heavyweight	1986	Michael Tyson	Heavyweight
1968	Bob Foster	Light-Heavyweight	1988	Michael Tyson	Heavyweight
1969	Joe Frazier	Heavyweight	1989	Pernell Whitaker	Lightweight
1971	Joe Frazier	Heavyweight	1990	Evander Holyfield	Heavyweight
1973	George Foreman	Heavyweight	1991	James Toney	Middleweight
1974	Muhammad Ali	Heavyweight	1992	Riddick Bowe	Heavyweight
1975	Muhammad Ali	Heavyweight			
	Joe Frazier	Heavyweight			
1976	U.S. Olympic Boxing Team (Howard Davis, Jr., Sugar Ray Leonard, Leo Randolph, Leon Spinks, Michael Spinks)				

JAMES J. WALKER AWARD RECIPIENTS
(Given by the Boxing Writers Association for "Long and Meritorious Service to Boxing")

Year	Name
1967	Joe Louis
1982	Eddie Futch
1984	Muhammad Ali

AL BUCK AWARD RECIPENTS
(Given to the "Manager of the Year")

Year	Name	Year	Name
1969	Yancey Durham	1980	Emanuel Steward
1971	Yancey Durham	1981	Janks Mortan (co-winner)
1974	Herbert Muhammad	1989	Emanuel Steward
1975	Eddie Futch	1992	Rock Newman

JOHN CONDON AWARD RECIPIENTS
(Given to the "Trainer of the Year")

Year	Name
1989	George Benton
1990	George Benton
1991	Eddie Futch

AFRICAN AMERICAN BOXING OFFICIALS
(as of July, 1993)

1) Robert Lee, President, International Boxing Federation
2) Larry Hazzard, Commissioner, New Jersey Athletic Commission

Index